Motherless Families

International Library of Sociology

Founded by Karl Mannheim

Editor: John Rex, University of Warwick

Arbor Scientiae
Arbor Vitae

A catalogue of the books available in the **International Library of Sociology** and new books in preparation for the Library, will be found at the end of this volume

Motherless Families

Victor George and **Paul Wilding**

Department of Applied Social Science
University of Nottingham

Routledge & Kegan Paul

London and Boston

First published 1972
by Routledge & Kegan Paul Ltd
Broadway House, 68–74 Carter Lane,
London EC4V 5EL and
9 Park Street,
Boston, Mass. 02108, U.S.A.
Printed in Great Britain by
Cox & Wyman Ltd, London, Fakenham and Reading
© Victor George and Paul Wilding 1972
No part of this book may be reproduced in
any form without permission from the
publisher, except for the quotation of brief
passages in criticism

ISBN 0 7100 7305 4

Contents

Tables

Acknowledgments

This book is about the problems and issues surrounding motherless families. It is based largely on long interviews with fathers who bring up their children without the help of a wife. Clearly the book would have been impossible without the generous co-operation of these fathers. We are, indeed, grateful to them for all their help.

The Department of Health and Social Security financed the project. The Family Allowance Branch of the Department and individual members of the Department's research section and supplementary benefit section have also helped us in different ways at different stages of the project. Our gratitude to them is acknowledged.

Research assistants are a neglected body of workers for while they do most of the work they enjoy few of the benefits following the publication of a book. We are very grateful to our two research assistants – Alison Jones, who worked on the project for a year and Ann McKay, who nursed the project from beginning to end, in fact for the whole two-year period that the project ran.

We owe a special debt of gratitude to our wives for their support and forbearance especially during the writing-up stage of the research when, together with our teaching commitments, life became extremely hectic.

This has been a corporate effort between the two authors from beginning to end. Chapters 1, 2 and 7 have been written jointly; chapters 3 and 6 predominantly by V. George; and chapters 4 and 5 predominantly by P. Wilding. We the authors alone share, of course, the responsibility for the views expressed in all parts of the book.

1 The study of motherlessness

The changing context of motherlessness

Families left without a mother are not a new phenomenon. Before the days of censuses and statistics numerous contemporary sources give evidence of the high maternal mortality rates which were common to all classes. The Book of Common Prayer stresses on various occasions 'the great pain and peril of childbirth'. The plight of the orphan is one of the great themes of Victorian literature. Samuel Butler writing of nineteenth-century family life recorded that most mothers wrote letters bidding farewell to their families shortly before their confinements and '50 per cent kept them afterwards'.[1] The best estimates we have of maternal mortality in the mid-nineteenth century suggest that one birth in every hundred resulted in a mother's death.[2] The ritual and solicitude which surrounded Victorian childbirth were the product of the very real risks involved.

High maternal mortality rates mean motherlessness for many families, but while the fatherless and the orphan have been the subjects of concern and the objects of charity for centuries, little has been heard of the plight of the motherless. The reasons for this are fairly easy to see. In the past the extended family absorbed the motherless. There were reserves of unmarried womanpower ready to step into the breach and become substitute mothers for nephews and nieces, cousins and younger siblings. Or the children would be parcelled out among willing and less willing relatives.[3] If there were no relatives available to help, the middle-class father could cope with the help of faithful maids and governesses.[4] If all else failed children could be taken into the care of the parish or the union.

Today the situation has changed. In 1969 the maternal mortality

1

rate was 0·19 per 1,000 births – a fall of over 80 per cent since 1948.[5] But while the number of families left motherless through the mother's death is smaller than in the past the number left motherless as a result of divorce or separation seems to be on the increase. The causes of motherlessness have changed but the problem of providing adequate care for the motherless remains. As a result of social and economic change the old solutions are no longer so readily available or so acceptable.

Today it is not so easy for the extended family to assume responsibilities which it assumed without question in the past, whether for the old, the mentally or physically handicapped or for the motherless. The increase in geographical mobility means fewer families have relatives to hand. Working wives mean fewer women at home with time and energy to spare. The increased popularity of marriage and earlier marriage means that the labours of maiden aunts and elder daughters are less frequently available as a source of help. Perhaps it is not only the ability to provide help but the willingness too which has declined, though when we asked a random sample of people in Nottingham whether they felt that relatives should normally be expected to help a man left to bring up children on his own, more than 70 per cent said they should.

In the past society could take it for granted that the extended family would absorb the motherless. The harshness of the alternatives to family care helped enforce the excellence of this principle. Today society cannot so easily take it for granted that the extended family will cope – though it often does.[6]

There have been other changes too. The importance of family life to the emotional stability and development of the child has become part of the conventional wisdom of social policy makers and social workers. In the Children and Young Persons Act 1963, it became a duty for local authorities to give such advice, guidance and assistance, as might prevent the break-up of families and the reception of children into the care of the local authority. This responsibility has been assumed by local authorities with varying degrees of enthusiasm and conviction. There are great variations both in the proportion of working time which child care staff devote to preventive work[7] and in the use which departments make of their power to use cash payments to avoid the necessity of taking children into care.[8] Society is much more convinced of the fact that family life is important and that families should generally be kept together, than it is of how or to what extent society can involve itself in achieving this. Wynn's important study[9] shows just how confused and inconsistent society is about the nature and extent of its responsibility for 'other people's children'.

Another very relevant factor is the changing roles of men and women in our society. A number of studies have shown increasing participation by men in the care of their children. Gavron found that in the middle-class families in her admittedly small sample, 44 per cent of the fathers would, and did, 'do everything' for their young children. Only 4 per cent of fathers were judged to be 'non-participant'.[10] John and Elizabeth Newson found 79 per cent of their Nottingham mothers, a mixed social class group, received or could call on substantial help from their husbands in caring for their babies. The Newsons rated 52 per cent of fathers as highly participant, 27 per cent as moderately participant and only 21 per cent as non-participant.[11]

These changes have made it less unthinkable than it once was for a man to contemplate trying to bring up a family on his own. Indicative of this change in attitudes is the fact that some 65 per cent of a random sample of Nottingham people thought a father quite capable of bringing up children on his own. A generation ago it would have seemed almost out of the question for a man to try to look after his children by himself. Now many more men regard it as their duty to do so, if faced with such a responsibility. This trend is likely to continue for there are signs that the roles of men and women will be increasingly interchangeable in the future.[12] Evidence in social policy for this change in roles is the increasing discussion of how the courts should decide which parent should have custody of the children in divorce cases. In the past custody almost automatically went to the mother and there was little scope for discussion. Today it is increasingly recognized that there is a genuine decision to be made, a decision described by Lord Simon of Glaisdale as 'the most important and difficult jurisdiction a judge has to exercise'.[13] Further evidence of this change in attitudes is the fact that the Supplementary Benefits Commission is prepared to pay an allowance to fathers left to care for their children so they can, if necessary, stay at home to look after them.[14]

The situation, therefore, is a rather complicated one. There are conflicting trends in the causes leading to motherlessness. While maternal deaths have declined there has been an increase in divorces and separations. Whether the final result is more or less motherless families it is impossible to ascertain. There have also been conflicting

3

trends in the factors making for the survival of motherless families as independent units. A number of factors have combined to make it less possible for the extended family to provide the support and help it provided in the past. In contrast to this, greater male participation in child rearing, the wider ownership of washing machines and the development of convenience foods have made it less unthinkable for a father to attempt to bring up children on his own. We cannot say whether the increased willingness and ability on the part of fathers to continue to care for their children on their own has compensated for the declining ability of the extended family to help and support its motherless members.[15]

In the past, however, the efficiency of the extended family at providing substitute mothers concealed the nature and extent of the problem of motherlessness. Today motherlessness is much more obvious as a social problem. Fathers caring for children on their own are more visible than motherless children absorbed into other family units or cared for by unmarried female relatives.

The size of the problem

Although precise information about trends in the numbers of motherless families is not available there are certain pointers. One example is in the figures for the reception of children into the care of local authority Children's Departments because of the mother's death or desertion. In recent years there has been a considerable increase. In the year ending 31 March 1960 the number was 3,954.[16] In the year ending 31 March 1970 it was 5,991.[17] The number of children received into care because of the death of the mother has increased a little from 609 in 1959–60, to 750 in 1969–70, but the real increase has been in receptions into care because of the mother's desertion – from 3,345 to 5,241. This does not, of course, necessarily mean that motherlessness due to desertion has increased. It may simply indicate a greater willingness by fathers to use the services of Children's Departments or the increasing inability of families to help. In view, however, of the increased emphasis in Children's Departments on taking steps to prevent children coming into care this trend is suggestive. In the year ending 31 March 1970 there were a further 1,458 children who came into care because of the mother's long-term illness.[18]

There are also other motherless children received into care who appear elsewhere in the official statistics because motherlessness is

4

not the immediate precipitating factor. There is no official information, however, about how many of the children in the care of local authorities are motherless or for how many motherlessness was the real underlying reason for admission. Once can, however, gather some useful evidence from relevant research. Packman studied the reasons for applications for children to be received into the care of the local authority and committals to care in a sample of authorities in a six-month period in 1962. In 10 per cent of cases the prime reason was the mother's desertion, in 2 per cent the mother's death.[19] This figure of 12 per cent of admissions to care as due to motherlessness compares with a figure of under 10 per cent of admissions as being due to the mother's death or desertion in the official figures for 1961–2.[20] So it suggests that the official figures may underestimate motherlessness as a reason for reception into care.

The 1966 Sample Census showed that there were 104,480 motherless families in England and Wales containing a total of 174,510 children or 1·67 per family.[21] In 58·8 per cent of the families there was only one child and in 30·1 per cent there was a child under the age of five. Table 1 shows the marital status of the fathers.

TABLE 1   Motherless families according to the marital status of the father (1966 Sample Census)

Single	10,030
Married	41,320
Widowed	39,090
Divorced	14,040
Total	104,480

The weakness of the census statistics on one-parent families is that they fail to distinguish between unmarried parents living with grandparents and those who are cohabiting. It seems that a high proportion of the 10,000 unmarried fathers live in households with another adult – possibly the child's mother. If in the census a cohabiting couple do not describe themselves as husband and wife, any children are inevitably classified as being in a one-parent family – fatherless if they are described as the children of the mother and motherless if described as children of the father. Thus some of the one-parent families identified by the census are in fact two-parent families. On the other hand many genuine one-parent families with unmarried mother or father are not identified as separate families if they live with grandparents.

There are other sources from which information about the extent of motherlessness can be gleaned. The national survey of a representative group of 5,386 legitimate children born between 3 and 9 March 1946 looked at their familial situation in 1950.[22] By then 6·8 per cent of the children lived in broken families but this included families which were parted by work or illness. If this group is excluded the proportion of children in broken homes falls to 4·4 per cent. Of the total number of children living in broken families, 84·1 per cent were living with their mothers, only 6·5 per cent with their fathers. The rest were with relatives, foster parents or in institutions of one sort or another. Only a tiny minority – a dozen or so – were motherless according to our criteria.

Rutter quotes unpublished figures from the national survey of the numbers of children who had lost a parent by death at certain ages.[23] At age six years three months, 2·66 per cent of children had lost one or other parent, at eight-and-a-half the figure was 3·65 per cent, by ten years nine months it was 4·75 per cent. At all ages paternal deaths were found to exceed maternal deaths by between 50 per cent and 100 per cent. The fact that the mothers of something like 1·5 per cent of these children had died by the time their children left primary school is perhaps surprising.

More recent information about the family situation of primary school children is available in the research done for the Plowden Committee on Primary Education.[24] In a random sample of families one or both natural parents was missing from at least 8 per cent of the homes in which interviews were conducted. This is likely to be an understatement, if anything, because respondents may not always have told interviewers whether either or both parents were not the child's natural parents. The broken homes fell into the following categories (percentages):

Natural mother only – no father or father substitute	4
Natural father only – no mother or mother substitute	1
Natural mother – substitute father	1
Natural father – substitute mother	1
Neither natural parent	1
	8

If 1 per cent of primary school children are in motherless families the figure for all children will probably be considerably higher. What is interesting is that the proportion of motherless families in the United States is very similar to the situation in this country. The 1960 Census showed that 12·5 per cent of families in the United States were headed by a single parent; 10 per cent of these – 1·25 per cent of all families – were headed by a father on his own.[25]

The meaning of motherlessness

Motherlessness means very different things to different families. The factors which affect its meaning and implications are very varied. Much depends on the age of the children and the size of the family, on the cause of motherlessness and the events which preceded the mother's death or departure. Equally important are the proximity of kin and their ability to help, the quality of relations with neighbours, the availability of social services and the degree of understanding of employers. The father's income, the nature of his job, the length and stability of the marriage are also relevant. Motherlessness will unite some families; it will divide others. It may bring blessed relief to the father and a chance of a fuller life for the children or it may be unrelieved tragedy. To some it will mean a combination of these – relief to the father and tragedy to the children, for example – and the result will be ambivalence and uncertainty of feeling. Some fathers are able to continue in employment and the pattern of the family's life remains outwardly unaltered. Some find it a struggle to combine work and the care of children but manage to do so. Others find themselves compelled to give up work thus suffering a drop in income, and often weakening their own self-respect and risking the good opinion of their friends and neighbours who fail to understand their problems.

To the children it may mean a rougher, harsher life without a mother's gentleness and care. It may mean drabness or poverty. It may mean a father so busy with combining work and domestic duties that he is always tired and impatient and without time to relax with his children. For girls it means the absence of a model in the family. The loss of one parent, say Glasser and Navarre, 'produces a structural distortion in the communications between the child and the adult world and, since such communication is a factor in the development of the self image, of social skills, and of an image of the total society, the totality of the child's possible development is also distorted'.[26]

7

Research in the past concentrated on the social problem aspect of broken homes, with the result that studies tended to explore whether delinquency, emotional instability, mental retardation and so on were more prevalent among children coming from broken homes than from normal homes. Bowlby, referring to this literature, concluded that 'the concept of the broken home is scientifically unsatisfactory and should be abandoned. It includes too many heterogeneous conditions having very different psychological effects.' He recommends the replacement of the concept of the broken home by 'the concept of the disturbed parent-child-relationship which is frequently, but not necessarily associated with it'.[27] Other writers have maintained that in spite of the differences among the various types of broken families there are enough common elements in the social situation in which they find themselves to warrant generalization about their situation. Marsden discusses the 'common bond of fatherlessness' which creates an underclass of fatherless families who 'felt trapped and desperate, and . . . had ceased to look to society for their standards, seeking comfort where they could find it.'[28] Schlesinger refers to the 'uncertain, not-married-and-not-unmarried status' of one-parent heads of families and concludes: 'They don't seem to fit any of the normal social patterns. They are the self-styled "fifth wheels" of society.'[29]

Whatever else it may mean, motherlessness results in a family pattern which is atypical. This affects not only relationships within the family but also relationships between the family and the outside world. It creates a new social situation full of ambiguities which places one-parent families outside the normal stream of life. Marsden discusses this problem in relation to fatherless families. Without a man, he says, 'the mother no longer fitted into patterns of behaviour in the family nor could new patterns easily evolve'.[30] Fatherlessness involved a shift in all the family's relationships with kin and community. The mothers he studied frequently reported this feeling that relationships had changed. They felt stigmatized and ostracized. In part these feelings were the product of their anomalous family status, in part the product of their dependence on National Assistance. In part, too, they may have been the outcome of the mother's own self doubts and uncertainties but Marsden found considerable evidence that they were firmly based on real changes in the behaviour of other people towards the mothers and their children.[31]

Goode reports the same social ambiguity in his study of divorced women. When a relative had been bereaved there were fairly clearly defined patterns of behaviour expected of the rest of the family. In the divorce situation there were no comparable patterns hallowed by convention and simplified by shared expectations and attitudes on both sides.[32]

Similarly there are no established, accepted patterns of behaviour which the motherless can adopt or which other people – kin and the wider society – can adopt towards motherless families. Depending on the reason for motherlessness public attitudes may vary from ostracism to sympathy, from admiration to condemnation. It is the loose and undefined nature of the new social situation which creates problems of ambiguity and isolation.

Problems of method and interpretation

In our study we set out to collect data on five types of motherless families – widowed, divorced, separated legally or otherwise, families where the wife was hospitalized for at least six months and families where the wife was committed to prison for at least nine months. We did not interview fathers where there were no children under sixteen at home nor did we interview where a father had a stable cohabitee, i.e. someone who has been living with him for the last year or more. The families were from the East Midlands, i.e. Derby and Derbyshire, Leicester and Leicestershire, Nottingham and Nottinghamshire, Rutland, Lincoln and Lincolnshire (Lindsey, Kesteven and Holland) and Grimsby – an area with a total population at the 1966 Census of 3·6 million.

The problems of obtaining a sufficiently large and representative sample in studies of special population groups are well known to researchers.[33] With little idea of the extent of motherlessness we had to cast our net fairly wide to be sure of securing a reasonable number of interviews. From the start we had to accept the fact that we could never secure a sample which we could prove to be representative, owing to our ignorance about the incidence of motherlessness and the characteristics of the motherless. So there was no way of knowing what a representative sample of such families would look like. We have attempted to show how typical our families are of the population as a whole in income, standards of housing, size of family and so on, but this tells us nothing of how typical our particular sample is of motherless families in general. We can only hope that nearly 600 families from such a wide and varied area, who differ so much one from another, are not too atypical of motherless families as a whole.

In August 1969 we wrote to all Children's, Education, Health and Probation Departments in the East Midlands explaining the nature and purpose of our study and asking for information about any motherless families known to the department. In the weeks which followed we visited all the departments and explained in more detail the help we were seeking. Almost without exception, departments expressed their interest in the study and agreed to help us by providing names and addresses. We also contacted likely voluntary agencies such as the NSPCC and at a later stage we wrote to long-stay hospitals asking for the names of any families which were motherless according to our definitions.

The danger, of course, in a sample collected from social welfare agencies is that it will be overloaded with families with problems, and that families who are coping satisfactorily on their own will be under-represented. In spite, however, of the new emphasis on preventive work with families in the Children and Young Persons Act 1963 this very vulnerable group of families was not well known to Children's Departments. We found Health and Education Departments a more fruitful source of information, and it is reasonable to assume that their referrals would be less likely to be families with problems than names submitted by Children's Departments. In theory at least Health Departments should know through Health Visitors of all motherless families with children under five, not just those experiencing difficulties. Similarly most schools should know any motherless children on their books, though such children would not always be known to the Education Department as well.

So the families referred to us by local authority departments are likely to be a biased sample but this bias should be limited because of the proportion referred by 'universal' services rather than 'social work' services. We also got names of motherless families from the Department of Health and Social Security. The Family Allowance Branch of the Department extracted for us the names of all fathers in our area whose names appeared on Family Allowance Order Books. At first sight this looks like a good sampling frame. Though it helped to give us a better balanced sample it has certain weaknesses. All one-child families or families where there is only one child under compulsory school-leaving age are, of course, excluded, because they are not eligible for family allowances. As there is often also a considerable time lag in altering Order Books when the mother has died or departed, this sample would be unlikely to include many families which had recently become motherless. There is also no guarantee that all Allowance Order Books are altered when renewed, and as we found, the fact of a father's name appearing on the Order Book was no guarantee of motherlessness.

The Department of Health and Social Security also made available to us a list of all fathers in the area drawing Supplementary Benefit in order to stay at home and look after the children. This was obviously an up-to-date and reliable list. Table 2 shows the number and type of cases referred to us by different agencies.

TABLE 2   Number of families referred as motherless according to referring agency and reason for motherlessness

Referring agency	Number of referrals	Widowed	Separated, divorced	Hospital, prison, not known
Family Allowance	526	203	322	1
Supplementary Benefit	130	43	80	7
LA Education Department	234	112	116	6
LA Health Department	192	100	76	16
LA Children's Department	83	26	57	0
Probation Department	20	6	13	1
Other	38	11	27	0
Total	1,223	501	691	31

Our original aim was to have two samples – a retrospective one of families which had been motherless for two years or more and a current sample of families made motherless in the three months immediately before our study began. Our idea was to interview the current sample six months or so after they had become motherless and again a year later. We hoped in this way to be able to examine in detail the problems these families faced at the beginning, and to follow them through their early difficulties. Then a year later we

11

could see what changes had taken place and how the family had adapted. The retrospective sample would, we felt, give more perspective on the problems of motherlessness.

In fact our current sample never accumulated to a satisfactory size. Local authorities, as well as the Department of Health and Social Security, were eager to help us by a once for all search through their records for all motherless families known to them. This was easy to authorize and relatively easy to execute. To ask these agencies to refer any motherless families as they became known to them over a three-month period was to ask for something much more difficult. It depended on busy individual field staff remembering that this information was required. Because our study covered such a wide area we were not able to make the frequent visits to local offices or establish the personal relationships with field staff which are probably the prerequisites of such continuing referrals. When the non-accumulation of the current sample became clear – this was before we started interviewing – we decided to put the two samples together and use the same interview schedule for all fathers.

In so doing we almost certainly lost a valuable element in the study. Goode supports this view. In his study he describes it as 'a major failure in the research design' that he used a true cross-section instead of a time panel. What he should have done, he says, was to follow up a cohort of mothers and interview them repeatedly over the period of the study. That he didn't do this was the result of 'simple impatience and lack of money'.[34] Our ideas were sound but administrative difficulties defeated us. Even though we analyse the material according to length of motherlessness and so get some perspective on the changing nature of the problems, this is really no substitute for the detailed information we might have gathered about the immediate problems, the decisions which were taken in the first days and weeks, and the fathers who decided that they had no alternative but to let the children go into the care of the local authority.

Our study as it stands is a study of fathers who have managed or are managing to cope with the problems of motherlessness, and have preserved the family unit. The current sample would have given us valuable information about the fathers who found that the situation was beyond them. What we recount is a success story – mostly of fathers who are successfully living with problems, or overcoming them or who *have* overcome them and can look back reflectively on their considerable achievements. We have no information on the misery of motherless families where the fathers did not try to care, or tried and failed; families where the children suffered and will suffer from the complete break-up of the family.

The fact that we relied on such a large number of agencies to refer motherless families to us meant that we could not lay down one single system for departments to follow when contacting fathers and referring them to us. Three different approaches were used. First, the contracting-out method: departments wrote to fathers informing them of the research project and asking them to reply only if they did not wish to be interviewed. Second, the contracting-in method: departments wrote to fathers, or sometimes visited them, asking them if they wished to take part in the research. Third, the no-obligation method; where departments wrote to fathers explaining the purpose of the research and informing them that their name had been given to the research team but they were under no obligation to take part if they did not wish to be interviewed.

In view of the length of the interviews, averaging two-and-a-half hours, the distance our interviewers had to travel to contact fathers, and the fathers' family commitments, we felt that it was right for interviewers to make appointments rather than simply arrive and try to secure an interview there and then or secure an appointment for a future occasion. Interviewers therefore wrote to fathers suggesting a time and fathers had to reply to the letter only if the appointment suggested was not convenient. If the interviewer heard nothing, she was instructed to call and ask for an interview. It was agreed with interviewers that if there was no reply they should call on three occasions at different times of day before classing the father as a non-contact. On the whole the system worked well.

Inevitably in a study such as this the response rate will tend to seem low. The issues to be explored are delicate and seem likely to be painful. Many respondents will be unwilling to be reminded of experiences which they have tried to forget. The postal approach, which was the way in which some fathers were approached initially, seldom produces a good response. An approach by social service workers known to the fathers may well have encouraged them to participate but on the other hand busy field workers with many other concerns are unlikely to urge the value of the exercise with quite the eloquence which the researcher himself might bring to his request for an interview.

Table 3 shows the nature of our referrals and the number in each group actually interviewed. Of 1,223 names referred to us a substantial number were, in fact, not motherless according to our definition. Table 4 gives an analysis of the fathers we did not interview. A total of 183 families were not motherless because the father had remarried, the mother had returned or because the father had a stable cohabitee.

TABLE 3   Referrals and interviews according to reason for motherlessness

	Referred	Interviewed
Widowed	501	281
Divorced or separated	691	303*
Other	31	4
Total	1,223	588

* 217 separated cases and 86 divorced.

TABLE 4   Analysis of non-response

Reason	Number of fathers
Family not motherless	183
No children at home	68
No children under sixteen	22
Father gone away/not known	85
Non-contact (three visits)	47
Father refused	208
Other	22
Total	635

In sixty-eight cases there were no children at home – they were in care or at boarding school and in twenty-two cases there were no children under school-leaving age. In eighty-five cases the father had moved and there was either no known address or only an address

14

outside the East Midlands. In these cases we did not feel it was worth-while in terms of time and expense to pursue the fathers. Excluding these groups our response rate was 62 per cent. It therefore compares quite favourably with Marsden's 56 per cent rate.[35] Marris in his study of widows did rather better with a rate of just over 70 per cent.[36] He had, however, the advantage that his study was a local one. It also seems that the widowed produce a higher response rate than other comparable groups. This was certainly our experience.

We cannot say at all precisely why fathers refused to be interviewed. From their doorstep comments to our interviewers, however, it seemed that there were both those fathers who had settled down so well that they did not want to discuss a situation which was not problematic to them, and those who had not come to terms with motherlessness and did not want to expose themselves to an interview which they anticipated would be painful.

We used some twenty-five interviewers scattered over our area. Most were captive wives and had been social workers before domesticity claimed them. Most were graduates or had social work qualifications of some kind. All were interested in the research for what it was seeking to find out, not just for the pin-money it offered. They were carefully briefed before they started interviewing and in addition were all given a set of notes explaining possible points of difficulty in the questionnaire. We saw most of them in groups of three or four for this briefing and we saw the groups again a month later to discuss problems and reactions. After this we kept in close touch with them by telephone and letter.

The use of social workers as research interviewers is fraught with difficulties. It can be argued that because of their training and experience in interpersonal relationships they are very suitable as research interviewers. On the other hand it can be argued that because they are professionally committed to providing help to people, they find it difficult to restrict their relationship simply to gathering information. This is particularly the case with practising social workers and with certain types of action research projects involving experimental groups who are denied casework support.[37] Though our interviewers were not full-time practising social workers, we discussed these possible risks with them. To deal with possible situations where fathers needed advice on practical problems, interviewers carried with them various pamphlets explaining people's rights to social service benefits which they gave to fathers. Where interviewers felt strongly that a family was in dire need of help, material or otherwise, they could refer the family to the appropriate department provided they got the father's consent and our agreement.

The actual interview required skill, patience and sympathetic understanding. Many of the questions explored areas which were likely to be painful for the fathers. At the end of many of the interviews, however, fathers thanked the interviewers for giving them the chance to talk about their situation in a way which they had not been able to do before. For some fathers the interview was clearly a genuinely therapeutic experience. Goode found the same in his study, that for many the interview 'served as a cathartic experience allowing them a release of emotion and the opportunity of discussing matters which had long been troubling them, but which they could not ordinarily discuss even with relatives and close friends'.[38] A number of our fathers had so much to say that the questionnaire was only completed after two or three lengthy sessions sometimes amounting to six or eight hours in all.

At the end of the interviewing we were left with an uneasy question in our minds. Can people interview successfully in a study of this kind unless they are deeply and continuously involved in the planning and thinking behind the project? We asked lots of open-ended questions. We knew what we were getting at and we explained to the interviewers the point and purpose of the questions and what they were to 'probe' for. However good the questionnaire design, however good the briefing, however good the interviewers, there is a vast difference between using a questionnaire which *you* have helped to design for purposes which *you* have helped to clarify and using someone else's questionnaire to explore their hypotheses. This was a problem which we felt very keenly. It was not a fault in the technique of our interviewers. It is a weakness, we suspect, in all studies which depend on the infrastructure of large research projects and seek qualitative information. The progress of science, Darwin once observed, is hampered more by incorrect observation than by poor theory. The truth he was expressing is very relevant to the social sciences. Too often 'interviewing' in social surveys is seen as a routine task which can be safely delegated while the experts sharpen the tools of analysis. It depends, of course, on what the survey is about. If it is seeking to explore complex areas of individual and family behaviour and reactions, then it demands a clarity of purpose and a consistency of approach which cannot reasonably be expected of a large team of interviewers. Such a task can only be carried out by a small group who are deeply involved in the study and working closely together, who know each others' minds, who can talk frequently together and are clear about their aims. The ideal perhaps is the one-man study – of which Marsden's, of course, is an obvious example – but if the study seeks quantitative as well as qualitative information then the sample almost inevitably will be larger than one man can hope to tackle.

Our study is in many respects a study not so much of the problems of motherless families as of the fathers' appreciation of the problems. We do gather objective data about the families but a lot of our information is the fruit of the fathers' interpretation of the situation. We have, for example, no objective measurement of the children's adjustment, only the fathers' views – views which are more likely to be favourable than unfavourable. One admits more readily to success even if with qualifications, than to failure. Most fathers, generally quite rightly, felt a certain pride and satisfaction at what they had accomplished. This difficulty occurs in many areas of the study.

Closely connected with this problem is the question of what constitutes deprivation. Is a family to be classed as deprived if the father expresses no feeling of deprivation? Many of our fathers expressed themselves satisfied with conditions which, objectively considered, were examples of severe deprivation. Many, for example, expressed no views about vast drops in income due to motherlessness.[39] This acceptance of things as they were did not only apply to material deprivation. Many fathers assumed crushing domestic burdens and accepted narrowing restrictions on their own and their children's lives without a murmur. Runciman's discussion of relative deprivation is obviously and clearly relevant to this kind of deprivation as well as to more obvious material inequalities. His argument is that a sense of deprivation is less likely to arise when deprivation is seen as unavoidable. What is needed for contentment is not ease, but an acceptance that things cannot, could not and will not be otherwise than they are.[40]

Another difficulty which arises in a study of this kind is that questions which are significant for the investigator are often meaningless for the respondent. This is more than a problem of questionnaire design. Behaviour which to the specialist may be indicative of maladjustment or deprivation may be incomprehensible to the layman and may therefore be ignored or not even noticed, or if noted it may not be seen as significant. We asked fathers how their children had adjusted to motherlessness. It was a difficult question to put in a way which was likely to be generally meaningful. To answer it fathers had to have both some idea of what they considered good and poor adjustment, and to make certain generalized assessments of their children's adjustment on the basis of specific items of behaviour. This was something many simply did not or could not do. They mentioned examples of behaviour which were clearly indicative of stress or disturbance and yet they replied in positive terms to general questions about the children's adjustment. The fathers' concrete way of looking at their children's behaviour and their inability to generalize made it difficult for them – and us – to make the kind of assessment which we were seeking.

A problem common to any study which asks about the past is the fallibility of people's recollections. This is a problem on at least two levels. People may quite simply be unable to remember details of feelings and situations which happened months or even years before – particularly when connected with conditions of extreme stress. The respondent may not know the truth well enough to tell it. There is the further point which Goode makes that 'a major element in the adjustment process, for any type of emotional crisis, may be the restructuring of reality into a new form that is more acceptable to the new life patterns the individual is working out'.[41] Our questions may not be able to pierce this interpreted reality and find the underlying reality of how things were seen and felt at the time. In the replies to his questions to ex-wives about their feelings towards their ex-husbands, Goode talks of a 'bias towards indifference' in the answers. Some feelings are difficult to admit to one's self and we were asking about areas of past life where this bias was very likely to be present.

This is perhaps an area where social work interviewing is more likely to get the father to talk freely about his past experiences than social research interviewing. The social worker has no structured questionnaire to adhere to, no need to make notes during the interview and is not attempting to get answers to a multitude of very different questions in one interview. In their comments, our interviewers occasionally referred to the father 'struggling to hold his emotions back', to the father's difficulty in expressing his 'true feelings to the full' because of the structured interview situation. Marsden was attempting to deal with such problems by adopting a freer line of approach to his mothers: no notes were taken during the interview apart from factual information and no structured questionnaire was used apart from the fact that certain areas were to be covered in all interviews. Because of the large sample and the number of interviewers involved, this approach was not practicable in our survey. We would have no guarantee that our interviewers would cover all the areas fully, that their probing would not reflect their views and prejudices (thus affecting the father's replies), and that they would be able to record accurately later on what was said during an emotionally charged interview lasting two-and-a-half hours. These problems obviously exist, but perhaps not to the same extent, even when the number of interviewers used is very small.

The use of a large number of open-ended questions was inevitable in a pioneering study which attempted to explore fathers' feelings and adjustment to motherlessness. The coding[42] of the replies to open-ended questions presented us with one of the major problems in this research. We had first of all to design a coding frame that coped satisfactorily with the replies of most fathers and secondly to ensure that our coders understood and applied the coding frame correctly. We based our coding frame on the replies of a cross-section of fifty fathers, tested it and re-drafted it several times before it was ready for use by the coders. We briefed our coders on the purposes of the research and we discussed with them problems of coding. The first week of coding was used for training purposes and for testing our coding frame with people who had not taken any part in drawing it up. Because of the length of the questionnaire we felt that we would achieve greater accuracy by training our coders to specialize on either the first or the second half of the questionnaire. Having considered the proposition that every questionnaire should be double-coded and having rejected it mainly on financial grounds, we arranged that every coder's fourth questionnaire should be checked by another coder. Differences of opinion were resolved by one of the four members of the research team who also acted as general supervisors and advisers.

In the early stages of the project when we were formulating our ideas and drafting the questionnaire we used radio and the Press to invite motherless families to write to us about their problems and experiences. Anne Allen of the *Sunday Mirror* also helped us by writing a feature, 'When a man has to bring up children on his own', and inviting readers to write to her so that she could pass their letters on to us. From these accounts we were able to get ideas and guidelines and a greater understanding of some of the issues which needed to be explored. Subsequently we gathered some further information from fathers who had written to us, much of which was extremely useful.

As the interviewing programme progressed and we studied the completed questionnaires it became very clear that the way fathers viewed their problems and what they felt should be done to help them were coloured by the values and attitudes which they thought existed in society at large. It seemed to us that it would be a useful exercise to find out what community attitudes were towards mother-less and fatherless families, how other members of the community saw the problems, what they thought fathers or mothers should do when left to care for children on their own, whether they felt a lone mother or father could provide for all of a child's needs and so on.

To gather this information we interviewed a random sample of the population from three areas in Nottingham, a predominantly middle-class area, a pre-war council estate and a redevelopment area of old terraced houses. We drew a sample from the electoral roll and interviewed 359 people – a response rate of 67 per cent. Most of the interviewing was done by students from the Department of Applied Social Science, University of Nottingham, as a post-examination exercise. The sample is not truly representative of the general popula-tion. Women are over-represented and so are social classes I and II. Men and classes IV and V are correspondingly under-represented. Nevertheless the study gave us useful background information on a number of issues.

Finally, a brief account of the issues and problems involved in projects such as this where government departments finance research may be of interest to other researchers. Our research was financed by the Department of Health and Social Security. The interest of the Department in this study, however, extended beyond the normal interests of a sponsor and paymaster. When we began work a Govern-ment Committee on One-Parent Families was about to be set up to look into the problems of such families and make recommendations.[43] This research was therefore seen very clearly by the Department of Health and Social Security as having the aim of providing the com-mittee with information about the circumstances of motherless families.

The first question that had to be clarified was the precise aim of the research. The Department saw the aim primarily in practical terms – to provide information on the financial, occupational and housing circumstances of fathers which could be of use to the One-Parent Committee. Since it was the first study of its kind, we had no hypotheses to test. We saw the research in much broader terms as an investigation into a previously unexplored type of family situation. With the death or desertion of the mother, a new structural situation in the family is created which makes new demands upon the various family members. It also creates a situation which requires a redefinition of the relationships between the new family unit and individuals and groups in the community. The central figure in this new structure of relationships is the father and we wanted to know how he felt, how he reacted and how he coped in his new role.

We felt that it was only through a close study of the fathers' feelings and reactions that the other issues could be understood. In this belief we were following what Marris found in his study of widows. 'As soon as I began to plan the study in detail', he writes, 'I became convinced that emotional reactions to bereavement must profoundly affect her attitude to all her problems.' He goes on to argue that unless account is taken of the widow's feelings, 'any insight into the social consequences of widowhood would be very superficial'.[44]

It was possible to reconcile these different approaches to the study but it meant that a number of questions were added to the questionnaire which from our point of view were not strictly necessary. This meant that the questionnaire was not only very long but that its questions ranged from the detailed and practical to the broad and theoretical. Depth had to be sacrificed to breadth. It was possible to deal with the problem of the length of the questionnaire by asking our interviewers to use their discretion whether to interview the father in one or more interviews. We have no way of knowing what the effects of the wide range of the questions were on the fathers' responses. We suspect, however, that detailed practical questions may have added to the structured nature of the questionnaire and in this way may have had an inhibiting effect on fathers' responses.

The next practical question was how best to maintain the 'very delicate and continuous contact between the department and the researcher' which Sir William Armstrong has described as essential if government-commissioned research is to be of maximum value.[45] A two-tier system was set up: a steering committee made up of members from the various sub-sections of the Social Security section of the Department of Health and Social Security, the researchers and Professor D. C. Marsh. The aim of the committee was to discuss matters of policy and generally to act as a watchdog on the progress of the research. This committee proved useful during the first three months when the project was being designed and then gradually receded into the background as the project ran fairly smoothly. The second tier of the administrative arrangements for on-going contact was between ourselves and the research section of the Ministry. We found the advice and help of the research section extremely valuable,

c

particularly on technical matters regarding the workings of the Supplementary Benefit scheme. Basically, however, the research was planned and carried out by us and we are, of course, responsible for all its shortcomings.

As regards publication, the Department of Health and Social Security recognizes the freedom of researchers undertaking research sponsored by the Department to publish their findings. It does, however, ask them to afford the Department the opportunity to see and comment on their work before publication though the researchers' obligation is limited to considering the comments. In view of the fact that considerable departmental time and money had been expended on this project it is only right and proper that the Department should have this right and the final draft of the report has benefited from its comments. The only two points on which the Department insisted were that no comments should appear in the book that would identify individual respondents and that it should be made clear that a certain procedure was followed in the survey work to avoid pressure on respondents and to ensure confidentiality – in fact two of the basic canons of research methodology.[46]

In trying to present the answers given by our fathers in a systematic and readable form, we have had to impose some order and synthesis which may have resulted in certain distortion of the picture. The problem is a fundamental one for the scholar trying to give literary form to his findings.

> The aim of writing [says Matza[47]] is to create coherence. The risk is that coherence will be imposed on an actual disorder and a forgery thus produced. No way of avoiding that risk exists since to write is to take on the task of bringing together and organizing materials. Thus the only legitimate question about a work is the *measure* of imposition, or the amount of forgery, the only offsetting compensation, the possibility of entertainment or illumination.

2 General characteristics of motherless families

We said in chapter 1 that this study presents in many ways a success story – the story of those fathers who have succeeded in caring for their children without the help of a wife. Ours is a retrospective study of fathers who on a certain date were caring for their children. The study does not cover the plight of those fathers who from the start gave up any idea of caring for their children alone, or who tried and failed. For this we needed to collect a sample of families as they became motherless and as we explained in chapter 1 we were unable to obtain such a sample. We consider this bias in our sample very significant and we ask our readers to bear it in mind all through the book. In this chapter we look briefly at some of the general characteristics of our motherless families and then we examine their housing conditions in more detail.

The vast majority of our fathers, 91 per cent, were born in Great Britain, 4·1 per cent in Ireland and the remaining 4·9 per cent were born abroad with Poland and the West Indies contributing half of this proportion. Interestingly enough the fathers born abroad had been in the country for a considerable number of years prior to the interview. None of them had been in this country for less than four years, 3·8 per cent had been here for four to nine years and the remaining 96·2 per cent for ten years or more.

Marital history

Like the rest of the population, the majority of our fathers had married young – 48 per cent before the age of twenty-five and 82 per cent before the age of thirty. A greater proportion of the separated and the divorced than of the widowed were already married by twenty-five. Also fathers in social classes I and II were less likely to marry before the age of twenty-five than fathers in other social classes. These figures reflect general trends in the population. Family break-up through separation and divorce is more common among people who marry young than among those who marry later;[1] and the higher the social class the later the age of marriage.[2]

Widowers had not only married at a later age than the separated and the divorced but their marriage had also lasted considerably longer. Of the widowers 57 per cent had been married for fifteen years or more before their wife died or left compared with 30 per cent of the separated, 23 per cent of the divorced and 42 per cent of the whole sample. This meant that they were older when they lost their wife; 62·3 per cent were over forty compared with 34·1 per cent of the separated and 25·6 per cent of the divorced. It also meant that their families were more likely to have been completed and so were likely to be rather larger. As we shall be seeing later in the book widowers differ in many respects from the other two groups in the way they view and cope with their situation and these demographic differences may be some of the many interrelated factors that account for this.

Married life involves the establishment of a pattern of relationships between the two partners which, with the passage of time, increasingly dominates their life. Thus Elliott and Merrill suggest that the effects of divorce on the family 'may be less severe in a short marriage because the habit patterns have not become deeply incorporated in the personalities of the spouses. In marriages that have continued for a long time, the habits may be so strong that it is more disorganizing to break the marriage than to continue it.'[3] This may help to explain why the divorce rate is at its peak in marriages which have lasted between five and nine years and falls thereafter. It also suggests that when it does happen it may have widespread and profound effects on the family. There is no good reason why the same argument should not be applied to marriage break-up through desertion or death. In brief, then, the emotional effects of the loss of the wife are likely to have been felt more strongly by the widowed than the other fathers, not only because of the fact that death is more traumatic than divorce or desertion but also because widowers were an older group and had been married longer than the other fathers at the onset of motherlessness.

TABLE 5   Years of marriage prior to motherlessness (per cent)
(n = 586)

Under 1	0·8
1–3	3·9
4–6	10·4
7–9	13·8
10–14	28·7
15 and over	42·4

Motherlessness is not necessarily a permanent condition. Some motherless families remain so indefinitely; others, however, return to the normal two-parent family unit either through the mother's return or the father's cohabitation or re-marriage. There are strong economic, child care and social pressures for the normalization of the family unit which we shall be discussing later on in the book.[4] On the other hand there are child-care problems in re-marriage in the sense that children may find it difficult to accept the new parent and vice versa.[5] Still other motherless families disappear altogether as units when the father gives up and the children are cared for by others. These pressures towards the re-establishment of the two-parent family unit on the one hand and towards complete family disruption on the other may help to explain the fact that the average number of years for which families in our sample had been motherless was only 3·7. Almost 60 per cent of our families had been motherless for less than four years and only 4·7 per cent for ten years or more. The length of the period of motherlessness was highest among the divorced and lowest among the separated. It is difficult to be certain about the reasons for these variations. The explanation for the shorter length of motherlessness among the separated, however, probably lies in the spontaneous recreation of the two-parent family unit resulting from the mother's return. Separation between parents is often temporary; divorce and death, on the other hand, result in a permanent break. Widowhood comes later than divorce and therefore the period of motherlessness for the widowed is likely to be shorter than for the divorced since our definition of motherless families excluded those where all the children had left school.

25

TABLE 6   Years of motherlessness (per cent) (n = 588)

Under 1	15·0
1–3	44·7
4–6	23·0
7–9	12·6
10 and over	4·7

Children

The average number of children, single or married, at home or away from home, in our sample was 3·5 per family at the time of motherlessness. No strict comparison with the average size of family in the general population is possible because of a number of biases in our sample. Social classes I and II who generally have smaller families than the rest of the population are under-represented and this will tend to exaggerate the size of the families in our sample. Another bias in the same direction is the under-representation of one-child families. On the other hand our families had not run the twenty-year period of marriage which is usually accepted as the period before which families cannot be taken as having been completed. Had our families run this full twenty-year period, they would probably have been larger. The average number of children for completed families in Great Britain is estimated at 2·22.[6] This figure, however, is based on all families, including childless families, whereas our sample included no such families.

Widowers had slightly more children than the other two groups of fathers but this was most probably due to their longer period of marriage rather than to any other factor. A relationship also existed between social class and the number of children. While 54·5 per cent of fathers in classes I and II had one or two children, the proportion in class III was 37·5 per cent and in classes IV and V, 34·0 per cent. At the other extreme, the proportion of families with five or more children was 6·3 per cent in classes I and II, 22·0 per cent in class III, 26 per cent in classes IV and V and 52·5 per cent for the unemployed. These social-class trends reflect similar social-class differences in the general population and they are due to the same reasons rather than to any special reasons relating to the motherless situation.[7]

What is more important for our study, however, than the total number of children per family is the number of children who were at home when the mother left or died and for whom the father had to bear some responsibility. Very young children are more dependent on the father physically but older children can cause more behaviour problems which make equal, if not greater, demands on the father. Any age limit is arbitrary to an extent and we decided to include all children in the family under the age of eighteen because this is the age of majority and because we felt that the first few years in a young person's working life can make demands on the father though these are perhaps not as great as those of school or pre-school children. Table 7 shows that 2·5 per cent of the fathers we interviewed had no children when their wife left, the reason being that the children were at the time cared for by someone else, mainly the mother or relatives. 45·5 per cent of fathers were left to care for one or two children, 52 per cent for three or more. No fathers in classes I and II were left to care for five or more compared with 15·1 per cent in class III and 17·1 per cent in classes IV and V.

TABLE 7　Number of children at home at the time of motherlessness (per cent) (n = 588)

	Under Eighteen years	Under Five years
None	2·5	46·7
One	9·8	31·0
Two	35·7	17·2
Three	25·3	5·1
Four	11·6	—
Five or more	15·1	—

The presence of children under the age of five makes it more difficult for a father to continue full-time employment because of the scarcity, or sometimes complete absence, of day nursery or other child-minding facilities. Slightly more than half our sample were left with the responsibility of caring for children under the age of five when their wife left or died. Bearing in mind what has already been said about the age of widowed fathers and the length of their marriage vis-à-vis the fathers in the other two groups, it was not unexpected that they were less likely than the other groups to be left with children under five to care for. Social class was again a significant factor; 38·1 per cent of fathers in classes I and II were left to care for children under five compared with 57·2 per cent in class III and 55·2 per cent in classes IV and V. Whereas only 9·4 per cent of fathers in classes I and II had two or more children under five the figure for class III was 24·8 per cent and for classes IV and V, 23·6 per cent.

Obviously the number of children at home at the time of interview was lower than at the time of motherlessness because in the intervening period some ceased to be dependent by our criteria and others left home. Equally important is the fact that the children who were still at home were older at the time of the interview than at the time of motherlessness. Both these changes may have influenced the fathers in such a way that they painted a less problematic picture of motherlessness than actually existed at the beginning. Several fathers indicated in their replies that they had got over the worst period now that their children had grown older. Though we have tried to take account of this factor in our discussion by examining the relationship of the length of motherlessness to our data, we may still have underestimated the seriousness of the situation.

Class and mobility

Our discussion in subsequent chapters shows that our fathers received a great deal of help from their relatives and friends in coping with their situation. This might not have been possible had our fathers been geographically mobile. Over three-quarters of our fathers had lived in the same district for ten years or more and only 7 per cent had lived in the same district for less than four years. Bearing in mind the social class bias of our sample they were not different in this from the general population.[8]

Table 8 shows that compared with the general population our sample contained a lower proportion of classes I and II respondents, a higher proportion of class III and an even higher proportion of unemployed fathers. The under-representation of classes I and II in our sample is most probably due to our sources of referral rather than to any other factor. There is no evidence to show that motherlessness affects classes I and II less than the rest of the general population. It is true that it is more likely for fathers in classes I and II to place their children in boarding schools with the result that they would not appear in our sample. On the other hand it is more likely for children of classes III, IV and V to be received into the care of the

TABLE 8   Social class distribution of fathers at the time of
motherlessness and at the time of interview[9] (per cent)
(n = 587)

Social class	At motherlessness	At interview
I	1·5	1·7
II	9·4	9·4
III	51·9	42·6
IV	25·9	17·9
V	3·9	3·2
Other	1·5	1·9
Unemployed	5·9	23·3

local authority with the same result as far as our sample is concerned.
Both at the time of motherlessness and at the time of interview the
social-class distribution of the widowed and the divorced was similar
and it was higher than that of the separated. This is important for, as
we shall see in subsequent chapters, social class and the reason for
motherlessness are significant factors in the fathers' circumstances
and attitudes and it has not been possible to disentangle their differential effect because of the smallness of our sample.

It was to be expected that motherlessness would, on the whole, lead
to downward social mobility. For 70 per cent of the fathers there was
no change in social class between the time of interview and the time
of motherlessness, for 23 per cent there was downward mobility and
for 7 per cent upward mobility. For upward mobility the change was
between adjacent classes but for downward mobility this was not the
case – more often than not it meant unemployment. It was also true
that fathers in classes I and II were less likely than fathers in other
classes to become unemployed as a result of motherlessness. The
social class of these fathers was less likely to be affected by motherlessness and when it was the effect was not so dramatic as in the case
of fathers in other classes.

Housing

We used five criteria to assess the housing conditions of motherless
families – the tenure of housing, the extent of overcrowding, the

possession of basic amenities, of household consumer goods, and the personal impressions of our interviewers. 'Motherlessness generates conflicting forces which have conflicting effects on housing. In the first place, society does not expect fathers to look after their children when their wife dies or leaves and it may well be that fathers in the most inadequate housing are less likely than other fathers to continue caring for their children. If this selective process is in fact true, then our sample of fathers would have better housing conditions than a truly representative sample of families becoming motherless. On the other hand, motherlessness can have an adverse effect on the tenure of housing and on the physical standards of the house in view of the reduction in earnings that follows motherlessness and the fact that the father has less time and skill to keep the house clean and tidy.

The tenure of housing of our sample showed that motherless families occupy a middle position between the general population and fatherless families. If one considers tenure of housing in economic or in social prestige terms then our fathers' housing was not as good as that of the general population since a smaller proportion of motherless families lived in owner-occupied accommodation. If, however, one considers tenure of housing in terms of security then our fathers were not in a worse position since the proportion that lived in privately rented and other accommodation was not greater than that of the general population.

TABLE 9   Tenure of housing (per cent)

	Owner-occupier	Council housing	Privately rented furnished	unfurnished	Other†
Motherless families	34·5	40·6	2·2	12·4	10·3
East Midlands – general	46·8	25·5	1·9	19·2	6·6
Fatherless families*	27·6	46·2	5·8	19·3	1·0

* Ministry of Social Security, *Circumstances of Families*, HMSO, 1967, Table A.14, p. 152.

† The two main categories were housing rented from relatives and housing provided rent free by employers.

Our measure of overcrowding is the one adopted by the Ministry of Social Security in its study of poverty among families drawing Family Allowances.[10] It is, therefore, disturbing that such a high proportion of motherless families are overcrowded. On one hand one would expect our sample to be less overcrowded than the general population since the Ministry's study did not include one-child families whereas ours did. On the other hand the larger size of our families would have the opposite effect. The explanation of the greater extent of overcrowding among motherless families is possibly

TABLE 10   Extent of overcrowding (per cent)

Motherless families*	27·4
Fatherless families†	31·0
England and Wales†	12·0

*The absence of the mother did not affect the degree of overcrowding since the measure we adopted allocated one room to the parent or parents.
†*Circumstances of Families*, Table VI.9, p. 57.

due to economic and social factors. The father's financial position may make it difficult for him to move to a larger house as the children grow older. His dependence on help from relatives and friends to cope with his situation must also restrict his ability to move to other accommodation. A move to another house, particularly in another district, would mean increased difficulties and possibly result in the father being unable to combine full-time work with the care of his children. Three-quarters of the fathers had not moved house since the loss of their wife. The only significant variation among the various groupings of fathers was that the divorced were more likely to move house than the other fathers, mainly in order to be nearer their friends or relatives. The other main reason for moving given by all fathers was emotional – a desire to leave the house which had so many memories for them.

The fact that a higher proportion of our sample than of the general population in the East Midlands lived in council accommodation, helps to explain the slightly better position of our fathers with regard to the elementary housing facilities shown in Table 11. This may exaggerate the quality of the housing of our fathers since it does not tell us anything about the state of these facilities or the general physical standard of the accommodation. This would have necessitated a detailed study of housing which was beyond us. We confined

TABLE 11   Percentage of families with some facilities

	Bath	Hot water	W.C.
Motherless families	88·7	93·6	98·6
East Midlands	87·6	83·5	97·5

ourselves to asking one further question – were there any structural inadequacies which, in the father's opinion, rendered the accommodation unsuitable for children? A very similar picture emerged – 83 per cent of the fathers said there were no such inadequacies and the remainder who said 'yes' referred mostly to dampness. There were also a few who referred to leaking roofs and the absence of play space for children.

Our criteria for measuring the quality of housing were very basic – in line with other studies on housing and family life. This is also true of our question regarding household consumer goods. We asked fathers whether they possessed any of a list of consumer goods most of which are considered as essential to the good life in our society. The replies show clearly that the unemployed fathers were worse off than other fathers but this is a point we shall pursue at greater length later in this chapter. There were many fathers who lacked more than

TABLE 12   Percentage of fathers having various household consumer goods

	Employed fathers	Unemployed fathers	Total
Washing machine	80·5	66·0	76·7
Spin drier	61·2	41·2	40·5
Electric iron	97·2	88·9	95·0
Vacuum cleaner	84·7	51·6	76·0
Refrigerator	50·7	32·0	45·8
Telephone	21·9	1·3	16·5
Television	98·4	92·1	96·7
Radio	90·7	77·8	87·3

one item and a few who had only one (2·1 per cent) or two (3·8 per cent) of the items. Such cases, few though they were, presented a picture of Dickensian poverty in an age of affluence. The lack of basic consumer goods was indicative of the low financial standing of the family and inevitably made tidiness and cleanliness a difficult, if not impossible, task.

To supplement this information about physical conditions and amenities and the fathers' feelings about their housing we asked our interviewers to rate the material standards and the cleanliness of the house. There were obvious difficulties in this not only because of the subjective nature of such assessments but also because our interviewers saw only part of the house and their visits were expected by the fathers. These assessments are likely to present a picture of housing which is brighter perhaps than everyday reality. Of the houses 65·4 per cent were rated as very good or good on material standards, 17·4 per cent not so good and 17·2 per cent shabby. On cleanliness, 86·0 per cent were rated as very clean or clean, and 14·0 per cent as dirty. Most of our interviewers had had some experience of social work and they had, therefore, seen inadequate housing standards before. They were not middle-class persons blatantly imposing their own standards on working-class housing conditions. Personal bias is inevitable in subjective assessments but we feel that this risk was lessened because of our interviewers' background. That such a high proportion of houses were rated as being unsatisfactory, particularly with regard to material standards, i.e. carpets, lino, chairs, tables, wallpaper, etc., is another indication of the deprivation that motherless families suffer. There were instances where even our experienced ex-social worker interviewers were shocked, as these two extracts show:

'Filthy – especially children's clothing. Half-empty tins of food lying around. The table laid for breakfast was covered with crumbs and sticky. Poverty-stricken. I have never seen such conditions. Children had only sleeveless cotton dresses with nothing underneath although no heating.'

'Poor. Lino on floor was old and cracked. Only half the room nearest the fire was furnished and used. They seem to live on one sofa, two chairs and use one table. All very old and worn. Walls in bad state of repair.'

Perhaps we should let our fathers have the last word with regard to their housing. The vast majority, 90 per cent, were satisfied with their housing and the minority who were not satisfied were divided almost equally between those who felt that their house was too small, or that it was too old and dilapidated, or that the council or landlord had been dilatory with repairs or that the house was in a rough area or too isolated from the rest of the community. Most of the dissatisfied fathers had more than one complaint about their accommodation which suggests that housing conditions must have been quite inadequate before complaints were voiced to the interviewers. The fathers judged their accommodation in the light of their own housing experiences and the limits set by their financial and social position on the type of housing they could possibly have. They were judgments made within the context of the father's relative position in the social structure and their value lies more in indicating the father's subjective feelings than in presenting an accurate picture of the objective housing situation. We are not suggesting that public opinion on social and economic conditions is not useful to policy makers; we are merely asserting that this opinion cannot be the one and only guide. The three quotations we give here are typical of many others showing multiple housing inadequacies.

'Beggars can't be choosers. The house is in a poor state. It is damp in winter. There's ants in the living-room and you can't get rid of them.'

'We are overcrowded. The toilet facilities are very poor – it is cracked and it leaks. I am unable to get any repairs done because the house has a time limit set on it. It is due for demolition in eighteen months.'

'There is no bathroom in the house and the toilet is outside. The house is very damp. It is due for demolition. The ceiling was so bad it had to be renewed. It would be better if we moved to another area and the kids could go to a white school. Here all the coloureds hold up our kids from learning.'

As might have been predicted, social class was an important factor in housing. A higher proportion of fathers in classes I and II than other fathers were owner-occupiers, had all three essential housing facilities, had more consumer goods, were not overcrowded and were satisfied with their housing conditions. The most deprived group as regards housing consisted of those fathers who were not at work and consequently relied on the social security system for financial support.

Not only were they worse off than the other fathers as a group but they were also worse off than fathers in classes IV and V. They were more dissatisfied with their housing conditions than other fathers and our interviewers rated their housing lower than that of other groups.

Two possible explanations suggest themselves for the housing conditions of the unemployed fathers: first the amount of benefit is not adequate, especially over a long period of time, to replace household goods which the father may have possessed when he was at work. The official policy of the Supplementary Benefit Commission distinguishes between non-essential consumer goods as in Table 12 and essential goods such as bedding and furnishings. For non-essential consumer goods the official policy is that 'specific payments of Supplementary Benefit are not normally made unless there are exceptional circumstances' although a man 'may manage to pay for them out of his weekly income or any resources which are disregarded for Supplementary Benefit purposes'. On the other hand, when a claimant is unable to provide essential major items such as bedding and furnishings, official policy is that 'consideration would be given to making a lump sum payment of Benefit for the purpose'. Second, in view of the high proportion of unemployed fathers in council accommodation (65 per cent) it appears more than probable that for various reasons they were housed in older council properties. Otherwise it is difficult to explain why a higher proportion of the unemployed than the other fathers lived in housing with structural inadequacies or which lacked basic facilities.

Deprivation is many-sided and is cumulative in its effects. The housing conditions of the unemployed must, therefore, be seen in conjunction with such other aspects of life as income, diet, health, etc. The income and diet of the unemployed will be discussed in subsequent chapters where it will be shown that they are worse than those of other groups. The health of the unemployed also appeared worse than that of other fathers. Of all fathers 70·2 per cent considered their health good, 18·7 per cent fair and 11·1 per cent poor. There were clear social-class differences with 84·1 per cent of fathers in classes I and II considering their health good while the corresponding proportion in class III was 74·2 per cent, in classes IV and V 66·3 per cent and for the unemployed it was 38·2 per cent. We are not implying that receipt of social security benefit has an adverse effect on health. We are merely stating the fact that people drawing

35

social security benefit are a deprived group in many ways and that their deprivation is in some measure the cause and in some measure the result of their reliance on social security benefits. There is no study, to our knowledge, that has examined the long-term effects of reliance on social security benefit and until this is done we can only guess what these effects are.

3   The children

The father's decision whether to care for his children without the help of his wife is clearly affected by many considerations one of which concerns the role of men and women in society as workers and parents. Wynn wonders whether society all too readily assumes 'that the mother of a family can be both mother and bread-winner' and maintains that fathers 'are never expected, and only a very few manage, to carry the double burden unaided by a woman'.[1] In our society there is a greater incidence of fatherless than motherless families and a larger number of children are received into the care of local authorities as a result of the mother's rather than the father's desertion of the family.[2] Our own study of community attitudes towards motherless and fatherless families provided indirect support for this thesis. The general public assigned different roles to fathers and mothers with regard to child upbringing and full-time employment. Respondents felt that work was crucial to a man's dignity and well-being but it was not so to a woman. They were prepared to accept mothers' financial dependence on society without loss of self-respect but not the fathers' dependence.

Society and work

Our society sets a high value on the virtues of work. A person's position in society is largely determined by his economic standing, which means his work and the income it affords him. To have any standing in society a man must work, not only because work provides him with money for the essentials of life, but also because it provides him with a socially recognizable status and thus a basis from which to form relationships with other people. This attitude may be the result of residual Calvinism which originally 'taught people to regard work as a form of prayer and the growth of possessions as the evidence of the state of grace'.[2] Whatever its origins the feeling is certainly strong. 'With a job there is a future', wrote Bakke, 'without a job there is slow death of all that makes a man ambitious, industrious and glad to be alive.'[3]

In their study of the meaning of work Morse and Weiss found that 80 per cent of their random sample of men at work said they would continue at work even if they inherited enough wealth to enable them to live comfortably without working. The men were questioned about their reasons for wishing to leave or remain at work and though attitudes do not always coincide with action, the writers felt justified in drawing the conclusion that 'for most men working does not simply function as a means of earning a livelihood. Even if there were no economic necessity for them to work most men would work anyway. It is through the producing role that most men tie into society, and for this reason and others, most men find the producing role important for maintaining their sense of well-being.'[4] To be an economic provider is 'virtually the only way to be a real man in our society'.[5] Without work, said Camus, all life goes rotten.

Perhaps the emphasis on hard work is not so strong or so obvious today as it used to be but it is still very much a part of our value system. Equally and obviously part of our value system is a belief in the value of the family and a concern for the well-being of children.

In our survey of community attitudes we sought to explore a situation where these sets of values conflict. We asked respondents what a father should do to provide the best care for his children when his wife died or left, distinguishing between fathers caring for children under school age and of school age. Respondents were asked whether the father should work or stay at home and draw Supplementary Benefit and for their reasons for thinking so. Of the sample 78 per cent thought that a father with children under school age should go to work and 96 per cent thought the same of a father with children of school age. Table 13 shows that there is a relationship between social class and the reply given. The higher the social class of the respondent the more likely he or she was to support the view that a father with children under school age should go out to work. This may be due to the fact that middle-class men work less hours than working-class men and to the better conditions of employment regarding holidays, sick pay, etc., enjoyed by the middle classes.[6]

TABLE 13   Should a father with children under school age go out to work or stay at home? Replies according to respondents' social class

Social class	Should go out to work		Stay at home	
	No.	%	No.	%
I ⎫ II ⎭	82	87·2	12	12·8
III	107	79·9	27	20·1
IV ⎫ V ⎭	28	63·6	16	36·4

$\chi^2 = 10.346$ $P < 0.01$

The same picture emerges when the respondents' views are analysed according to their school-leaving age. Those who left school at the age of nineteen or after were more likely to say that the father should go out to work than respondents who left school at the ages of sixteen, seventeen or eighteen; they in turn were more likely to express that view than respondents who left school at the age of fifteen or earlier. Another interesting relationship was that women were less likely than men to expect a father to go out to work and the same was true, though the difference was smaller, between respondents with and without contact with motherless families. It seems as if a knowledge of what it really means to care for children has a sobering effect on expecting someone to fulfil two roles adequately – being a wage-earner and a housekeeper.

This belief in the man's place being at work was expressed variously by respondents. There were those who expressed the view in a matter-of-fact way. 'A man can't take on a woman's role – he can't become a mother' or 'A man should be encouraged to go out to work. After all he is not a woman and he should not be expected to fill a woman's role.' There were others who felt that going out to work would benefit the father socially or psychologically. 'It is better psychologically for the father to work since he is used to it', or 'The father must at all costs maintain social contact which is provided by going out to work'. There were also those who feared that the father's character would suffer by staying at home. 'It is not a man's place to stay at home. He will get lazy and would not want to return to work when the time came' or 'A man should never lose his job. It makes him feel inferior to other men if he cannot work'; or 'Work preserves a man's dignity, he needs to work', said a working-class respondent.

For some the belief in a man's place being at work was linked with the bogy of the scrounger and the featherbedding of the welfare state. 'Most men would want to work – it's their role in life. But there are scroungers who would want to stay at home and not work if they felt they could get something for nothing'; or 'People should be encouraged to provide for themselves rather than live off the state. It is made too easy at the moment to get benefits. No incentives'; or 'Taking responsibility from people erodes their sense of responsibility. Too much help encourages idleness, scrounging'. There was clearly a feeling of resentment in these replies for what respondents saw by implication as working-class malingering though this feeling was not restricted to non-manual respondents, as Runciman suggests.[7] And finally for a few the receipt of Supplementary Benefit has a permeating ill-effect for the whole family because 'children grow up in an atmosphere of charity'.

What is interesting is that respondents made little mention of the problems of combining work and the care of children. Few people mentioned the fairly obvious difficulty that the school day is shorter than most working days and somehow the father has to make arrangements for the periods at either end of the day when the children are at home and he is not. Little mention was made either of the problem of school holidays, or when the children were ill or the difficulties of finding domestic or child-minding help on a long-term basis. This illustrates perhaps the very limited value of a study such as this. It may be useful and interesting to know community attitudes but they are of little practical value for policy unless respondents have experience of the issues being explored. Social problems cannot be solved on doorsteps.

British society, along with most other societies, has long cultivated the belief that a mother's love is very important to the emotional well-being of young children and also that mothers need to look after their young children to satisfy their 'maternal instinct'. Perhaps more implicitly than explicitly, the father's relationship with his young children has not been seen to be so important for either himself or the children. These cultural beliefs have somehow been loosely related to biological 'needs' and 'instincts'. Hence Oakley's polemic that 'Child-rearing is regarded as necessary for real satisfaction in life if one is biologically female – but not if one is biologically male'.[8] Galbraith is sceptical about the validity of these beliefs and about the motives behind them. 'For some reason women are supposed to be more suitable than men for looking after children and supervising their upbringing. This is nonsense. It is a suggestion propagated by men who surrogate the responsibility because they do not want it themselves.'[9] These beliefs are clearly reflected in the social and economic structure of the country. Wages for men are higher than those of women; men who stay at home to look after their children while their wife goes out to work are considered odd to say the least; a woman is expected to put her children before her job; a man is expected to do just the opposite, etc. That these cultural values exist is generally accepted. What is not clear is the extent to which they prevail and the rate and manner in which they have been changing in recent decades. There has certainly been more discussion in recent years of the role of the father in the family and there is considerable evidence too of greater participation by fathers in the care of their children.[10]

Though our study is not primarily concerned with male and female roles, public attitudes in this field are relevant to our discussion. We asked our respondents whether mothers or fathers on their own with reasonable incomes could provide adequately for all the needs of their children. Table 14 shows that more respondents felt the mother on her own could provide adequately for her children. We did not specify the ages of children but we feel certain from comments and from

TABLE 14　Can mothers or fathers on their own provide *Craig* adequately for their children?

	Yes		No	
	No.	%	No.	%
Mother	242	71·6	96	28·4
Father	217	64·4	120	35·6

$\chi^2 = 3·702$　$0·05 < P < 0·10$

replies to other questions that had we referred to young children only, the proportion of respondents considering the mother competent would have been greater and the opposite would have been true for the fathers. The two main reasons given for the father's inability to provide adequately for his children were a general belief that he cannot replace the mother and that he cannot provide for the emotional needs of children. On the other hand, the two main reasons given for the mother's inability to provide for her children were a general belief that she cannot replace the father and that she cannot discipline the children satisfactorily. In a sense these respondents saw the roles of father and mother in child rearing as complementary, with the mother specializing in providing for the children's emotional needs while the father's specialized contribution was in discipline matters – a difference between expressive and instrumental roles. What is perhaps more interesting and unexpected is that the majority of respondents – about two-thirds – felt that either the mother or the father could provide for all the needs of the children if the financial situation had been taken care of.

This generally held belief in the greater ability of a mother to provide for her children was supported by both men and women. The proportion of both male and female respondents who felt that a mother can provide adequately for her children on her own was greater than the proportion who felt the same about the father. Another interesting point was that a larger proportion of female than male respondents felt that a lone father or a mother could provide adequately for the children. Perhaps this is due to the fact that women today are more likely than men to find themselves doing both paid work and caring for children. Married women at work tend to carry most of the responsibility for running the home as well. Girls at school are prepared for a career as well as for motherhood. Boys, however, are usually prepared for a career and rarely for fatherhood.

Social class proved a very important variable in this question. A greater proportion of all social classes said that a lone mother could provide adequately than felt the same for a father in a similar situation. The lower a respondent's class or school-leaving age the more likely he was to feel that a lone parent of either sex could provide adequately for the children.

This finding about class also supports our idea that it is because women have experience of combining work and the care of children that they are more likely to say that a mother on her own can provide. For recent evidence shows that the wives of men in social classes IV and V are more likely to work than wives in classes I and II and are therefore more likely to have had this experience.[11] It is also rather unexpected that men in classes IV and V who take a smaller role in the care of their children than men in social classes I and II should be more confident that a father can provide adequately on his own.[12]

TABLE 15 Can a father provide adequately for his children?
Respondents' replies according to social class

Social class	Yes		No	
	No.	%	No.	%
I and II	43	42·5	58	57·5
III	95	67·4	46	32·6
IV and V	31	70·4	13	29·6
Total	169		117	

$\chi^2 = 17·752$ $P < 0·001$

TABLE 16 Can a mother provide adequately for her children?
Respondents' replies according to social class

Social class	Yes		No	
	No.	%	No.	%
I and II	57	58·2	41	41·8
III	101	77·7	29	22·3
IV and V	32	84·2	6	15·8
Total	190		76	

$\chi^2 = 13·991$ $P < 0·001$

Perhaps the explanation for the caution which social classes I and II showed in their replies is their belief that fathers cannot provide for the children's emotional needs; 32 per cent of them compared with 25 per cent of respondents in social class III and 10 per cent in social classes IV and V said that although a father can provide for the children's physical needs he cannot provide for their emotional needs. This view is corroborated by the answers to another question regarding the problems which motherless children face. Of respondents in classes I and II 80 per cent thought that the lack of a mother's love and consequent emotional disturbance was a problem while the corresponding proportion for classes IV and V was only 25 per cent. The popularized theories of Bowlby and Spock may have been absorbed more by the professional than the working classes.

Our fathers were not as certain as our sample from the general public was about the father's ability to provide on his own for all the needs of the children, as Table 17 shows. The vast majority of those who felt the father could not perform adequately the parenting role for both mother and father explained it by the conventional reason that the father has not the mother's patience and gentleness with children. Others saw practical problems in looking after very young

TABLE 17 Can a father alone provide for all needs of his children? (per cent) (n = 510)

No	62·7
Depends	12·8
Yes	24·5

children which the father would find difficult in view of the fact that he had not been prepared for such tasks. Still others saw difficulties in looking after older girls because of the problems involved in buying underclothes for girls and in explaining adequately questions relating to sex. Others still saw problems in one person performing satisfactorily the two seemingly conflicting parental tasks of providing affection and disciplining the children.

'No he can't. There are things which a mother can give – mother love, it's a different love – and a father can't. Little things like buckles of shoes, mothers notice things like this.'

'He can't be both and there is a possibility of spoiling. He can't provide all the affection all the children need. With John being the youngest I fussed a lot over him. I now see I may have neglected Arthur a bit in this way.'

'No, it is hard to be strict and give children the type of affection usually shown by the mother.'

Those fathers who could not give a clear yes or no reply consisted of those who felt that the father's ability to care for his children alone depended on whether he possessed adequate domestic skills, on whether he has relatives to help him out, on how much he loved his children and on his job and income.

Those who felt a father could perform adequately both parenting roles were very brief in their replies though there were the exceptions.

'Men can cuddle and love children nowadays more than ever before. I don't feel out of place with female things such as shopping. Daughters may be easier in some ways. You don't kiss your son and so on, with girls it's easier to do this.'

'It would be a poor father who can't. The young ones are growing up and it is good to see that. It also keeps you young. You have fun and you joke and a bit of a dance around. The children have friends in and I get as daft as them. I can never be down in the dumps – always jovial.'

There were no variations according to social class but there were differences according to the reason for motherlessness. Widowers were more likely than divorced or separated fathers to reply that the father cannot provide adequately for his children. Since this is not a social-class difference it is probably attributable to the quality of married family life which fathers experienced before motherlessness.

We have already discussed respondents' views about whether the father should be expected to go out to work or stay at home receiving Supplementary Benefit to care for his children. We posed the same questions with regard to unsupported mothers differentiating again between families with children below school age and families with children of school age. The different roles of men and women became apparent in the case of families with children below school age as Table 18 shows. Whereas the majority of respondents felt such fathers should go out to work the opposite was true for mothers. When each respondent's replies to what a father and what a mother should do

TABLE 18   Should a father or mother with children below school age go to work?

| | Yes | | No | |
	No.	%	No.	%
Father	267	78·3	74	21·7
Mother	49	14·0	301	86·0

$\chi^2 = 285 \cdot 149$ $P < 0.001$

are compared, it is interesting that 70 per cent thought the man should go out to work but the woman should stay at home. This is one of the clearest indications that separate roles are still allocated to mothers and fathers in families with young children. The two main reasons given for the mother staying at home were that it is better for her to be with her children and it is also better for the children to be with their mother. In the words of an electrician, 'Children need their mother around all day – otherwise her absence could have adverse effects on the children'; or in the words of an engineer's wife, 'Children need their mother to care for them more than their father at this age. It fits in with the child's views of the role of his parents. A child considers his father should go out to work, whereas the mother should be at home.' What is the position, however, with families with children of school age? There is clearly a convergence of views favouring fathers and mothers going out to work though the proportion is still lower for mothers as Table 19 shows. There are, however, important qualifications to this convergence of views. Of the respondents who felt the mother should go to work, 42·2 per cent suggested that this should be on a part-time basis. Moreover, the

TABLE 19   Should a father or mother with children of school age go out to work?

	Yes		No	
	No.	%	No.	%
Father	331	96·2	13	3·8
Mother	287	87·0	59	17·0

$\chi^2 = 31·111$ $P < 0·001$

reasons given why the mother should go out to work showed very little trace of the harsh punitive attitudes that were predominant in the case of fathers. Mothers were expected to go out to work because it was felt that the children are at school and she has the time; or because it is good for the mother since it gives her interests and social contacts; or because the amount of social security benefit is not adequate. No one felt that she should go to work because it is her place in society or that she should not sponge on the state though a small minority felt that she will lose her self respect if she relies on Supplementary Benefit. Clearly these were more tolerant and understanding attitudes than those expressed in the case of fathers. Generally then there are still different roles assigned to mothers and fathers in families with children of school age though they are not as sharply divided as in the case of families with children below school age.

We asked our fathers in the main study a similar question: should a father left with the care of his children be given Supplementary Benefit and stay at home to look after his children, or should he continue at work and try to care for his children with the help of relatives, home help service, day nurseries, etc., or should he give up the care of the children and let them be cared for by the local authorities or voluntary organizations? Only a minute proportion of fathers opted for the third alternative. It would have, indeed, been extraordinary if many of the fathers had agreed to the suggestion that children should be removed from their family. Ours is a child-centred and family-oriented society and our fathers had already taken the decision to care for their children. The few who considered extra-familial care best for the children were those who found caring for their children too demanding or those who felt that their place was at work and they could not fulfil a mother's role.

'If I had to do it again, I'd put them into a Home. You're so tied with them you don't get any freedom.'

'I would know then the children are all right and have some sort of mother image and I would be able to continue working. It's not really a man's place to be in the house all the time.'

For most fathers it was a matter of faith that children should not be taken away from their family because 'it's not right', because 'it's not good for them' or because 'it's certainly not for me'. The implication of these brief replies was that not only would the children suffer but the father, too. As one father put it, 'I would never think of that, I'd die first. It would break their hearts.'

TABLE 20   What should fathers do when left on their own to bring up their children? (per cent) (n = 537)

Receive Supplementary Benefit	19·6
Combine full-time work and care for the children	71·3
Allow children to be received into care	1·1
Other	8·0

The reasons which fathers gave for wishing to combine full-time work and care for the children rather than rely on Supplementary Benefit reflected the public attitudes to man's place in society. The main reasons that emerged from the fathers' answers were that a man's place is at work, to receive Supplementary Benefit undermines one's independence, the amount of Supplementary Benefit is inadequate and reliance on Supplementary Benefit for a period of years will make it impossible for a man to find a job when the children grow up.

'Man first and foremost should be at work. He is the breadwinner. Security Benefit is not enough to live on. It brings you to a lower class of living. There is no future to look forward to – it is depressing living on social security.'

'It is not correct for a man to lose ten years or so of his working life staying at home. He might have difficulty getting into work later when he is older. In fact I know he will. Employers don't like giving jobs to men who have been out of work for years and lived on social security.'

There were no differences among the three groups of fathers in the emphasis they placed on work though there were variations according to their social class. The division of opinion related to whether the father should go out to work as well as care for his children or whether he should stay at home and care for his children with the financial support of Supplementary Benefit. All social classes rejected equally strongly other forms of coping with the situation. The lower the father's class, particularly the unemployed, the more likely he was to agree to the idea of Supplementary Benefit. This is to be expected for it is fathers from the working classes that are likely to lose or are forced to give up their jobs in order to care for their children. The prospect of relying on Supplementary Benefit is not for them simply a theoretical question but a likely possibility. What is perhaps more interesting is that the unemployed who relied on Supplementary Benefit were divided equally on this issue. It is an illustration of the problems involved in the congruence between a person's value system and his behaviour. In this case the harsh reality of the situation forced some fathers to accept a solution to their problem which in principle they disagreed with. How the fathers drawing Supplementary Benefit felt about this and how they viewed their relationship with the Supplementary Benefit officers will be discussed in chapter 4.

TABLE 21   What should fathers do when left on their own to bring
up children; by social class at time of interview

Social class	Receive Supplementary Benefit		Go out to work	
	No.	%	No.	%
I and II	4	7·0	53	93·0
III	23	11·2	181	88·8
IV and V	21	21·4	77	78·6
Unemployed	57	50·0	57	50·0

$\chi^2 = 72·98$ P < 0·001

Family diet

One would expect the diet of motherless families to be worse than
that of two-parent families. If the father is at work, the time and
energy he can devote to meal preparation must be limited; if he is not
at work, the amount of Supplementary Benefit he receives will be
enough for a basic standard of living only. He has, moreover, to
carry out so many other functions which in a two-parent family are
shared between husband and wife that, as Glasser and Navarre have
said,[13] the fulfilment of any one parental task is likely to suffer in one
way or another.

> Even if the remaining parent is able to function adequately, it
> is unlikely that one person can take over all parental tasks on a
> long-term basis. Financial support, child care, and household
> maintenance are concrete tasks involving temporal and spatial
> relationships, and in one form or another they account for a
> large proportion of the working life of two adult family
> members. A permanent adjustment then must involve a
> reduction in the tasks performed and/or a reduction in the
> adequacy of performance, or external assistance.

Apart from these difficulties that stem out of the structure of one-
parent status, there is the additional difficulty that men are not, on
the whole, well prepared in their upbringing to cook and serve meals.
We must be careful, however, not to exaggerate the differences
between one-parent and two-parent families with regard to the diet
of the family. Not all two-parent families are in the position where

one of the parents is at home and the other earns wages which are adequate for a standard of living above the basic. In many two-parent families both the husband and the wife are at work, in other families where only one parent is at home, the other's wages are not higher than the amount of Supplementary Benefit while in other two-parent families both parents are out of work. Moreover, with the widespread use of prepared, tinned food, cooking for the family becomes easier, and it requires less skill and time.

In spite of the annual reports of the National Food Survey Committee for the last thirty years, there is concern among experts concerning the state of our knowledge about the 'nutritional status of the community'. The coverage and the methodology of the official surveys have been questioned with the result that it is not possible to state precisely what sections, if any, of the population are undernourished. The Office of Health Economics in its recent study of the problem called for more thorough studies and concluded that[14]

> Until such studies are undertaken uncertainty as to the precise nature of the position will remain and with it not only the inability adequately to isolate and deal with potentially vulnerable groups but also perhaps an over-readiness to discount any suggestion of malnutrition.

McKenzie's review of the literature led him to the conclusion that[15]

> The evidence at present available concerning the United Kingdom indicates that there is a major restriction of food choice of those with low incomes or with large families. The fact that the evidence is too imprecise to indicate whether or not malnutrition still exists should not lead us too readily to assume by inference that because of this the case for no malnutrition has been conclusively proven.

We did not attempt in our study to measure the standard of nutrition among motherless families simply because we were not qualified for such a task. Instead we accepted Marsden's suggestion and looked 'for signs of any major departure from ordinary food customs or restrictions in diet'.[16] This is also the approach adopted by Land who also stated explicitly its limitations – 'Without a full nutritional analysis', she writes, 'of the food bought, methods of preparation and variable consumption within the family, it is impossible to assess the full nutritional implications of variations in diet.'[17] We have since found, however, that in the absence of sociologically established 'ordinary food customs' among the general population it is not possible to tell to what extent and in what ways the eating customs of our families deviate from the norm. Though we can guess at 'major departures' from the general norm it is impossible to make any more precise comparisons. What we have studied, therefore, are the types of meals of motherless families and how they compared with those prior to motherlessness.

Though most motherless families experienced changes in their meals there is no general trend. While one-third of the fathers felt that their meals were worse at the time of interview than before motherlessness, one-quarter felt they were better. Those fathers who felt their meals were better attributed the improvement to one main reason – their wife was not a good cook and sometimes it was coupled with the fact that she could not budget either. They were, in other words, better cooks and better managers than their wives.

'Definitely better. She wasn't a good manager or cook at all. I don't think she could boil water right. She's not here to defend herself, I know, but it's true. Even no proper dinner on Christmas Day – she would be out.'

The fathers who felt their meals had deteriorated since motherlessness attributed it either to their worsened economic position or to the fact they didn't have much time to devote to cooking or that their wives were good cooks or, with a touch of emotion, that meals tasted better when their wife cooked them.

'She was a good cook, I'll say that for her. I'm pretty handy at cooking myself. I can bake bread but it's not just the same as she made. Somehow it tasted better.'

'We don't get the little extras. My wife was a damn good cook and mother. There are always little things missing now and, of course, I don't cook as well.'

These are subjective judgments and they may reflect to some extent the father's relationship with his wife. Only 5·4 per cent of the widowers compared with 38·6 per cent of the separated and 42·8 per cent of the divorced felt that their meals had improved. Vice-versa, 47·3 per cent of the widowers compared with 21·4 per cent of the separated and 14·7 per cent of the divorced felt their meals had worsened. There may well be an element of truth in the views of the separated and divorced fathers that their wives were not good cooks

51

or managers but there may also be an element of rationalization and bravado that they could cope just as well if not better than their wives who 'left' them for some other man.

TABLE 22   Comparison between meals at the time of interview and meals before motherlessness (per cent) (n = 578)

The same	43·3
Better	23·5
Worse	33·2

To assess the family diet we asked the father to tell us the meals he and the children had on the day prior to the interview or, if the interview took place on a Monday, the meals they had that day. We wanted to avoid confusing week-day and week-end meals for we felt the latter would be better in spite of Marsden's finding to the contrary, explainable by the bias in his sample.[18] Our findings showed that week-end meals compared very favourably with week-day meals – 69·2 per cent of the fathers said they were better, 1·0 per cent that they were worse and 24·7 per cent that they were the same. Land also found the same trend among her large families. 'However restricted the meals eaten during the week, a major effort was made to provide a "Sunday dinner" such as was enjoyed by other families. A family unable to have a Sunday joint with the accompanying vegetables, and a pudding to follow felt very poor.'[19]

The classification of meals into the categories shown in the tables of this section proved quite satisfactory from the research point of view. We feel that though there may have been a few borderline cases where meals were classified into one rather than another category, the overall picture we present of the motherless families' meals during week-days is correct. Such borderline cases were few and mistaken classification could have upgraded as well as downgraded them. Several points stand out from the three tables comparing the fathers' and children's meals: The children's meals are better than the meals of the fathers not only as two separate groups but also within the same family. Several fathers commented that they went out of their way to ensure that their children had adequate meals. One unemployed father commented: 'They don't do bad. I see that they have good meals. I don't believe in children going to school on an empty stomach. The only trouble is walking around looking for the cheapest stuff. It's the only way we can manage.' We did not en-counter any cases, however, where fathers starved themselves in order to provide an adequate diet for their children as Marsden found in the case of mothers. 'Of three mothers who had had special national assistance discretionary allowances for food because they were ill, only one had spent it on food for herself. Another said, "Well, I ask you. How could I sit down with a piece of chicken when the kids are wanting things." '[20]

Breakfast is the least adequate of the three meals for both fathers and children, very much in line with the findings of other studies. Marsden found that half of the mothers[21] and Land found that 24 per cent of the fathers[22] had no breakfast at all. It is difficult to know whether the decline of breakfast is due to financial or to cultural and social factors. The large proportion of children, for example, who rely on cereals for breakfast may be due to the fact that the fathers have little time in the morning to prepare breakfast and in some cases the children are left to prepare their own breakfast. There is, however, some evidence that this is a problem which affects children from two-parent families as well. Lynch found that 25 per cent of a sample of school children in the East End of London 'regularly fasted for eighteen hours each school day. They generally had their last meal – generally a snack – before 6.30 p.m., went without breakfast, and so ate their next meal at the following lunch time.'[23]

The importance of school meals to children in motherless families is abundantly clear. The proportion who were having school meals was higher than the national average, 70·1 per cent in 1969,[24] and very similar to the proportion of fatherless children, 85 per cent,[25] and children of large families, 78 per cent.[26] The evening meal of the children compared favourably with the evening meal of the small group of working-class school children investigated by Lynch. He found that 4 per cent of the children had no evening meal and only 37 per cent had a 'main course meal' while the remainder had a snack, sandwiches or titbits.[27]

Since fathers' meals are worse than those of the children we looked at all three meals of each father together and compiled Table 26. It presents a more accurate picture of the diet of each father than the three previous tables separately or together. In the absence of any substantial sociological evidence of meal patterns different inter-pretations can be given to the figures. We would like to suggest, however, that on a moderate estimate all those fathers who had no meals, one snack only, one cooked meal only or two snacks only, a

E

TABLE 23 Breakfast of fathers and children (per cent)

	Father (n = 568)	Children (n = 529)
Nothing	29·9	3·7
Drink only	10·2	2·7
Toast or bread or biscuits	12·5	8·2
Cereal	15·1	39·6
Cereal and bread or biscuits	5·8	18·4
Cooked breakfast	18·3	12·7
Cooked breakfast and cereal or fruit	6·4	14·2
Other	1·8	0·5

TABLE 24 Mid-day meal of fathers and children (per cent)

	Father (n = 562)	Children (n = 580)
Nothing	9·4	—
Sandwiches or snack	31·7	4·2
Cooked meal	31·3	11·4
Cooked snack	10·3	3·6
Canteen/school meal	17·1	80·7
Other	0·3	0·2

TABLE 25 Evening meal of fathers and children (per cent) (n = 565)

	Father	Children
Nothing	2·7	—
Sandwiches or snack	15·2	17·8
Cooked meal	55·0	51·2
Cooked snack	25·3	29·4
Other	1·8	1·6

total of 13·9 per cent of all fathers, had inadequate meals. The diet of our fathers was certainly better than that of Marsden's mothers where 'One in ten mothers maintained, in spite of detailed questioning, that they had eaten literally no solid food on the day before the interview'.[28] Nor did we come across the same harrowing instances which he so vividly describes. This is not to say that we did not meet

TABLE 26   Fathers' three meals (per cent) (n = 562)

No meals at all	2·8
Father has one snack (cold or cooked) only	1·8
Father has one cooked meal a day only	3·3
Father has two snacks a day only	6·0
Father has one cooked meal and one snack only	29·0
Father has two cooked meals only	10·9
Father has three snacks	4·5
Father has two snacks and one cooked meal	18·9
Father has one snack and two cooked meals	17·8
Father has three cooked meals	5·0

cases of hardship. We came across fathers who said they 'couldn't afford a hot dinner every day'; fathers who maintained that they had to economize by sharing the food with the children. 'We have chips and we share a piece of fish between us two. I can't afford a piece of fish each'; and fathers who insisted that they lost their appetite, 'I never eat breakfast and rarely a mid-day meal now. I just don't feel like it.' On the whole, however, the answers to our questions and the impressions of our interviewers, while not making us complacent about the problems of this group of families, have provided evidence for concern about the diet of only a small minority.

The adequacy of the meals was positively related to social class. The proportion of fathers who had three cooked meals a day or two cooked meals and one snack was 50·8 per cent for classes I and II, 39·6 per cent for class III, 36·2 per cent for classes IV and V and 24·3 per cent for the unemployed. There was no social-class relationship, however, with the diet referred to above as inadequate, apart from the fact that the proportion of the unemployed who had such a diet was much higher – 28·7 per cent – than fathers at work – 9·1 per cent.

It is worth repeating the warning that ours was not a study of dietary standards and though the meals may seem adequate from a layman's point of view they may be totally inadequate from an expert's point of view. Thus Lynch, using the dietary allowances recommended by the Department of Health and Social Security, reached the conclusion from a national study of school children's diet, that '32 per cent qualified as being satisfactory, 57 per cent by our definition qualified as being unsatisfactory and 11 per cent were seen to be extremely poor'.[29] The high proportion of children having unsatisfactory diet was due to the fact that they had meals which did not contain adequate nutritional value. It was not due so much to poverty as to feeding habits, for the study showed that children in the South-East fared worse than children in the North and secondary school children also fared worse than younger children.

The loss of the mother

One of the first hard tasks facing a father after his wife leaves or dies is what, if anything, he should tell his children. It is a topic shrouded by emotional attitudes towards marriage, sex, death and parental adequacy all of which make the father's decision difficult. As Gorer has said, 'British parents find it embarrassing to talk to their children on subjects of deep emotional disturbance; and traditionally they try to hide their own deep emotions from their children's observation.'[30] In his study of death, Gorer found that of 156 parents, half 'did not tell their children anything at all, nor discuss the subject with them. Thirty-five told their children the truth as they saw it; forty-two employed some form of euphemism.'[31] Marris, in his study of widows in London, found that mothers had ambivalent feelings on this matter. On one hand they 'tried as far as they could to protect them (their children) from awareness of death' but on the other 'most of the widows realized that it was wiser to break the news gently themselves, than to risk their children making a much more brutal discovery of the truth from neighbours or school mates.'[32] Morris in her study of prisoners' wives found that 38 per cent of wives said that their children did not know of their father's imprisonment and 12 per cent that only the older children knew.[33] Marsden found that 'Mothers differed widely in their approach. Many had still to face the problem, and for various reasons of shame, or a misreading of the child's emotional defences, or lack of the right words, had avoided the explanations altogether.' He gives no figures apart from the fact that 'probably a quarter of the families'[34] had children who were too young to understand the absence of a father.

The vast majority of the replies of fathers, 83 per cent, showed that some explanation had been given to the children about the mother's absence while the remaining 17 per cent of the replies stated that no explanation was given. These percentages refer to fathers' replies and not to fathers themselves. Though the two are very similar they are not quite identical since there were some fathers who gave more than one reply indicating that though the matter had been explained to some of the children it had not been explained to others. There were significant variations among the three groups of fathers but not among the various social classes of fathers. An explanation was more likely to be given to the children of the widowed than to the other children.[35]

Where an explanation had been given, this had been done by the father in 64 per cent of the families and in the remainder the children had been told by their relatives (7·5 per cent), by their own mother in the cases of separation and divorce (5·1 per cent), by someone else (4·0 per cent), and in the remaining 19·4 per cent the children either knew all along of the impending loss of their mother or found out themselves before anyone told them. As one would expect the main group of children who had not been told comprised under-five-year olds though surprisingly there were about twenty-two children over the age of fifteen years who had not been told. They were some of the children who lost their mother when very young, grew up without a mother and where presumably the father never brought himself to tell them, though this does not mean that they did not know of their mother's loss. The explanation to the children had generally been given promptly – in 61·3 per cent of the families on the day the mother left or died, in 14·7 per cent of the families within a week, in 5 per cent of the cases later than a week but before the end of one month, in another 5 per cent later than one month and in the remaining 14 per cent of the families it was not possible to establish the time limit.

Most of our fathers, 79·3 per cent, felt that their children had been told the truth about the death or departure of their mother. In the case of desertion, where the truth was told, fathers varied in the way they presented the mother's action to the children. They ranged from the gentle and forgiving explanations to the harsh and punitive.

'I told them plainly that mummy stopped loving daddy and would like to live elsewhere for a time.'

'I told them the truth. She went off with another man because she was fed up with us. No point in telling lies.'

The way the truth was told about death appeared also to be rather harsh sometimes.

'The children found her. The twins (aged seven years) were at school but John (aged four years) was at home. She went to lay down in the morning and John couldn't wake her up at lunch time. He lay down near her. The twins came home from school but they couldn't wake her up. When I got home they were trying to get tea. They said, "Go and see mummy". I went and knew she was dead. I went back and said to them straight out – "your mummy is dead". No tears from any of them.'

The remaining 20·3 per cent of the fathers said that their children had been given an explanation which was untrue because the truth was too hard to tell or that their children had been given an explanation which was a 'euphemism' because it was the only explanation the children could understand because they were so young. The usual explanation given to young children in the case of death was that the mother had gone to heaven, or that she had gone to Jesus. Such explanations were not very meaningful to children but they were the only possible explanations. Gessel's work in the United States, Nagy's work in Hungary and Anthony's in this country have provided enough evidence that children under the age of three years cannot understand death; children of five years can only understand death as a temporary event; and it is only at about the age of seven that children begin to appreciate the finality of death and its relationship with illness, hospitalization, accidents, etc.[36] As Rutter has said, 'The child's ideas of death at different ages reflect his general picture of the world, physical causality, language and thought, and are an aspect of his physiological and psychological maturation.'[37] One of our fathers explained that the children (aged seven years and five years) 'were told that mummy had gone to heaven and they appreciate she is dead. But they do say "Is mummy going to come down again when we grow up?".' It is not only death that is difficult to explain to young children. Separation can be just as difficult especially if there is no contact between mother and children afterwards. Bearing also in mind that some fathers felt resentful about their wife leaving them, it is no wonder that the children are told falsehoods.

'How does one tell small children that "Mummy has decided to leave us". I told lies to them – "Mummy has gone to look after her sick sister in London" – and this was sufficient explanation for quite a long time.'

Sometimes parents, finding it shameful to tell their older children of the separation, resort to uniquely untruthful stories. One mother told her ten-year-old daughter that 'she was going for a shilling for the gas and she never returned.' According to the father, the daughter 'has never forgotten this'.

Contact with the mother

In some of the divorced and separated families, the mother was still in the picture maintaining some contact with the children. We tried to measure the degree of contact between mother and children but found it difficult to be precise for a variety of reasons: some children of the same family saw the mother more frequently than others; the frequency and regularity of contacts changes; children and mother can meet without the father knowing; fathers cannot always remember how often the mother had been seeing the children over a long period. Bearing all these qualifications in mind, 39·3 per cent of the fathers said their wife had not seen the children at all since they parted; at the other extreme, 12·4 per cent of the mothers saw the children once a week or more. In the remaining cases visits were infrequent or irregular and we grouped them into those where the mother and children met, on average, more than once a month but less than once a week (11·4 per cent); those where they met less than once a month (24·8 per cent); and those (the remaining 12·1 per cent of families), where the arrangements varied, with some children seeing their mother more often than others.

Our impression from the fathers' answers is that there is a tendency for visits to diminish in frequency and regularity with the passage of time. As one father said: 'They were happy to see her then but the visits have been so few and far between and other times she hasn't come at all and I have had to console them. Now they don't want to see her, not encouraged by me, might I add.' Another father said: 'They used to like going but now it doesn't really bother them now. The periods are getting longer now. When they visit her they just go in the front room and play with the toys.' Marsden found the same thing in the case of fathers visiting their children: 'The usual story appeared to be that visits which began well have tailed off.'[38] Goode found the same in the case of divorced fathers visiting their children. He explained this by the existence of a 'set of structural elements in the post-divorce situation, which in turn creates a set of cost-demand processes: the cost of very frequent visits will ordinarily be great, and the visits will decline in frequency unless there are unusual counter-factors at work'.[39] In other words, mothers, fathers and children find that visits make demands on them all which generate stresses and conflicts that eventually tend to reduce the frequency of visits. The parent caring for the child finds that the visiting parent is not always punctual or doesn't turn up at all for justifiable or unjustifiable reasons; visiting parents may give children money, toys or presents intentionally or unintentionally making the caring parent's task more difficult especially when he or she cannot be so generous to the child. The visiting parent may find that visits cost a lot in terms of time, money and convenience; visits expose the visiting parent, particularly the mother, to the charge that he or she failed as a parent. Our society disapproves more of the mother's desertion of her children than of her desertion of the husband. Both the caring and visiting parent may use the visits at first as a means of seeing each other; with the lapse of time, however, one or both parents develop new friendships with the result that they feel less need for such encounters. The children, too, may find that they have to give up what they are doing in order to see the visiting parent or to go out with the visiting parent. As the child grows older and develops its own personal friendships, such visits, if they are infrequent, may lose their emotional attraction and if they are too frequent they may cause irritation or inconvenience.

A majority of the fathers, 56·2 per cent, felt that contacts with the mother had no visible favourable or unfavourable effects on the children. As one father said: 'They don't show anything and they never mention it at all when they get home. It makes no difference to them.' Other fathers, 16·6 per cent, felt that the children were more difficult or more disturbed after the visits. The most common explanations given for this were that the mothers tried to get at the father through the children, or that the children couldn't understand why they couldn't stay with the mother or that they found it difficult to adjust to two persons. As one father expressed it in the third person: 'The children become upset, first at leaving the father and going to the mother and then when they have to leave the mother and return to the father.' Only a small proportion of fathers, 3·7 per cent, felt the children benefited from such contacts and even then the benefit was expressed in very vague terms – 'it is good for them to know that she is there and they can see her'. It was a rare father who saw a positive value in such contacts: 'I think the major benefit of such visits is to acquaint Matthew and his mother and the situation as far as he can understand, otherwise at a later stage his curiosity and reaction will be more intense, perhaps leading to hangups. It is a preventive measure.' A sizeable proportion of the fathers, 23·5 per cent, found it difficult to decide what the effects of such contacts on the children were. Our findings on this issue are similar to Goode's who found that half the mothers felt that the father's visits made no difference to the children's behaviour; 25 per cent felt that the child became more difficult to handle after the visits, 2 per cent that the children were easier to handle and 14 per cent said that the father never saw the children.[40] The proportion of fathers who never saw the children is much lower than in our study and it is due possibly to the fact that Goode's study covered only divorced families where visiting is regulated by the court, and to the fact that we are dealing with mothers who may find it more difficult than fathers to visit, as a result of the greater cultural stigma attached to 'deserting' mothers than to 'deserting' fathers.

Fathers were much more explicit about their own attitude towards mother–child contacts, as Table 27 shows. The fathers who objected to such contacts usually expressed strong feelings.

TABLE 27   Fathers' attitude towards mother–child contacts (per cent) (n = 166)

Objects	31·3
Does not mind	46·4
Approves	16·3
Other	6·0

'I don't like them. If I could change the legal access I would. I hoped her mother would have got tired of seeing Yvonne but this hasn't happened. I personally don't like seeing her. I used to love her but now I hate her. It interrupts our lives especially at week-ends when I could spend more time with the children. It's an intrusion and breaks up the running of things.'

As the quotation shows, divorced fathers can have very strong feelings against visits irrespective of the court's decision. There was, in fact, no difference between the replies of separated and divorced fathers. Some fathers were particularly incensed when the mother visited with a male friend especially if there were any signs that the male adult threatened the father's status with his children. One of the more accommodating fathers who felt he did not mind his wife visiting, felt very strongly about her new husband's overtures to his son. He could not stop the visits but he said, 'When I see them [his son and the mother's husband] walking away hand in hand I feel terrible. Something inside me makes me want to kill him [mother's husband].'

The small proportion of fathers who approved of the visits were less likely to express strong feelings to support their attitude than those who opposed visits. For most of them it was simply a belief that such contacts were 'essential for the children's happiness'. Among those who approved of such contacts were some who, though not themselves liking them, felt from personal experience that the children would benefit.

'I don't like it for myself but they have a right to see her. I've never known a mother but I still miss one.'

'Well, I don't want Billy to stop seeing her. I try to put myself in his boots. As a child my mother meant more to me than my father.'

The impression gained from the fathers' replies was that most of those who approved of such contacts did so because of the benefit to the children and not out of any consideration for the mother's feelings.

The largest group of fathers said they had no particular feelings about mother–child contacts. They would do nothing openly to discourage or encourage such contacts but because of the nature of the situation they are not so neutral as it appears at first. When things go wrong with mother's visits and the child goes to the father for advice, he is more likely to influence the child against rather than in favour of further contacts. Discussing father–child contacts, Marsden observes that 'Repeated contacts with the father only served to dramatize and exacerbate the conflict of affection, and by active discouragement – or by an equally eloquent display of "neutrality" when the child appealed to her for a decision about writing to or seeing the father – the mother worked to bring the relationship to an end'.[41] In emotionally charged situations, it is very difficult for a member of a small group to remain neutral and objective when relationships between the other members affect him as well.

Children's reaction to motherlessness

The nuclear nature of the British family with its close and intense relationships is a source of strength and a source of weakness to its members. At its best the family provides physical and emotional support for all its members but at its worst 'the family, with its narrow privacy and tawdry secrets, is the source of all our discontents'.[42] The consequences of family crises, such as death, divorce or separation, are much greater for members of nuclear families than for members of families where attachments are culturally not so exclusive. It was, therefore, to be expected that most fathers would feel that their children missed their mother when she left or died. What was not so expected was the high proportion of separated and divorced fathers who felt that the children did not miss their mother in any way. Some fathers interpreted their children's silent feelings as satisfaction and contentment with their new situation while others went further and claimed that the children 'seemed pleased that she'd gone'. This different attitude towards the mother between the widowed on one hand and the separated and divorced on the other, is a recurring theme which can be interpreted in more than one way, as was found in the discussion on meals. With the passage of time many fathers felt that their children had got used to their one-parent status with the result that the proportion of fathers who felt their children still missed their mother at the time of interview dropped to 47·2 per cent. As one would expect, the decline was much sharper

TABLE 28   Did children miss their mother when she left or died?

	Yes No. %	No No. %	Doubtful No. %
Widowed	207 81·2	27 10·6	21 8·2
Separated and Divorced	146 49·1	92 40·1	59 19·9
Total	353 64·2	119 21·4	80 14·4

$X^2 = 61·254$ P < 0·001

in the case of the children of the separated and divorced than in the case of the widowers' children. Thus while 70·5 per cent of widowers felt that the children still missed their mother at the time of the interview the corresponding proportion for the separated and the divorced was only 27 per cent.

Children missed their mother in a variety of ways but the most common type of loss was emotional both at the time of the interview as well as during the immediate period after motherlessness. This is in line with the generally held public belief discussed earlier that the mother's unique contribution to the children's well-being is mainly emotional and affectional. The same picture emerged when we put a similar question to the fathers: in what ways were the children worse off and in what ways better off without their mother? Of the fathers 53·2 per cent replied that the children were not better off, 30·1 per cent that they were not worse off and the remaining either found it difficult to answer or felt that the children were better off in some ways and worse off in others. Again there were the expected variations according to the reason for motherlessness but no social-class variations. The vast majority of fathers, 77·4 per cent, who felt their children were worse off without a mother gave loss of the mother's love and affection as the reason; only a small proportion, 6·7 per cent, gave material reasons in terms of money, clothing, etc.; an even smaller proportion, 3·3 per cent, referred to the uneasy feeling and experience which children have of being different from other children, and the remaining gave other reasons.

'They just miss the affection. I tried to make up for it but it's not the same.'

'They are certainly worse off. For example, I've just had the girls' hair cut. They used to have plaits and they said I didn't do it like mum. I was not as gentle. They say I am rougher washing them than was mum.'

'Worse off, definitely. They are without a mother's presence. I have to try and be mother and father to them. I try to spend more time with them now than before. The three hours from four in the afternoon to seven in the evening are allocated to the children solely.' [Father was a vicar.]

'When he is with other kids and they talk about their mothers he says "I haven't got one" and it is upsetting for him.'

The two main reasons fathers gave for their children being better off without their mother were that the children were now better clothed, fed and generally better cared for and that the children did not have to put up with the bickering and squabbling between the parents, the inconsistent discipline and the often unbearable tension that prevailed in the family before.

'They are better off. They are kept clean and generally better looked after. The wife never bothered. She let them fend for themselves although Stanley was still a baby then. She never kept the place clean and she neglected the baby.'

'They are better off in as much as there was friction between us before she left. The children didn't know what to do for the best. Now it is only me they have to answer to and they know where they stand and are more manageable.'

'They are better off in the emotional atmosphere. There is no parental friction and there is only a single outlook to get used to. Therefore life is calmer and less confusing.'

The few who felt that the children were better off in some ways and worse off in others gave a variety of replies which are difficult to classify. They did not give any new reasons but simply a combination of the reasons already discussed.

'Better off in some ways. Andrew is happier now. When she was at home she tended to be harsh with him. He was getting on her nerves. Now he gets smacks just the same but not the cruel parts. He is worse off though because he misses a mother's love – female love, not *the* mother's love but *a* mother's love.'

The various studies of fatherless families confirm the view that the reaction of children to one-parent status depends on the reason for fatherlessness. Marris in his study of widows[43] reports that

the young children's reactions ranged over an extreme variety. Some became violently hysterical, and cried for weeks afterwards; some refused to speak of their father or hear him mentioned; or they became withdrawn and unsociable. Others showed an extraordinary self-possession. Many, specially of the youngest children, did not seem to react at all.

Goode's study of the divorced,[44] however, concluded that 'almost all these mothers thought that the children were no worse off after the divorce than before'. Kriesberg's study of separated and unmarried mothers[45] similarly reached the conclusion that

> most of the mothers do not feel that the child suffers because of the absence of the father. Among those mothers who do feel that the child would be better off if the father were around, the majority explain that the father would help discipline the child, and several mention the value of the father's companionship: only one mother mentioned that there would be more money for the child's care. Among the mothers who thought the child would be worse off, nearly all of them talked about the father as a bad example, or of poor father–child relations.

Effects of motherlessness on the children

Our study is not directly concerned with the effects of motherlessness on the children since we did not interview or examine any children. It is concerned rather with the father's perception of the situation and it is more than likely to be different from the objective situation. Our questions regarding the effects of motherlessness on the children may have been not only difficult but also threatening to the fathers. They were difficult in the sense that the fathers had to recognize any changes in the behaviour of the children since motherlessness and to be able to say that these changes were the result of motherlessness. They were threatening because admission that the children's behaviour or well-being suffered may have been seen as a censure on the fathers as caring parents. Our findings are not therefore comparable with those of the numerous studies which looked at the behaviour of the children from 'broken homes'. No good purpose would be served in reviewing this literature apart from pointing out that different studies reach different conclusions because of the complex nature of the 'broken home' concept and that the effects of 'broken homes' on children are far from clear. Rutter's review of the literature[46] concluded that:

> although probably most children from broken homes are normal, among delinquent or maladjusted children there is unduly often a background of disruption of the home. Disruption because of parental separation or divorce may be somewhat more important than disruption as a result of death, although deaths too are considerably more frequent than

expected. Break-up of the home may be less important than the factors which lead to the 'break-up' and less so also than unhappy and discordant homes which have not 'broken'. In so far as they are relevant, 'broken homes' tend more often to lead to delinquency than to neurosis in the child.

The same confusion exists in the literature on the effects of maternal deprivation. Bowlby's initial thesis was that infant–mother separation can lead to the child being deprived of his mother's intimate care and this deprivation, especially when total and prolonged, can have 'far-reaching effects on character development and may entirely cripple the capacity to make relationships'.[47] Partial deprivation can have less serious effects. Later studies, including one by Bowlby himself, have shown that the claims made for the effects of maternal deprivation had been exaggerated. The theory overlooked the effects of unsatisfactory care by the mother, the effects of the substitute care on the children, the importance of the father to the child, and the capacity of children to recuperate from stressful experiences, and generally oversimplified a very complex situation. As Ainsworth said, events following Bowlby's monograph 'have clearly shown that research into the effects of maternal deprivation is extremely difficult and complex, and that the problems and findings are not as simple as they may have seemed to the reader of *Maternal Care and Mental Health* in 1951'.[48] This is not to say that mother–child separation does not have significant effects on the child's well-being. It merely asserts that it is one of many interlocking factors affecting the life of the child before, during and after separation. Wolff's recent summary of the situation[49] is characteristic of the more involved thinking on the problem that now prevails:

In summary we can say that between six months and three years of life, the baby depends for his future emotional and intellectual development on stimulation and affectionate care from people he knows well and who know him as an individual. Whether such needs can be met in the absence of a continuous mother figure is not yet known. What is known is that loss of the mother, especially if followed by care in an impersonal institution, is likely to have long lasting and perhaps permanent adverse effects.

Table 29 shows that the majority of fathers felt that motherlessness had no immediate effects on their children. This is in line with Marsden's finding that 'At the widest estimate in only a quarter of

TABLE 29 Immediate effects of mother's loss on children's mental and physical health (per cent) (n = 574)

None	72·1
Emotional disturbance	18·1
Physical health – worse	4·3
Physical health – better	5·5

the families were any kinds of emotional stress apparent, such as nightmares, hysteria, or very withdrawn behaviour. Violent partings in several instances had brought on attacks of temporary enuresis.'[50] Those who felt that the emotional health of their children suffered consisted of two groups: those who said that the disturbance started before the mother left or died but got worse after, and the much larger group who thought that the disturbance appeared for the first time after the mother left or died. There were no differences in the responses of the fathers according to social class or reason for motherlessness. There were, however, small social-class differences in the fathers' ability to handle the children. While 75 per cent of fathers in classes I and II found no problems, or found the children easier to handle, the corresponding proportion in class III was 69 per cent and in classes IV and V, 65 per cent. Examples of fathers who reported their difficulties ranged mainly from those who felt that as the children got older they became more difficult in behaviour, and those who felt that it was difficult dealing with problems of teenage girls, to those who found the responsibility of the children inevitably

TABLE 30 Has father found any of the children difficult to handle since mother left or died? (per cent) (n = 644)

No, no problems as a rule	64·0
No, children easier to handle/ better behaved	4·1
Yes, children more difficult to handle/ worse behaved	22·5
Yes, children delinquent/ being before the court	7·1
Other	2·3

a harder proposition to deal with alone than when shared with the wife. We did not, however, come across the feeling bordering despair that some of Marsden's mothers faced with regard to discipline. Perhaps this was due to the father's greater ability to enforce discipline as well as to the children's greater willingness to accept discipline from the father than the mother. After all, this is what society seemingly expects of parents – the father to be primarily the disciplinarian and the mother primarily the gentle counsel to the children.

*There is some evidence to show that children of atypical families, including one-parent families, do not achieve educationally as well as those from normal families. The Plowden Report referred to this problem[51] and Kellmer Pringle's study showed an association between poor reading ability and atypical parental situation highly significant for boys and significant for girls.[52] Marsden was doubtful about the effects of fatherlessness on the children's education and he observed that 'In this field of school results where the mother knew so little anyway, it appeared that often her stories of the children's struggles were oblique expressions of her own feelings about the father, and justifications of her behaviour'.[53] Marris found that the financial difficulties of widows jeopardized their children's chances of staying on at school beyond the school-leaving age. 'While they did not want to thwart their children's ambitions', he writes, 'the prospect of having to support them for several extra years was very discouraging.'[54] Those of our fathers who felt that their children's education suffered attributed it to a variety of reasons: the emotional ill-effects of the mother's loss on the children, the fact that the mother was no longer there to help and encourage the children with their school work, the father's lack of time to help the children the way his wife did, and sometimes financial difficulties.

TABLE 31   Has motherlessness affected children's progress at school?

	No		Yes – improved		Yes – deteriorated	
	No.	%	No.	%	No.	%
Widowed	195	65·7	7	2·3	95	32·0
Separated and divorced	180	59·0	60	19·7	65	21·3
Total	375	62·3	67	11·1	160	26·6

$\chi^2 = 48\cdot052$ $P < 0\cdot001$

'Oh yes it did affect Bill. He had just passed his 11 plus and got to the Tech. Grammar. Then his mother died; he never got on after that. The shock seems to have upset him.'

'The eldest boy was top in the A stream but now he is at the bottom. My wife used to encourage him. I haven't got the time and I don't think I am good at it.'

'John and Brian are bright enough to go to Grammar School. The headmaster told me but I can't afford it. The same with the girl. She is three years ahead of her age.'

⁴ Fathers who felt their children's school progress improved attributed it to better school attendance and a more stable home life more conducive to school work. This explains the fact that a much smaller proportion of widowers than separated or divorced fathers said that the school progress of their children improved. The crucial factor was the stability of marriage prior to motherlessness, for there were no social-class differences in the fathers' replies. There was very little evidence from the interviews either that parents informed the school of their new situation or had any discussion with the staff on how best to help the children at the beginning before the children's problems were manifest. One widower, however, said: 'I do have talks with the various teachers who try very much in school to make my children feel at home. So they are getting on alright at school.'

The types of secondary schools attended by the children in our sample are different from those attended by children in the general population in the East Midlands though this may be due to the under-representation of classes I and II in our sample. Of the children in motherless families, 17·1 per cent went to grammar schools, 54·5 per cent to secondary modern schools, 20·3 per cent to comprehensive schools and the remaining 8·1 per cent to other types of schools. The corresponding proportions for children in the general population in the East Midlands are 22·8, 45·1, 23·2 and 9·1 per cent respectively.

Effects on the family

Interaction within the family is a dynamic group process and the withdrawal of any one member (but particularly the father or mother) inevitably affects the network of interactions among the remaining members. The absence of one of the parents inevitably affects the other parent hence Wolff's remark that in fatherless families 'The children have lost their father but they have lost a part of their mother, too'.[55] The vacuum that is created by the absence of one parent creates for a time an unstable situation that the rest of the family members will gradually restructure and eventually stabilize into a new one in a number of ways. They may restructure their activities to fill the gap as much as possible with the result that they may all take on more responsibilities; they may decide or be forced to allow certain of the missing parent's functions to lapse or be modified; or a new mother or father substitute may be found; or they may rely more on the assistance of outside persons or agencies than they did in the past. Whatever solutions are found the important point is that the new family set-up is different from the one it replaced.

The mother's absence inevitably resulted in the children having to take on more responsibility in looking after themselves and helping the father to run the house as Table 32 shows. This was achieved in a variety of ways: in some families different duties were allocated to different children; in other families special periods in the week were used when special household tasks were performed with all the children in attendance; and more often than not children helped out without any formal organized plan as and when the need arose.

TABLE 32 Have the children helped or taken on more
responsibility since family became motherless?
(per cent) (n = 577)

No	26·2
A little more	44·5
A lot more	24·6
Less	4·7

Young children were not usually expected to help though there was a great deal of variation as to when a child was old enough to help.

Many fathers referred to children under school age as being too young to help in the house but some felt differently.

'John (seven years old) might wash up the pots but Keith (just five years) is too small.'

'Anthony (five years) and Lesley (four years) help with the washing, they clean their own shoes and they help tidy the house.'

'Janet (five years) and Ann (four years) can dress themselves completely without any help and they try and "mother" the baby (three years). They look after their own bedroom. They have become very independent.'

Older children, particularly teenage girls, were expected to help and sometimes to act as 'little mothers' to their younger siblings. They were highly praised for doing this but vice versa were strongly resented when they did not fulfil this role expectation. The position of the non-conforming eldest became impossible to tolerate when a younger sibling helped out in the expected manner. Thus one father, whose second eldest daughter was very helpful in the house, said 'the eldest girl though does hardly anything. That's why I am so disgusted with her. It's just not natural.'

Fathers were divided about the value of this extra responsibility to the children. Some felt that it made the children more independent and they thought it would stand the children in good stead one day. Others felt that their children suffered as they had less time to play, to do school work or other things they wanted to. The few fathers who thought that their children were doing less than if their mother had been at home consisted of those who said that their wife was too lazy to do any housework and either piled it on the children or the father or left the house untidy, and those who said that their wife, as a matter of principle, would have expected more from the children.

We said in chapter 1 that a number of families that had been referred to us as motherless were in fact complete when we called, either through re-marriage or cohabitation. This group of families would have merited a separate study in view of the problems which a new parent would have to face in being accepted by and accepting the other members of the family. Marris found that though re-marriage of widows helped to solve many of their problems it created others, particularly resentment of the stepfathers by the widow's own children. We asked fathers whether there was a woman whom the children had come to accept and to use as mother substitute and 52·7 per cent of them, irrespective of social class or reason for motherlessness, agreed, and the remaining 47·3 per cent said there was no such person. Most family crises tend to centre on the mother with the result that she is more likely to seek help from her parents rather than those of her husband. It was, therefore, natural for our fathers to rely on their relatives for help with the result that it was more likely for a paternal than a maternal relative to be considered as mother substitute by the children. There were no social-class variations though there were significant differences according to the reason for motherlessness. Though the proportion who relied on both grandmothers as mother substitute was not very different – 36·9 per cent for the widowers and 42·7 per cent for the separated and the

TABLE 33   Which relation or friend do the children regard as mother substitute? (per cent) (n = 338)

Maternal grandmother	10·6
Paternal grandmother	29·3
Aunts	24·6
Elder sisters	8·6
Other relations	8·0
Non-related women	18·9

divorced together – a greater proportion of widowers than the separated and the divorced together relied on the maternal grand-mother – the proportions were 15·0 per cent and 6·7 per cent respectively. Vice versa, a smaller proportion of widowers, 21·9 per cent, than the separated and the divorced together, 36·0 per cent, said their children used the paternal grandmother as mother substitute. We did not differentiate between maternal and paternal aunts but our impression is that a similar picture would have emerged as for the grand-mother. This will explain the greater proportion of widowers than the rest of the fathers who said their children relied on their aunts. Clearly the children of the separated and divorced fathers, because of the stigma attached to marriage break-up, find it harder than the children of the widowed (where no such stigma exists) to approach the relatives of their mother and to use them as a mother substitute. This greater possibility that the children of the widowed will look for a mother substitute among their mother's relatives explains why a smaller proportion of them (13·1 per cent), than the separated and the divorced (24·7 per cent), find mother substitutes outside their kinship network.

▾ The absence of the mother from the family group inevitably threw the fathers and children into closer contact in their attempt to fill the vacuum created in inter-family relationships. It was therefore to be expected that the majority of the fathers would say that motherlessness had brought them and their children closer together. Of the fathers 68·0 per cent said motherlessness had brought them and all the children closer; 13·4 per cent said this was true for some of their children only; and for the remaining 18·6 per cent motherlessness had made no difference. There were no significant differences according to social class or according to the reason for motherlessness. Perhaps the most interesting group of fathers are those who said that in spite of the new structural family situation, relationships between them and the children had not altered. The replies of this group of fathers indicated two main reasons for this: inter-family relationships had always been close and yet free and easy, with the father and mother carrying out domestic and child-care duties jointly, with the result that interaction between the father and the children had always been frequent and intense; or the father had taken a very active part in the care of the children before motherlessness because of the mother's lack of interest. Both these sub-groups of fathers viewed their role as a slight extension of their pre-motherless role rather than a marked contrast to it. They were fathers with a 'joint conjugal role' rather than a 'segregated conjugal role relationship'.[56]

'No, we were always a close family. We did everything together, so it hasn't made any difference in that way.'

'No, I was always close with the children. It was always daddy who played with them and got them ready for bed even when their mother was here.'

This closer relationship between father and children is a two-way process. It is not only the children who have to rely on the father to a greater extent than they did before but the father, too, is more likely to discuss some of his problems and feelings with the children. The range of problems that the father could discuss with the children varied from day-to-day household duties to personal problems related to loss of the mother or re-marriage. There was a degree of similarity in the replies of some of our fathers to the replies of some of the widows described by Marris. A group of fathers found emotional problems beyond them and they relied heavily on their eldest daughter in the same way that they relied on her to 'mother' the children.

'Many a time I've broken down and Janet has had to deal with me and hear my feelings. I don't know what I would have done without her. She looks after the house and the children. She is like a mother to them.'

Marris found a similar dependency among some widows on their sons who were expected to take their father's place in the family and he speculated that this 'premature burden may cramp their development, and they may never feel free to marry and make a life of their own'.[57] This reliance of the solitary parent on the children for the satisfaction of his emotional needs 'may prove intolerable and damaging to the children, who are unable to give emotional support or to absorb negative feelings from this source'.[58] Bell and Vogel also refer to the fact that parents can and should be dependent upon one another but not upon the immature child for this will hinder the child's normal development. 'The child needs the security of dependency to utilise his energies for his own development. His development can be stunted if he must emotionally support the parent he needs for security.'[59]

TABLE 34   Can father discuss his feelings with any of his children? (per cent) (n = 579)

No, no reason given	25·0
No, not right to burden the children	1·9
No, I do not want to	1·2
No, children are too young	25·0
Yes, some feelings and problems	27·8
Yes, anything	29·1

Holidays and special days reinforce the solidarity of institutions as units by inculcating group loyalties and by developing closer bonds among the members of the institution. The family is no exception to this. Christmas or Easter, mother's or father's day, birthdays, wedding anniversaries and so on give families an opportunity to lift themselves above and beyond the everyday routine of family life. They are landmarks in the calendar that the family looks forward to with anticipation and looks back on with nostalgia. The mother has a central part to play on such occasions by the mere fact that she usually makes the necessary arrangements. Her absence is, therefore, bound to be noticed and it was no surprise that fathers said that such occasions, more than any others, reminded the family of its one-parent status. As Table 35 shows, only a small minority of fathers felt that there were no occasions when the family felt motherless. They were mostly the separated and the divorced who had been unhappy with their wives, or a few of the widowers whose wife had been ill for a long time before she died or some of those who lived with relatives. Almost half the replies of the fathers who said there were occasions when the family was aware of being motherless referred to special days, mainly Christmas.

TABLE 35 Are there any occasions when the family is aware of being motherless?

| | Yes | | No | |
	No.	%	No.	%
Widowed	253	94·1	16	5·9
Separated and divorced	221	77·8	63	22·2
Total	474	85·7	63	14·3

$\chi^2 = 28\cdot426$ P < 0·001

'We miss her particularly at Christmas. She was very jolly and used to play the piano and have a sing-song. We have not bothered with holidays since the wife died but we used to go regularly before. Birthdays also just come and go. There is no fun.'

'Christmas is the time when you feel it most. That's when I feel lost. It's terrible at Christmas. It's a family affair and there is something lacking.'

'We manage better at Christmas really. I cook the Christmas dinner and we all enjoy ourselves. I cooked it before so it makes no difference really.'

The remaining fathers included those who said that among the many occasions when they felt the absence of the mother were weekends, the evenings before the children went to bed, school holidays, when they came home from work, or sometimes when they had achieved something and wanted to talk to someone close, and when they met other families. For a small group, 13·6 per cent of the fathers, the question was irritating and daft as they felt the family was constantly aware of being motherless.

'It can be very miserable. Wherever you go, with or without the children – even to friends you are missing a partner. If you are at home you miss her even more. There is no answer to it.'

4　Occupation and income

When a family is left motherless it means that a father has to under-take the tasks which in most societies are done by two people – earning a living and caring for children. This means that his whole life must become child centred. He has to judge events, opportunities and possibilities in the light of his dual task of earner and carer. This chapter examines the impact of motherlessness on the two closely linked areas – occupation and income.

Our sample fell into two groups – those fathers who were at work and those who were not. The great majority of those who were not working were drawing Supplementary Benefit in order to stay at home and look after their children. Of our respondents 29·4 per cent had at some time drawn Supplementary Benefit to do this since their family became motherless and 19·4 per cent were doing so at the time of interview. Such cases, however, are almost certainly over-represented in our sample as the Supplementary Benefits Commission referred to us the names of all those men known to be drawing Supplementary Benefit for this purpose. No other source of referrals was as com-plete as this.

Fathers on Supplementary Benefit

The crucial question perhaps is why some men are able to continue to combine work and the care of children while others find this impossible. There are many factors which are relevant – the nature of the father's work and his hours of work, his health and his domestic skills, the age of the children, the presence and helpfulness of rela-tives, neighbours and the social services, the father's income and ability to pay for domestic help and child minding, and the availability of such help.

Our evidence suggests that certain generalizations can be made about these fathers who have to give up work and draw Supplementary Benefit. We have already seen that as regards health and housing they are worse off than the other fathers. There are also social-class differences. Fathers in classes III, IV and V were considerably more likely to apply for Supplementary Benefit than fathers in classes I and II. There are certain obvious explanations for this. As we shall see

TABLE 36 Did father draw Supplementary Benefit to look after the children following his wife's death or departure?

Social Class	Yes		No	
	No.	%	No.	%
I and II	7	11·3	55	88·7
III	92	30·8	207	69·2
IV and V	69	38·5	110	61·5

$\chi^2 = 15.995$ $P < 0.001$

later on, fathers in classes I and II not only work shorter hours, they also work hours which fit more easily round the school day. Because of their greater financial resources they are more likely to be able to afford to pay for domestic help and child minding and certainly more of them do spend on this. Classes IV and V, on the other hand, work longer and more irregular hours. They are less able to pay for help and it is less of a drop in income for them to rely on Supplementary Benefit than it would be for classes I and II and therefore, perhaps, less unthinkable. Their work and income makes it easier for fathers in classes I and II to continue to combine work and the care of children; on the other hand it is more difficult for classes III, IV and V to do so.

The proportion of widowed and divorced fathers who had received Supplementary Benefit to stay at home and look after the children was very similar – rather less than a quarter – but well over a third of the separated had received benefit for this purpose.

When the data are analysed according to length of motherlessness they suggest that those fathers who had been left on their own more recently are more likely to have received Supplementary Benefit.

This may, of course, reflect the fathers' better memory of more recent events – particularly in the cases where receipt of benefit was very short term. It may also reflect the greater publicity which the Supplementary Benefits scheme has received in recent years or it may reflect the Commission's increased willingness to pay benefit to fathers to stay at home and care for their children. It would seem very few fathers applied for but were refused Supplementary Benefit.

When we looked more closely at the group of fathers who were drawing Supplementary Benefit at the time of interview we found interesting differences in family size between them and the working fathers.

Fathers drawing Supplementary Benefit quite clearly had larger families. 69·3 per cent of them had three or more children compared with 47·8 per cent of the working fathers. Slightly more fathers on Supplementary Benefit were left to care for children under five. The biggest contrast between the two groups, however, was in the number of fathers left with children between five and eleven. 52·7 per cent of Supplementary Benefit case fathers had two or more children in this age group compared with 32·7 per cent of all working fathers.

A large family obviously means greater domestic burdens. The presence of children under five means that permanent day care arrangements have to be made. Children between five and eleven are safely at school all day but there is the problem of providing care before and after school and in school holidays and this is also the worst period for childish ailments and the day care problems this poses. So it is fairly easy to see why the particular family characteristics of fathers on Supplementary Benefit should make this solution of their problems more likely.

The larger a father's family the more Supplementary Benefit he will draw. The loss of income for the larger family which becomes dependent on Supplementary Benefit is likely to be less great than for the small family. When weighing up his situation this could well be a factor in the father's decision. The physical and emotional costs of continuing at work and the acute caring problems which this would pose are not worth the marginal gain in income. Given the current level of Supplementary Benefit it is perhaps only the father with a large family who has any genuine choice over whether to carry on at work or temporarily give up work to care for his children.

Of those fathers who had at some stage since their wife's death or departure received Supplementary Benefit to stay at home and look after the children the majority received benefit for a comparatively short period. Table 37 shows that 55·3 per cent received it for less than a year, the majority of these for less than six months.

TABLE 37 Length of time father was/has been drawing Supplementary Benefit since wife's death or departure (per cent) (n = 168)

Under 6 months	35·7
6–12 months	19·6
12–24 months	18·5
24–36 months	12·5
3 years plus	13·7

When we looked more closely at the group of fathers who were not working at the time of interview, it was clear that the proportion was greater among those who had been left motherless more recently. The proportion not working remained at just over 20 per cent for the first four years of motherlessness and then fell steadily to 4 per cent for those motherless for over ten years. The time of greatest need for the father to be at home is obviously when there are children under five. As children grow up so it becomes possible for fathers to return to work.

Those fathers who had drawn Supplementary Benefit to stay at home gave varied descriptions of their contacts with Supplementary Benefit officers, as Table 38 shows. Just over 60 per cent of fathers spoke of their contacts as very good, good or satisfactory.

TABLE 38 Fathers' descriptions of their contacts with Supplementary Benefit officers (per cent) (n = 146)

Very good/good	34·3
All right/fair	26·0
Some good officers, some unhelpful/ unreasonable	13·7
Most officers unhelpful/ unreasonable	12·3
Bad, unhelpful, terrible	13·7

'Have always been pleasant and helpful with me. It depends how you are with them,' was one father's view.

'Some of them that have come here have been real gentlemen. Haven't had any difficulty. Can't speak anything but highly of them. They've got a very difficult job,' said a widower.

'Very sociable and helpful. An officer calls once a month and suggests any extra help I might need. He is always very kind and talks man to man,' said another father.

13·7 per cent of fathers reported mixed contacts. 'All right at first. They get worse as you go on,' said a father who had drawn Supplementary Benefit for fifteen months. 'Mostly fair, occasionally a bit shirty. Last Tuesday one got officious', said another. 'Not too bad', was another father's verdict. 'One bloke was trying it on, but most of the blokes have been quite nice.'

26 per cent of fathers spoke of contacts which were generally bad, unhelpful or unsatisfactory. 'I didn't really like their attitudes,' one father explained, 'they act as if they were paying out of their own pockets.' 'We'll see what we can do . . . but I wish I could afford the suit you're wearing,' was one officer's response to a request for help. 'They try to go too far into one's business. He suggested selling various articles to get extra money', was another complaint. 'Horrible – the odd one that is' – was one father's response, 'he told me to get rid of the telly. When I say horrible I really mean the system, not the ones doing the job.'

Altogether 9·6 per cent of fathers mentioned pressure put on them to get back to work. 'I try to explain the situation to them,' said a father with two children aged three-and-a-half and two years, 'but they're always trying to get you to work. I'd prefer to be at work but I've tried explaining to them. I don't know whether they understand or not or whether it's their job to get you off their back.' 'One of them told me . . . that it was time I got a housekeeper and went out to work, and stopped living off the community,' said one man who was keeping house for his seven children, six of them at school. 'You again – about time you got a job' was the greeting another father received at his last visit to the Social Security office. 'They are always telling me to get a job – and I can't work. I've been in and out of hospital but they don't understand,' a widower said bitterly.

This last point about pressure to return to work is one which it is difficult to evaluate. There comes a time when it will be in the father's and the children's interest that he should return to work. A little judicious encouragement from the Supplementary Benefit officer may reasonably be seen as part of the officer's welfare function. What would be quite intolerable is that pressure should be brought to bear on a father to return to work where he has pre-school children and little possibility of making adequate arrangements to provide for their care.

In our study of community attitudes to motherless and fatherless families we asked respondents whether they themselves had claimed any social security benefits in the previous ten years and whether they had experienced any problems or difficulties in so doing. Only 35 per cent had claimed benefits and had personal contacts with social security officers while doing so. 82·3 per cent of these had found the officers pleasant, helpful and understanding. The remainder had complaints about the officers ranging from their rudeness and authoritarianism and milder complaints about impersonality. What was particularly interesting was that 97·2 per cent of respondents aged sixty and over found their contacts with ministry officials satisfactory compared with 70 per cent of the under-sixties. It is difficult to know, of course, whether the difference reflects a better attitude on the part of officials towards the elderly or a more accepting attitude on the part of the elderly to lower standards of service or a low incidence in the case of the elderly of features that could give rise to dissatisfaction such as uncertainty about the continuance of benefit.

The opinions and attitudes of Supplementary Benefit officers are likely to reflect to a greater or lesser extent the attitudes current in the community. They are, therefore, likely to be more sympathetic to some groups than others. Marsden describes very different attitudes to the different groups which made up his sample – the unmarried, the widowed, the separated and the divorced. Pressure to return to work was greater on unmarried mothers than on the others.[1]

In general the fathers in our sample were less critical of their contacts with Supplementary Benefit officers than were Marsden's mothers. Their position, of course, was less dubious. Clearly most had no other source of support whereas Marsden's mothers were frequently suspected of having secret cohabitees. Most of our sample who were drawing Supplementary Benefit would have clearly preferred to have been at work. They were so clearly worse off on Supplementary Benefit that it was difficult for anyone to believe that they were drawing benefit from anything but sheer necessity.

The majority of our fathers were unhappy about drawing Supplementary Benefit. Table 39 shows their feelings.

'I hate receiving it,' one father told our interviewer, 'you're always pestered and I don't like having it on my conscience at being paid by the government for not doing the job. Still if it wasn't for that what would you have?'

TABLE 39 Fathers' feelings about receiving Supplementary Benefit (per cent) (n = 176)

Doesn't like it/ Didn't like it	*Ester*	63·6
Not bothered/ It's a right	*9·42*	23·3
Other		13·1

'To be quite candid,' said another, 'I feel very sensitive about it. A lot of people class it as a stigma and that's how I feel about it.' 'I asked for something which was my right and they made me feel I should have been better off begging in the street for it,' said a third. Fathers' feelings on this were clearly the product of a number of influences. Most felt that they *ought* to be at work. Without a job they were less than men. They realized that there was no alternative to Supplementary Benefit if they were to keep their children but they resented their sense of dependence. In part their feelings were the product of the system. As the last father quoted put it – benefit was a right and yet the system aimed to deter – or so he felt. Fathers resented having to ask. They resented the 'pestering' which is an inevitable part of a means-tested system. They resented, too, the attitude of some officers who failed to understand their situation and to sympathize with them. Fathers also felt that the community classed them with the mighty stage army of scroungers abusing the Welfare State.

Only a small minority positively asserted their right to Supplementary Benefit. 'Thought I was entitled to it. Felt no guilt at all,' said one widower. 'I didn't feel it was charity.' 'It was something that should be done although the way it was dealt out, sometimes you felt you were being given charity,' said another. 'To begin with I thought it was degrading,' said one respondent, 'but my doctor said it was my right – that I shouldn't feel this way so then I didn't mind.'

What is interesting is that feelings about dependence on Supplementary Benefit varied slightly according to the reason for motherlessness. The widowed were in general happier about it. They were less likely to express dislike of having to draw Supplementary Benefit, more likely to express a feeling of entitlement, that they had a *right* to benefit. These feelings are obviously related to the different status which widowers, the separated and the divorced feel they enjoy. Society sympathizes with the widowed, they are not culpable, they are the victims of circumstances, they deserve help. The separated and the divorced are partly to blame for their plight and are stigmatized to some degree. They, therefore, feel less able to ask for or receive help.

Fathers' comments about the adequacy of the level of Supplementary Benefit were predictable. 72 per cent of those who had received benefit to stay at home and look after their children described the amount as inadequate. This is in line with the findings of our community attitudes study where 65 per cent of the sample thought the level was too low.

'Only adequate for marginal living,' was how one father summed it up. 'I thought if they gave me £20 a week I could manage and was saving the state the cost of having them in care,' said another conscientious father. 'But when I started it was £12.65. I couldn't believe it.' What came through a great many replies was that the level was adequate for minimum day-to-day needs – 'Adequate for existing' was how one father put it – but it provided no margin for any extras, for replacing things which had got worn out or broken. 'Definitely wouldn't have done if we had had to live on it permanently,' said one father who was back at work at the time of interview. This helps to explain, of course, why the non-working fathers were so much worse off as regards household consumer goods and housing in general.

Most of the 25·7 per cent of fathers who spoke of the Supplementary Benefit they received as adequate hastened to qualify their answers. It was adequate for day-to-day needs but not for the replacement of things which had worn out. It was adequate some weeks but not others. It was adequate for meagre necessities but not for extras. 'On the whole O.K.,' said one widower. 'It depends what you want to get out of life. I have resigned myself to the fact that I will live a day-to-day existence. No point in complaining.' 'Adequacy' in fact meant a grinding narrowness and restriction of life superimposed on a situation where family circumstances tended to produce that in any case.

Very few fathers were benefiting from any additions to the basic level of Supplementary Benefit. Only 4·5 per cent of fathers drawing Supplementary Benefit at the time of interview told us that they were getting any additional special allowance – for diet, extra fuel, etc. Most fathers expressed complete ignorance of the fact that there were such special allowances though the longer a father had been dependent on Supplementary Benefit the more likely he was to know of the possibility of this additional help.

When we asked about exceptional needs grants – occasional grants given for bedding, furniture and the replacement of items of capital equipment – we found that less than a quarter of fathers drawing Supplementary Benefit had ever received such grants. Of those who had never applied for such a grant most knew nothing of the possibility of this addition.

'They're not helpful in that way,' said one father, 'they'll not tell you what you can receive. People get to know from their mates.' Ignorance was an effective rationing device.

The main object of the fathers we interviewed was to continue to care for their children. Supplementary Benefit was an unpopular means to this end. Most fathers would have sooner been at work. What they would have preferred was help which enabled them to work rather than help which enabled them to stay at home.

Job changing

In the case of fathers who continued in full-time employment we tried to explore the impact of motherlessness in three areas – job changing and job mobility, hours worked and attitudes to work.

Where fathers were in the same job as before the wife's death or departure – this was the situation for 58·3 per cent of fathers – we asked whether they had had to stay in the same job because of their home situation. We had no illusions about the problems involved in asking this kind of question. We were asking about events which for many fathers had happened some years before. We were asking about decisions which for many came in the aftermath of a traumatic experience. We were asking fathers for explanations of their behaviour at a time which, from a distance, must have seemed one of immense confusion. To disentangle one motive from another is not easy at any time. What we were asking of our fathers was something peculiarly difficult.

Just over 8 per cent of fathers said they had had to stay in the same

G

job because of their family situation. The replies fathers gave covered a range of reasons. Some fathers had stayed in jobs involving shift or night work so that they could be at home during the day. Some had had to give up jobs involving irregular hours so that they could be at home when the children were at home. Others had stayed in the same job because of their nearness to relatives and parents. Understanding employers, too, sometimes discouraged movement.

'My employer understood the situation and lets me have time off when necessary,' was how one father explained his non-movement. The heavy burdens of combining work and the care of children also discouraged movement to new and better-paid jobs which might turn out to be more demanding. 'I've just been offered a better job with more responsibility,' a father told the interviewer, 'and I can't take it because it would mean longer hours and I can't manage that with the children.' Fathers who had managed to work out viable types of substitute care or who had helpful relatives, friends or neighbours, were understandably reluctant to disrupt such networks. The costs of immobility sometimes seemed considerable – though rarely precisely calculable.

The number of fathers not moving because of their home situation varied slightly according to the reason for motherlessness. Widowers were a little more likely to stay put than the others. The more recently motherless, too, were likely to be more affected than those who had been motherless for longer. In the early years the presence of very young children – which was the situation in over half the families in our sample when they became motherless – will make the father acutely dependent on the help of others. This lasts until the youngest children are safely at school when the problems of combining work and the care of children ease a little.

We also asked those fathers who had changed or left their job since their family became motherless for their reasons for changing. Of the reasons given, 42 per cent related to caring for the children. 'Sacked because couldn't keep hours – i.e. shifts. Hours in haulage better – i.e. 8 a.m. – 5 p.m.,' one father explained. 'I couldn't work any shorter than the full day because we had all to go out on the same transport, so I left,' said a former building worker. 'I couldn't carry on when she died. I couldn't set off in the morning and leave the children,' said a widower whose job involved a lot of travelling. Some fathers tried to work out satisfactory arrangements – not always to the satisfaction of their employers. One father was working on a near-by housing estate for the local authority housing department. 'I went first thing in the morning to order materials, etc.,' he related, 'then nipped home to get Ann up and off to school, then went back to work. This was fine till they found out and I got the sack.' Jobs which took fathers away for irregular and indeterminate periods could not be combined with the care of their children. The children had to come first. Even when fathers managed to combine work and the care of their children this sometimes involved very precarious child-minding arrangements as we shall see later.

The separated were more likely to mention caring for the children as the reason for leaving or changing their job than the widowed or the divorced. This is interesting because a greater proportion of the divorced than the separated had children under five. The social class differences between the divorced and the separated may be the explanation. The divorced had proportionately more fathers from social classes I and II and fewer from IV and V than the separated, and the shorter hours and higher incomes which this meant would have eased the situation for them.

This hypothesis is supported by the evidence about social class and the reasons for changing or leaving the job held at the time of motherlessness. Fathers in social classes I and II are in general less likely to change their job or stop work to look after their children than are fathers in classes III, IV or V. They are more likely to stress emotional reasons for job changing – an illustration perhaps of the argument that emotional feelings are a luxury to which only the better off can aspire. Similarly, ill-health and redundancy accounted for over 20 per cent of the reasons given by classes III, IV and V for job changes but they were scarcely mentioned by fathers in classes I and II. Health is less likely to affect the job performance of fathers in classes I and II and they are more secure against the winds of industrial change.

In very many ways the non-manual worker is greatly privileged in comparison with those in manual occupations. Wedderburn and Craig, for example, in their study of employment conditions in industry found that only 8 per cent of clerical employees were subject to loss of pay for late arrival at work compared with 90 per cent of manual workers. They found, too, that the vast majority of firms were willing to pay their non-manual workers when they had time off for domestic reasons whereas only a third of firms were prepared to do the same for manual workers.[2] These privileges and inequalities can be of crucial importance for the father struggling to combine work and the care of children. They may make it possible or impossible.

87

Hours of work

We asked fathers how many hours they normally worked each day. Table 40 shows fathers' replies according to social class. Nearly 46 per cent of fathers in classes I and II and classes IV and V work eight hours a day or less compared with 30 per cent of fathers in class III.[3] It is, therefore, that much more difficult for fathers in class III to combine work and the care of their children.

TABLE 40   Hours worked daily by father (per cent) (n = 420)

Social class	7 hours or less	8 hours	9 hours plus
I and II	11·5	34·4	54·1
III	4·6	26·1	69·3
IV and V	19·5	27·1	53·4

We sought to explore the impact of the family's motherless situation on fathers' hours of work by asking them how the number of hours they worked at the time of interview compared with the hours worked before the family became motherless. 32 per cent of the fathers at work claimed to put in a shorter working day since the family became motherless. Fewer of fathers in classes I and II work shorter hours presumably because their hours were already shorter and because their jobs gave less opportunity for reduction – for example, giving up overtime or shifts.

Motherlessness made less impact on the hours of work and therefore on this particular aspect of earning capacity in classes I and II. With their previously existing higher incomes fathers in classes I and II were therefore in a better position all round to buy domestic help or help with the care of children. Fathers in classes III, IV and V are initially less able to afford help so they have to work shorter hours thus further reducing their ability to pay for help. There is a downward spiral of deprivation.

If the impact of motherlessness on hours of work is analysed according to length of motherlessness an interesting pattern emerges. Those motherless for less than a year seem less affected than those motherless for between one and six years. In other contexts, too, we found that motherlessness seemed to make a smaller impact on those motherless for less than a year. A likely explanation is that the early months of motherlessness are seen by the father and by relatives, friends and neighbours as an emergency. The situation is new; it is a crisis situation. Therefore more help is likely to be available. By the

TABLE 41 Comparison of hours worked by father before and after motherlessness (per cent) (n = 433)

	Fewer hours after	Same	More after
Under 1 year	28·0	67·0	5·0
1–3 years	35·0	55·0	10·0
4–6 years	31·5	58·3	10·2
7 years plus	27·6	62·1	10·3
Total	31·9	58·9	9·2

time the family has been motherless for a year or more the situation is no longer an emergency, the novelty has worn off. Those who helped in the early days are less willing and probably less able to supply help on what looks like becoming a permanent basis. The same is true, too, of the social services as we shall see later on in the study. There may well be, therefore, a trough in the experience of motherlessness which hits families in the crucial months or years between the novelty of an emergency situation wearing off and the situation easing for the father as the children grow older.

Attitudes to work

We attempted to explore whether motherlessness had affected the father's attitude to work. This demanded a feat both of memory and insight on the part of the fathers. Nearly a quarter of fathers spoke of being or having been less happy or less immersed in their work. There were those fathers who stressed the other job waiting to be done when they got home. 'Never seem to enjoy your work the same,' said a widower, 'always got it on your mind you've got to get it done and rush home.' 'I certainly don't put the same energy into work as I did before,' confessed another father, 'I make sure that there is some energy left by the time I get home. I have to make sure I enjoy the kids' company in the evening.' 'I've got to put children before work,'

TABLE 42   Effect of mother's death or departure on father's
attitude to work (per cent) (n = 405)

Same	61·7
Less immersed/ Less happy	15·3
More immersed/ More happy	10·2
Less happy at time, O.K. now	8·4
Other	4·4

was one simple reply. Other fathers stressed the lack of incentives provided by their situation. 'My job is to keep the children going – not interested in work as such now,' was how one put it. 'Unable to be single-minded or seek promotion,' was how another summed up his attitude. 'Lost ambition – not free to do work in the same way. Would have expanded farm but had no heart to do so,' said a farmer.

In contrast to this group, just over 10 per cent of fathers found comfort and a new satisfaction in work. 'I feel more dedicated to my work, it seems to help a lot,' was how one put it. 'Feel as if the job is all that matters at the moment. Reluctant to leave work and go back to an empty house,' said another. 'Before I had the two interests,' one father explained, 'now my main interest is work. Rapid advancement is probably due to interest in the job.' 'Yes, I've had the opportunity to concentrate more on my career because a few years' prior to her leaving I had a lot of other worries at home,' said another.

The impact of motherlessness on the father's attitude to work depended on a multiplicity of factors past and present – his involvement in his job, the attitude of employers and his fellow-workers, the ease of combining work and the care of children and the reason for motherlessness. We tried to look further at some of the variables involved. Widowers were more likely to describe their attitude to work as the same or less immersed and less happy. Only a tiny minority spoke of themselves as happier in their work whereas quite large numbers of the separated and the divorced spoke of greater contentment at work since parting from their wives. For the widowed there are no compensations. As we found at many points in the study, widowers were more likely to see work, domestic arrangements, care of the children, etc., as less satisfactory since their wife's death. Loss of their wife coloured their whole attitude to living and the problems of motherlessness. On the other hand, the separated and divorced saw their situation as part loss, part gain. Many were keen to assert that things were better since their wife's departure.

When asked about their attitude to their workmates some 20 per cent of fathers said they felt less close, 9 per cent said they felt closer and friendlier, 71 per cent said their attitudes were the same. 'I more or less argued with my workmates over nothing when she left. I was very quick tempered at first,' one father confessed. Others said the same but said that things had improved with time. Some referred to changes of attitude which seemed to them at the time of interview to be permanent. 'I was a happy-go-lucky man,' one father said, 'and now nobody wants to know me.' Some described the sympathy and support they had received from fellow-workers; others described the opposite. 'People blamed me for my wife's suicide and took it out of me, especially the foreman,' one father complained.

On the whole the widowed were rather more likely than the other groups to say they felt less close to their workmates. Yet this is the group for whom one would have expected most sympathy. It is impossible to know, of course, to what extent it was the father's attitudes and expectations which created barriers – or seemed to the father to create them – and to what extent the father's feelings were the fruit of a correct perception of other people's attitudes.

We have already seen that motherlessness meant that many fathers had to give up work in order to care for their children. For some of those who did continue to work it meant job changes so that they could better fulfil their dual role. For others it meant that they could not change to better jobs when opportunities presented themselves. For others it meant shorter hours in order to combine work and the care of their children. What effect did motherlessness have on the family's financial position? We tried to examine this in four ways by looking at the impact on income, wages and expenditure and by studying the father's own feelings about the family's overall financial position. Asking people about changes in their financial position, often over a considerable period, can only produce a picture of rather general trends. These are clear and the picture needs to be viewed in these rather broad terms.

Impact on income

Just under 44 per cent said that their income had gone down since the family became motherless, 19 per cent said their income was the same, 37 per cent said it had increased. Anyone whose income has gone down at a time of generally rising incomes and general inflation has, of course, suffered a considerable relative fall in standard of living. This 44 per cent, of course, includes fathers who had had to give up work and rely on Supplementary Benefit but they only form about half the number.

TABLE 43   Impact of motherlessness on income

	Less now		Same		More now	
	No.	%	No.	%	No.	%
Under 4 years	177	52·1	70	20·6	93	27·4
4 years or more	68	31·1	37	16·9	114	52·0
Total	245	43·8	107	19·1	207	37·1

$X^2 = 36·312$ $P < 0·001$

As might have been expected from what we have seen so far, fathers in classes III, IV and V were more likely to report a fall in income than those in classes I and II. Those who could least afford therefore to suffer a drop in income were more likely to do so. As might have been expected too, those made motherless more recently are more likely to complain of a reduction in income than those who have been motherless for longer. 52·1 per cent of those motherless for four years or less said their incomes were less than before motherlessness compared with 31·1 per cent of those who had been motherless for four years or more. In time, of course, wage increases will make good any initial loss so the information given by those motherless for longer is less valuable. The true impact of motherlessness on family income is seen in its effect on the more recently motherless.

For many the drop in income was very considerable: 15·6 per cent of fathers said their income was less by £10 or more per week, 40·1 per cent of fathers complained of losses in excess of £3 per week. Those who lost most were those who could least afford to lose anything. 28·4 per cent of fathers in classes I and II reported a loss of £3 per week or more. For fathers in classes IV and V the figure was 37·5 per cent. This meant a relatively greater fall in income for classes IV and V – due largely to the greater number of fathers having to give up employment. Table 44 shows the main reasons which fathers gave for the fall in income. Far and away the most important was 'father not at work'. This is a reflection of the relationship between wage levels and the level of Supplementary Benefit. Many fathers who gave up work suffered a very considerable drop in income. 'I had to leave work for which I earned about £30 p.w. I had to leave to look after the children,' said one unemployed father who was drawing £10.30 per week Supplementary Benefit plus rent at the

TABLE 44 Reasons given by father for fall in income (per cent)
(n = 318)

Father not at work	34·6	
Loss of overtime	18·5	
Changed job	10·4	
Loss of wife's earnings	12·3	
Other	24·2	

time of interview. 'I was earning £35–£40 per week as a plasterer,' said another father drawing £12.50 Supplementary Benefit plus rent. Another father who had been earning £40–£50 per week complained sadly about the problems of adjusting to £8 per week Supplementary Benefit plus rent. Fathers give up work to keep the family together and avoid the necessity of the children going to live with relatives or going into the care of the local authority. The level of Supplementary Benefit is probably generally not a factor in the father's initial decision whether or not to care for his children but it may be a factor in his ability and determination to continue to do so. We can say nothing about this because our study is purely of fathers who were caring for children at a particular moment in time. It would be extremely interesting to know whether any motherless children come into the care of local authorities because fathers have given up work and found themselves unable to manage on Supplementary Benefit.

If a father is drawing Supplementary Benefit to stay at home and look after two children it is costing society about 60 per cent of what it would cost on average to keep two children in care. This illustrates the advantages of encouraging fathers to give up work rather than place the children in care. The basic level of Supplementary Benefit can hardly be said to provide such encouragement.

The affluence of many families – and the basic comforts of some – depend on the wife's earnings. In 13·3 per cent of our families the wives had been working. It was clear that the loss of her earnings was a considerable blow to the financial situation of many families. Evidence from other research shows that most working wives in fact spend most of their earnings on their families.[4] The loss of their earnings is, therefore, a loss to family income and necessitates considerable adjustments. Fathers mentioned to us earnings by their wives in some cases of £20 per week. Often, although the wife's earnings were small, they were nevertheless a crucial element in the family's economy. Commitments, too, had often been assumed in the light of the husband's and the wife's joint income. When one – or both – incomes ceased the economy was undermined.

The explanations which fathers gave for their reduced income varied slightly with social class. Fewer fathers in classes I and II gave up work so this was mentioned much less frequently by them than by those in classes IV and V. No father in classes I or II mentioned loss of overtime as a factor, whereas this was mentioned by some 20 per cent of other fathers.

Motherlessness almost inevitably means a loss of income in the short term if not in the long term. There is the loss of the tax allowance for the wife frequently mentioned by tax-conscious fathers in classes I and II. There is the loss of her earnings – and we know that nationally over one-third of married women with children under sixteen go out to work.[5] In around a quarter of the families in our sample the father had had to give up work to care for his children so leading to general reductions in standard of living. A large proportion of our families were hit by one or other of these factors. Three-quarters of the fathers in our sample, however, managed to continue at work. To gauge the wider impact of motherlessness on income it is necessary to look more closely at its impact on wages and earning capacity.

Impact on wages

We have seen already that the motherless father has to regard his work in a new light. No longer can he look at it solely from the point of view of its economic rewards, the satisfactions – if any – which it affords him and the other criteria by which most people assess their jobs. For many, a new and overriding criterion asserts itself – the compatibility of work with the care of children. It is because of this new concern that motherlessness makes an impact on earning capacity.

Table 45 shows that nearly one-quarter of the fathers in our sample who were in full-time work at the time of interview had suffered a fall in wages relative to their situation before motherlessness. This fall took place against a national background of unprecedented general wage increases. A drop in earnings was right against the general trend and meant a major change in standard of living. The losses too were frequently considerable. Half the fathers reporting a fall in wages had suffered a loss of £6 or more per week.

TABLE 45 Comparison between present wage and that before motherlessness (per cent) (n = 398)

Less by £6 plus	12·8
Less by £3–£5	8·3
Less by 50p to £2	2·0
Same	24·9
More	52·0

Just under a quarter of working fathers said their wages were the same. What this means depends, of course, on how long they had been motherless. For those recently motherless it may mean their wages have been unaffected. For those who have been motherless for longer it may mean that after an initial fall their wages have regained their former level.

The largest single group was the 52 per cent of fathers whose wages had increased. For most people frequent wage increases are now the norm, and it is only to be expected that this would be the largest group.

There were two main reasons given by those whose wages had fallen – loss of overtime and change of job. Loss of overtime accounted for 42·6 per cent of the reasons given, change of job for 37·7 per cent. Reduction in overtime was an obvious immediate adjustment to the extra burdens of motherlessness. 'Unable to work the number of hours required to bring income up,' said one father, so pinpointing a characteristic of industrial earning patterns in this country – that high wages are frequently 'brought up' by long hours of overtime.[6] Such a situation leaves the man who cannot work the extra hours in a relatively deprived position. 'Weekend working ceased,' said many fathers in response to our inquiry about the

95

reason for their reduced wages. 'Can't do any overtime and can't do the night shift so am on a lower rate on the regular day shift,' another father explained.

A considerable number of fathers had to give up work which involved a lot of travelling or irregular hours and take whatever jobs they could find which were more convenient. 'Do not travel so far to get good jobs,' explained a father who was a pipe fitter. 'Was able to travel around before and get more money – Manchester and London for example,' explained a transport driver. Other fathers had to give up lucrative second jobs at weekends or in the evenings. '£10 a week short,' one father summed up his situation. 'Before, this job wasn't a full-time job – I worked in the factory for Mr F. and did house repairs at night – now I do houses all the time.' Several fathers expressed their frustration at having to work below their full capacity and having this emphasized every week in their pay packets. 'I could get about £25 p.w. now in my present job,' a father who had changed his job once explained, 'but that would mean doing shifts again so I have to work below my earning capacity and I find this very, very frustrating to know I'm doing so.'

The impact of motherlessness on wages was by no means uniform. By the nature of their conditions of employment fathers in classes I and II were less susceptible to such losses. Their incomes were altogether more secure. This conclusion is supported by evidence from the Department of Employment and Productivity's earnings survey. It showed that over 90 per cent of non-manual workers' earnings are derived from their basic pay which means that in general their income is known and predictable. In contrast basic pay makes up only two-thirds of manual workers' earnings. Some 16 per cent comes from overtime and 7 per cent from payments by results. So their total earnings are much less predictable than non-manual earnings.[7]

Only 14·2 per cent of fathers in classes I and II reported a fall in wages compared with 25·7 per cent in class III and 21 per cent in classes IV and V. There was little difference between classes in the percentage of fathers reporting a loss of £6 or more per week. But whereas 2 per cent of fathers in classes I and II suffered losses of between 50p and £5, the figure for class III was 12·4 per cent and for classes IV and V, 10 per cent. This sort of loss is explicable in terms of lost overtime or shorter hours or the move to a more convenient but less well-paid unskilled job. For many low-paid men such sums make up the difference between subsistence and modest comfort.

Analysis of falls in wages by length of motherlessness in Table 46 is also fruitful. Those made motherless within the last twelve months are less likely to report a fall in wages than those who have been motherless for longer. This suggests that the impact of motherlessness on earning capacity is not immediate. These fathers have continued in work – presumably because they have been able to make arrangements for the care of their children during working hours. These arrangements enable most of them to maintain their earnings. For those fathers motherless for over a year, the situation has become permanent. It is a chronic rather than an acute problem which they pose. The fathers find that major adjustments are called

TABLE 46   Impact of motherlessness on wages, analysed according to length of motherlessness (per cent) (n = 398)

	Less	Same	More
Under 1 year	15·4	52·0	32·6
1–3 years	28·4	23·0	48·6
4 years plus	20·3	18·1	61·6
Total	23·1	24·9	52·0

for in their work. As mentioned earlier, initially satisfactory arrangements break down, perhaps under the stress of seeming permanency, and fathers have to bear a greater burden. This means a reduction in earning capacity during the children's period of greatest dependency.

Just under 14 per cent of fathers who had been motherless for seven years or more complained that their earnings were less at the time of interview than before motherlessness. The same number complained that their wages were the same – which is equivalent to a fall in real wages. As time goes on memory becomes less accurate. People are often reluctant to admit that their standard of living has improved when by all objective criteria it has. For some everything will seem worse since motherlessness. So the views of those who have been motherless for this length of time, when the time of comparison is so far away, need to be interpreted with some care. The important point, however, is that so many *felt* badly off. This was the reality of the situation to them.

There were interesting differences between social classes in the reasons fathers gave for falls in wages. For class III fathers far and away the most important reason was loss of overtime with change of job mentioned by only about half as many fathers. For fathers in classes IV and V the reasons were almost exactly reversed in importance. Change of job was mentioned by nearly twice as many fathers as loss of overtime. The significance of overtime earnings presumably reflects the shortage of skilled men. These fathers had pushed up their income through extra hours of work. When left to run a home and care for children they found it impossible to sustain the extra load which overtime had meant. Fathers in classes IV and V on the other hand moved to jobs which enabled them more easily to combine work and child care – at a price.

The explanations which fathers gave for their fall in wages alter with the length of the period of motherlessness. In the early days loss of overtime is the most frequently mentioned explanation. For those motherless for four years or more change of job becomes the most important single reason. Giving up overtime is an immediate response to the dual task imposed by motherlessness. Change of job is the response to a permanent problem.

The financial costs of motherlessness are, therefore, considerable. In a society where family affluence is largely dependent on the contribution of the wife's earnings, motherless families are almost by definition deprived – currently or over the life cycle. In those families where father has to give up work there are further financial costs. These are expected and explicable. It is not so obvious that substantial numbers of those fathers who continue in full-time work are also paying the costs of motherlessness in reduced wages.

Impact on expenditure

The result of motherlessness is to reduce income for many families. Changes in expenditure will follow from that, but such changes do not occur simply in those families where income has been reduced. Changes in expenditure are more than a response to a reduction in income. They are a direct result of motherlessness.

We asked fathers whether there were items on which they regularly spent more or less since the family had become motherless. This was obviously a difficult question to answer particularly for those who had been motherless for some time. Many fathers would not have known in detail the family's past patterns of expenditure. Inflation means that most people, motherless or not, spend more at any given moment than they did in the past. Children get older. Their food and clothes cost more. Patterns of expenditure alter. The question was clearly beset with difficulties. What we were trying to get was a picture of the father's feelings about the effect of motherlessness on the family budget. The answers we got and the explanations which fathers gave with their answers make up a consistent pattern.

We gained the very clear impression from various parts of the survey that motherlessness makes life more expensive but it is extremely difficult to give a precise figure for the extra expenditure involved. When a man loses his wife he no longer has to support her. On the other hand, he loses those services which are part of the role and function of a wife and mother to render. He loses the economic benefits of her ability to make and mend clothes, her ability to buy wisely and cheaply and to improve the value of what she buys by her labours. 'I think I do less well on the money I get than a woman can who knows how to make the money stretch,' one father pointed out. 'After nine years I have still not completely mastered the financial side of housekeeping,' another father said in a letter to us. A wife at home also enables a man to work longer hours and so increases his earning power.

Altogether 86 per cent of our sample said they spent more since the family had become motherless. Replies seemed relatively unaffected by social class, the reasons for motherlessness or the length of motherlessness. Of those who had been motherless for twelve months or less – the group whose replies are perhaps most reliable – 88 per cent said they spent more.

Just over 31 per cent of our sample said they were spending more on food. Many fathers told us that they had no time to shop around looking for bargains. They complained that they had to buy at shops which were convenient for home or work rather than seek out the cheapest supermarket. 'Not always possible to be selective in shopping. Just have to be quick,' one father summed it up. Another factor making for greater expenditure on food was that fathers tended to buy ready prepared food which did not require any great investment of time or effort. 'Food is bought for quickness, therefore it's often more expensive,' complained another father. 'I find myself buying expensive food if it is quicker to prepare,' said a father who had been motherless for nine years. A number of fathers complained about the extra costs of school meals compared with the cost of feeding children at home as had been the practice in the past. For a father just above the income limit for free school meals with two or three children at school this could be a very heavy burden though this is not peculiar to the motherless.

37 per cent of fathers said they spent more on clothing. 'My wife used to make all her own and the girls' clothes,' said a widower. 'Children's clothing costs are more because my wife was a good needlewoman,' said another father. When it came to buying new clothes for children many fathers ruefully confessed their lack of knowledge about what constituted a good buy.

There is little difference by social class in the proportions of fathers saying they spent more on food or clothing. On the other hand extra expenditure on domestic help was commoner among social class 1 and II fathers than among the rest of the sample. Surprisingly few fathers in fact said they spent more on domestic help or child care but such expenditure was clearly a function of ability to pay rather than of need. The reduction in income which many fathers suffered combined with the unavoidable increased costs of motherlessness severely limited their ability to spend on these other items – which might have helped to reduce the reduction in income and the other extra costs.

Another interesting area of increased expenditure was what we describe as compensating expenditure for father or children. By this we mean expenditure on minor luxuries – sweets and toys for the children, for example, cigarettes and drink for the father – in an attempt to compensate for the physical and emotional stress of motherlessness; 28·4 per cent of fathers spoke of spending more on their children and 31·7 per cent said they spent more on themselves. Several fathers mentioned such expenditure on the children – as well as on themselves – with a certain guilt. 'I don't suppose I should,' said one father, 'but I *do* give the children more to try and make up for their mother.' 'When the kids ask for something you will give it them for fear of feeling you have let them down,' was how another father explained it. Such expenditure tended to be characteristic of the early period of motherlessness and to fall off as time went by.

In contrast to the 86 per cent of fathers who described items on which they spent more since motherlessness, 37 per cent of fathers described items on which they spent less. It was in the field of semi-luxury items such as sweets, cigarettes, toys and outings or on items like clothing on which expenditure can always be put off for a time, that expenditure tended to be reduced. Some fathers were spending less because they were better managers, some because the pattern of family expenditure had changed, some quite simply because income had been reduced.

The absence of the mother should, other things being equal, reduce expenditure. There is one less mouth to feed and one less adult to clothe. We have already seen, furthermore, that motherlessness reduced the incomes of nearly half our families. A reduction in numbers or a reduction in income should logically lead to a reduction in expenditure. Apparently the opposite is true. While reducing numbers and income motherlessness at the same time increases expenditure. The main source of reduced expenditure is on luxuries. The most important items on which fathers spend more are necessities – food and clothing followed by compensating expenditure – a direct corollary of the motherless situation.

This was the broad picture – of generally increased expenditure. Individual replies, however, provide considerable insight into how particular families adapted to the problems of motherlessness. A number of the more affluent fathers mentioned increased use of cars to take children to school or day nurseries or to take them to and from daily minders. Some found a car a necessity to combine work and the care of their children – though an expensive one. A small minority of fathers mentioned the value of the telephone as an easy way of providing remote control of children during school holidays. The father and children would ring each other up at stated times to reassure each other that everything was all right. There were ways in which the problems could be eased – at a cost – but they were methods only really open to a small minority. Many fathers found themselves the victims of a situation which was all against them. They lacked the resources to buy the services which would have enabled them to maintain their incomes – and so buy the services they needed. Their situation was like that of a classical depressed economy which needed pump priming if prosperity was to be restored.

The overall financial picture

We tried to assess, too, the family's overall financial position, whether the father felt that the family was worse off materially because of motherlessness, the nature and extent of the financial problems which motherlessness brings and the changing nature of these problems over the years.

We asked fathers whether they felt that there were things which they or their children or their house ought to have but could not afford because of their wife's death or leaving. Just under half our sample expressed feelings of deprivation. Table 47 shows the percentage of fathers mentioning particular deprivations. Those who voiced a sense of deprivation about holidays, trips, etc., were concerned about the loss of extras and little luxuries – which in an affluent society most of the population take for granted. The other sources of deprivation are essentially in semi-capital items – types of expenditure which can always be put off for a time and *are* put off when budgets are tight. Few, if any, fathers mentioned food. They were not deprived

TABLE 47 Percentage of fathers mentioning particular deprivations (n = 565)

Satisfied	55·2
Deprived about holidays, trips, toys, sweets, etc.	8·5
Deprived of clothing	10·2
Deprived of furniture, bedding	16·4
Deprived re house decoration	12·3
Deprived – other	13·2

of basic necessities as were some of Marsden's fatherless families. Our fathers felt relatively deprived, cut off from the abundance and the opportunities they saw around them. House decoration is interesting because it is both a material deprivation in the sense of lack of money for materials in the face of other competing claims, and also the product of a shortage of time. This was one thing nearly all our working fathers were desperately short of. 'Never enough time. Could have done with fifty hours in the day,' was a typical comment by one father for whom things had eased. They could cope – just – with the necessary day-to-day chores – cooking, washing, cleaning, shopping – but they had no time or energy for more. Something like house decoration was always going to be done but in fact except on rare occasions the money, time and energy were just not available.

These felt deprivations show the general position of our fathers. They were not the victims of acute deprivation but most of them had experienced a drop in their standard of living or it had not risen in line with that of those around them. They were doing what they felt was right and best for the children. As some pointed out they were saving society £20, £30, £40 per week by their efforts in keeping the family together and the children out of local authority care. Most had the satisfaction of men who know they are doing what they ought to be doing. Yet in their unsought-for task many felt society had offered them little help or support. The drop in standard of living could be borne like the other burdens of motherlessness but it was a very real burden.

The divorced were more likely to be satisfied with their material position than the widowed or the separated. The separated were least satisfied. More of class I and II fathers were satisfied with their material position than were other fathers. The group which expressed the strongest sense of deprivation was the fathers drawing Supplementary Benefit. Less than 30 per cent of them were satisfied. Interestingly too, the longer a family had been motherless the more likely the father was to be satisfied with his material situation. There are two possible explanations of this. There is the first and obvious one that the deprivations had in fact eased over time, that the children had got older, the father was able to get back to work, do more overtime, etc. On the other hand it is possible that as motherlessness continued fathers got inured to deprivation and so less conscious of it. Time and habit make the intolerable tolerable remarkably quickly.

If we turn from the satisfied to the dissatisfied what is striking is the strength and the almost immediate nature of the sense of deprivation which motherlessness brings. Certainly some fathers might blame long-standing deprivations on their new family situation – consciously and unconsciously – but the replies to this question are really too consistent to be explicable in this way. Table 48 analyses recently

TABLE 48   Percentage of fathers wifeless for less than a year, mentioning particular deprivations (n = 102)

Satisfied	48·2
Deprived – holidays, toys, trips, cigarettes, etc.	10·8
Deprived – clothing	20·5
– furniture, bedding	16·9
– home decoration	16·9
– other	9·6

wifeless fathers' feelings of deprivation. The strong sense of deprivation of those wifeless for less than a year is partly explicable in terms
of the immediate financial problem posed for many fathers by the
wife's debts. These brought immediate financial stringency to many
families.

It is important, too, to realize the long-term implications of motherlessness for the family. It is easy to under-emphasize this as in so
many fields there are clear indications that things improve or at any
rate that the father feels less discontented after four to five years when
the youngest child starts school, the other children become more
able to do things for themselves, etc. Table 49 shows the connection
between length of motherlessness and the father's sense of deprivation. What is important to emphasize is that for many the deprivations are long-term and continue long after a *modus vivendi* has been
worked out. Nearly 40 per cent of those motherless for over seven
years expressed feelings of deprivation – and seven years is equivalent
to half a childhood.

TABLE 49   Fathers' feelings of material deprivation, analysed by
length of wifelessness

	Satisfied		Deprived	
	No.	%	No.	%
Under 4 years	169	50·1	165	49·9
Over 4 years	144	62·3	87	37·7

$\chi^2 = 7\cdot148$ $P < 0\cdot01$

In an effort to get some idea of the relative significance of the
various problems which motherlessness brings we asked our sample
a general question about whether there were any problems which
the father found particularly difficult at the beginning. Just over 13
per cent of fathers mentioned financial difficulties whereas 28 per cent
of fathers mentioned the difficulties involved in combining work and
the care of children and making arrangements for the children's care
and 27 per cent mentioned domestic problems. In the face of the other
immediate difficulties which motherlessness brought, financial problems were obviously less immediately pressing. Financial problems
tend to build up over time as bills come in, clothes wear out and so
on. The domestic and child-caring problems were immediate and
acute and had to be faced and solved in the aftermath of loss and

desolation. They were there from the start. They did not take time to emerge. They could not be put off.

In spite of this comparatively small proportion of fathers mentioning financial problems as particularly difficult at the beginning in comparison with the numbers mentioning other problems, many fathers were clearly faced with such difficulties as a result of the wife's death or departure. In all 56 per cent of fathers said they had immediate financial difficulties due to their wife's death or departure. As one would expect such difficulties were mentioned more frequently by fathers in classes III, IV and V than by those in classes I and II.

Fathers in classes I and II were more likely, as we shall see later, to have savings. They were less likely to have to give up work and rely on Supplementary Benefit. If their wives had left debts, for example, they were altogether in a better position to deal with them. What were difficulties to the other groups were not difficulties to them. Widowers were also at an advantage – but for other reasons. Some 13 per cent of them spoke of difficulties arising from funeral expenses but they were, it seemed, less likely to have to face the financial situations which were problems for the other groups. Far and away the biggest source of difficulty was debts left by the wife. These seemed to accompany marital disharmony and widowers did not have the debt burden which faced the separated and the divorced. 11·1 per cent of widowers mentioned difficulties resulting from their wife's debts compared with 56·2 per cent of the separated and 47·1 per cent of the divorced.

'There were debts of £200 left by the wife about which I knew nothing until the "club men" started to call for payments,' said one father. 'The worst thing was when I got to know about these debts,' another father told us, 'I received court summonses for outstanding fuel bills. I didn't know anything about them. The wife must have run them up. I had to pay £1 a month. Nearly cleared now but I was very upset at being taken to court.' 'About £300 in debts – various clubs and so on.' 'When she left me I was left with £400 of hire purchase debts.' 'She had debts of £215 I didn't know about,' said other fathers. Many were left with much smaller and less dramatic debts which took months or years to clear for a father on Supplementary Benefit. Of these fathers left with debts by their wives, 39 per cent of those motherless for one to three years and 22 per cent of those motherless for four to six years were still struggling to pay them off.

When we moved on from the initial problems posed by motherlessness to ask about the biggest continuing problems, financial difficulties emerged as the most common problem – mentioned by 25·2 per cent of fathers. They were mentioned far more frequently than any other specific problem. 'Money is always the biggest worry,' said one father. 'Can't save,' said another, 'I live from hand to mouth.' 'The biggest problem is not being able to live the life we used to before – holidays, etc.,' said a widower, 'and having to count every penny, having to be careful all the time not to misspend.' 'It's difficult to keep "afloat" and have something for occasional extras,' was how another father summed up his position. What emerges from the fathers' comments is a picture of continuous struggle rather than of desperate poverty. There was enough for basic necessities but little margin. Money was a continuous nagging worry because of the dual impact of motherlessness on income and on expenditure.

We went from discussing the biggest continuing problem to ask fathers whether there were any problems which they found particularly difficult at the time of interview. It is interesting to compare the replies to this question with the replies to the question about the biggest continuing problems. When asked about the present far fewer fathers reported any problems as being particularly difficult. 42·4 per cent of fathers had no particular problems at the time of interview compared with 22·7 per cent who said there had been no major continuing problems. On most fronts the problems had eased – in some cases very considerably. Only financial difficulties remained unaffected by the passage of time with the same proportion of fathers mentioning finance as a problem at the time of interview as mentioned it as a major continuing problem. This was true for all the fathers in the sample irrespective of social class or the cause of motherlessness. Finance was a continuing and present problem.

Finally we asked fathers for their general opinion on their financial position at the time of interview compared with their position at the time of motherlessness. Just over 40 per cent said their position was better in some way. The most frequently mentioned reasons for improvement were that the father was a better manager, that the father now had a better-paid job, that the wife spent too much on herself, that there were now fewer mouths to feed.

On the other hand 67 per cent of fathers said their financial position was worse in some way. (The seeming contradiction between this figure and the 40 per cent who said they were better off in some way is the result of some fathers saying they were better off in some ways and worse off in others.) 36 per cent of fathers said it was worse because housekeeping was more expensive without a wife, 28 per cent said it was worse because their income had been reduced because of shorter hours, change of job or dependence on Supplementary Benefit. No other reasons approached these in importance. The next largest group was that of 14 per cent of fathers complaining that things were worse because of the cost of domestic help or child minding.

Widowers were more likely to report that motherlessness had made housekeeping more expensive. On the other hand, they were less likely to complain of a reduction in income. Those made motherless more recently are more likely to say their financial position has deteriorated in some way. But of those motherless for seven years or more over half complained that they were worse off in some measure.

The majority of our sample felt themselves in some measure worse off financially than they had been before the family became motherless. This was partly due to reductions in income, partly to increased expenditure. A lot of the evidence we have gathered is, of course, subjective. It is the fathers' feelings about the situation uncorroborated by hard factual data. This is particularly true of the evidence we quote about the effects of motherlessness on expenditure. Whatever the objective reality the fathers' subjective feelings have a reality and validity of their own. Whatever the objective reality, many fathers *felt* worse off. For them this was the reality. And if we are to understand their social situation we must start from their perception of it.

In addition to information about the impact of motherlessness on income, wages and expenditure, we gathered information about the family's actual current financial position. We asked about savings. Of the fathers who answered the question – 95 per cent of the sample – 66·7 per cent had no savings, 21·1 per cent had some savings, but under £300, 12·2 per cent had over £300. As one would expect social classes I and II were more likely than classes III, IV and V to have savings and to have more. Similarly the widowed and the divorced were more likely to have savings than the separated.

We also gathered information about working fathers' take-home pay. For general comparative purposes it might have been more useful to have gathered information about gross earnings as published statistics use this as a base line. Had we collected information about gross earnings it would still not have enabled us to make meaningful comparisons between our sample and the general population or between motherless families and the general population. Our sample is not representative of the general population by social class. Whether it is representative of motherless families we cannot tell. Another obstacle to precise comparisons is the fact that our interviewing programme lasted nearly a year – a period when average earnings for full-time manual workers rose by over £3 per week.[8] Such an increase makes it virtually impossible to make the fine comparisons which are required for any worth-while evaluation.

For the benefit of the Department of Health and Social Security we compared the incomes of our working fathers with the level of Supplementary Benefit to which they would have been entitled. This produced straightforward comparative figures but if the object is to make some assessment of a family's level of living it is not very helpful. On a strict calculation very few fathers in our sample were likely to appear as at or below Supplementary Benefit level. A man, wife and two children aged between five and ten years would in early 1970 have been entitled to £11.15 plus rent – roughly £14 (less family allowances of 90p) as the average rent paid by the Supplementary Benefits Commission is about £3. We know that substantial numbers of men in full-time work take home less than this. The Supplementary Benefit entitlement for a man on his own with two children falls to £8.10 plus rent – say £11 (less family allowances of 90p). Very few men take home less than this. In fact we found eleven fathers were below this level – three as much as £3 or more below it. Another eleven had less than £2 more than basic Supplementary Benefit. If we take as a poverty line £2 above Supplementary Benefit, then some 5 per cent of our working fathers were below this. Because, however, of the absence of the wife's allowance in the general household income these families are likely to be considerably worse off than a two-parent – two-child family with less than £2 above Supplementary Benefit. Table 50 sets out in more detail the relationship between the earnings of our working fathers and their Supplementary Benefit entitlement.

Table 51 sets out the facts about the take-home pay of the working fathers in our sample. Just over 59 per cent of fathers took home £20 or less per week. The average take-home pay was £20.90. The widowed were the best-paid group, 52·5 per cent of them took home £20 or less compared with 59·1 per cent of the divorced (exactly the percentage for the sample as a whole) and 68·2 per cent of the separated. At the other end of the scale, more of the widowed had incomes over £30 per week.

If we examine the father's take-home pay and compare it with the length of time the family has been motherless certain patterns emerge.

TABLE 50 Working fathers' incomes related to the level of
Supplementary Benefit (per cent) (n = 429)

Below Supplementary Benefit	2·6
Less than £2 above	2·6
Over £2 and less than £4 above	7·4
Over £4 and less than £6 above	10·9
Over £6 and less than £8 above	16·1
Over £8 above	60·4

TABLE 51 Take-home pay of working fathers (per cent) (n = 421)

Under £14	10·2
£15–£17	18·5
£18–£20	30·4
£21–£23	11·2
£24–£26	13·3
£27–£29	4·0
£30–£32	5·7
£33 plus	6·7

It is quite clear that those fathers who have been motherless for less
than a year earn more than those who have been motherless for
between one and six years. Those motherless for seven years or more
are better off than the intermediate group but are still not as well off
as the most recently motherless.

This is a further piece of evidence for the argument that the
financial impact of motherlessness is not immediate. In the period
straight after the wife's death or departure the father somehow maintains his former job and his former hours. As the temporary situation
assumes a greater air of permanency he has to adjust. The adjustment
leads to the loss of earning power which is clearly evident in those
motherless for one to six years. The loss of earning power seems to be
long term if not permanent. A manual worker who is compelled by
domestic circumstances to take a lower-paid job or to restrict his

hours of work for a period of years is likely to find it extremely difficult to increase his income again when domestic circumstances would permit this.[9]

Motherlessness meant that over a quarter of the fathers in our sample had recourse at some stage to Supplementary Benefits. Of those who continued in work 40 per cent said their financial position was better in some ways, as one would expect at a time of rising standards of living. On the other hand, nearly a quarter complained that motherlessness had led to reductions in their income. As regards expenditure nearly 90 per cent of fathers said that motherlessness made life more expensive. Of all the many problems which fathers described, financial difficulties seemed the longest lasting.

5 The father's emotional and social adjustment

Crucial to an understanding of what motherlessness means to a family is a consideration of what motherlessness means to the father. He becomes the pivot on which the family's life rests. His feelings and attitudes are crucial to the way the new family unit functions. The impact which the loss of his wife makes is therefore a factor of major importance in the family's future. Marris argues that it is impossible to understand the social consequences of widowhood unless account is taken of the widow's feelings.[1] The same, we believe, is true of fathers left with motherless families.

The father's initial feelings

We began our exploration of the fathers' reaction by asking them how they felt when they knew their wife had died or left. It was a difficult question for different reasons both for the newly motherless and for those who had been motherless for several years. The overwhelming majority of fathers, as Table 52 shows, replied that they were shocked or very shocked or upset or very upset. Reactions varied, of course, in detail between the different groups in the sample but to the vast majority, widowed, separated and divorced, those who had expected it and those who had not, motherlessness was accompanied by shock and upset.

'I just did not think at all', said one widower in reply to the question of how he felt when his wife died. 'I didn't visualize that life was going to carry on.'

'End of the world as far as I was concerned', said another widower. 'If someone had put me against a wall and wanted to shoot me I wouldn't have cared.'

'The night she left I can never forget', said a father whose wife had gone off with another man. 'I contemplated suicide for myself and the three children.'

'It just felt as though the world had dropped out. It was entirely unexpected', said another father whose wife had left him.

TABLE 52   Father's feelings when he knew his wife had died or left (per cent) (n = 556)

	Not bothered	Relieved/ pleased	Shocked, very shocked/ upset, very upset	Mixed feelings	Other
Widowed	0·8	2·2	85·9	5·3	5·8
Separated and divorced	6·1	13·9	66·0	8·2	5·8

Table 52 shows how replies of the different groups varied. 85·9 per cent of widowers described themselves as shocked or very shocked and upset[2] compared with 66 per cent of the separated and divorced. What was noticeable, too, was that widowers described their feelings much more clearly and much more vividly than the others. Their situation, of course, was final, the situation of the separated at the time of the wife's leaving was not. The separated were much more likely to be confused and not sure exactly what they did feel. There was likely to be some element of relief or satisfaction in a proportion of cases. For the widowed the situation was stark and unrelieved. It was all loss without any compensations except for the few who were glad for their wife's sake that her suffering was over. Feelings about loss caused by death are deep and instinctive and reinforced by learning – one knows how one ought to feel. For those whose wives had left them, or who had left their wives, there is no such simple, basic response. Neither does convention help by prescribing a set of expected and acceptable feelings.

There is much stress in the literature on the uniform picture presented by people suffering from acute grief. 'I know of no other psychological illness which follows so stereotyped and predictable a course', says one authority.[3] 'Common to all,' says Lindemann expounding the same point in his classic paper, 'is the following syndrome: sensations of somatic distress occurring in waves lasting from twenty minutes to an hour at a time, a feeling of tightness in the throat, choking with shortness of breath, need for sighing, an empty feeling in the abdomen, lack of muscular power and an intense subjective distress described as tension or mental pain.'[4] He goes on to describe four other feelings characteristic of grief in addition to this physical distress. There is frequently a preoccupation with the image of the deceased and a strong feeling of his or her presence or nearness which makes for an inability to accept the finality of death. Often there is a feeling of guilt, of failure to do the best for the lost one and an exaggeration of minor omissions or negligence. Third, many recently bereaved display a loss of warmth, often amounting to near hostility in their relationships with other people. Finally, there is an aimless search for activity but accompanied by an inability to initiate and maintain organized patterns of activity.[5]

Marris[6] summarized the reactions of his sample of seventy-two working-class London widows as:

first, physical symptoms; second loss of contact with reality
and inability to comprehend the loss, brooding over memories
and clinging to possessions, a feeling that the dead man is still
present, expecting him home with every turn of the key in the
door and talking to him and of him as if he were still alive;
third, a tendency to withdraw – to escape from everything that
recalls the loss, from sympathetic friends and relatives, from any
interest in life at all; fourth, hostility – against the doctor,
against fate, inturned against oneself.

In normal mourning there seem to be three phases, a short period of numbness and shock, a period of intense grief and then a period of recovery marked by the gradual resumption of normal life. There are many aspects to the impact made by bereavement. Parkes found in one study that the number of patients admitted to a psychiatric clinic whose presenting illness had come on within six months of the death of a spouse, was six times greater than would have been expected had the bereavement not been a causal factor.[7] In another study he found a significant increase in visits to general practitioners during the first six months after bereavement – and the increase remained even when visits for sedatives, tonics and psychiatric symptoms were excluded.[8] Marris reports that 43 per cent of his widows thought that their health was worse from one to three years after bereavement than before their loss.[9]

In a sophisticated statistical study, Young, Benjamin and Wallis examined the mortality rates of a sample of 4,500 widowers aged fifty-five years or over. Their conclusion was that 'widowhood appears to bring in its wake a sudden increment in mortality rates of something like 40 per cent in the first six months'.[10] Their view was that 'the "desolation effect" of being widowed, may be at least a good part of the explanation'.[11]

The impact of bereavement on widows and widowers is clearly affected by many factors. The impact seems likely to be greater when death has been unexpected and the survivor has had no time to prepare for it.[12] Parkes also quotes evidence which suggests that women under sixty who lose their husbands are more likely to display complicated grief reactions than older women, presumably due to the fact that the loss was less expected.[13] This may go some way to explaining the strength of the reactions which Marris reports, in that his sample of younger widows was a particularly vulnerable group. It is also true that the excess mortality of widowed over married people is greatest for the younger age groups.[14]

Factors in the family situation of the bereaved clearly play an important role in the situation. 'If the mourner has people whom he loves and who share his grief,' says Klein, 'and if he can accept their sympathy, the restoration of harmony in his inner world is promoted, and his fears and distresses are more quickly reduced.'[15] Lindemann makes a further important point about the family situation. 'Not infrequently', he says speaking of his particular sample though the point has a wider relevance, 'the person who died represented a key person in a social system; his death was followed by disintegration of this social system and by a profound alteration of the living and social conditions for the bereaved. In such cases readjustment presents a severe task quite apart from the reaction to the loss incurred.'[16]

In many ways the fathers in our sample were a particularly vulnerable group. Very few were of an age when they might accept the loss of their wife as in any way natural. We asked fathers whether their wife's death was expected or unexpected; 41·9 per cent said they knew it was going to happen and exactly the same proportion said it was unexpected. The remaining 16·2 per cent said they suspected it would happen. Far and away the most important cause of death which fathers mentioned to us was cancer, which accounted for 42·5 per cent of all the deaths. This nearly always meant that death was expected. In other types of illness fathers were often taken by surprise. 'The doctor said no one ever died of asthma', said one father explaining why to him his wife's death was unexpected. 'The doctor was treating her for high blood pressure', said another, 'but I'd no idea it was so serious.'

Although the father might be prepared for his wife's death all the wives died unexpectedly in the sense that any death before old age is today unexpected. All died tragically, too, in that they left dependent children. The shock was heightened, too, for the father by the implications of her death. The wife was – to quote Lindemann – 'a key person in a social system'. In the families we studied, her death was not followed by the disintegration of the system but for many it meant 'a profound alteration of the living and social conditions'. Fathers had to face not only personal loss but the implications of a changed pattern of life. The detailed implications were not perhaps immediately obvious but the problems of maintaining the former patterns were clear.

Also relevant here was whether the wife had been away from her husband and the family before her death – whether the father had any prior experience of motherlessness. In fact, exactly two-thirds of the wives had been away from home before their death, nearly all for hospital treatment. Some of these absences were quite lengthy. Only 34·1 per cent of them were for under a month, 37·6 per cent were for between one and three months and 28·3 per cent were for three months or more. So substantial numbers of widowers had had considerable prior experience of managing the household, caring for the children and trying to combine these with work. Many would already have worked out ways of managing and organized new routines to deal with previous absences – or found that they could not satisfactorily combine work and the care of children.

The fact that substantial numbers were prepared for their wife's death and had had prior experience of running a motherless household may have lessened the shock which the wife's death brought, but as we have seen the shock was still very great. Many of our sample displayed classic responses to bereavement but not perhaps as frequently or intensely as Marris's widows. There were those who felt acute physical symptoms. 'I felt physically ill,' said one father describing his initial feelings, 'out of breath. I thought I was going to

115

die myself. I couldn't go to the toilet. I had nightmares. I was really shocked.' Several fathers spoke of the strong feeling of their wife's presence in the house after her death, of hearing her speak and of imagining her coming into the room. 'I couldn't believe she was dead,' one father explained. 'I used to imagine her coming into the bedroom.' Many fathers spoke of their initial inability to accept the death. 'I was so shocked I just walked about the streets. I just couldn't accept it,' was how one put it. 'With being with her so long waiting,' said a father whose wife had been ill for many months, 'the shock numbed you and you didn't have any feeling, not for months that she had actually gone.'

Several fathers expressed guilt about the past. 'I so wished I hadn't taken the wife so much for granted when all was plain sailing,' said one speaking for many. A number of fathers spoke of a feeling of not wanting to go on living. 'I could have put my head in the gas oven. Everything was finished for a time. There seemed precious little to live for,' was how one put it.

In this situation the children were both a problem and a support. Sometimes they could help in the way Klein described by virtue of their closeness to the father and by sharing his grief. Sometimes, of course, the children were too young to understand the meaning of death and to feel grief – which must make an acutely painful situation for the father. In other cases the children were old enough to suffer with the father but not old enough to provide comfort except by virtue of their presence.

On the whole the separated and the divorced were less shocked and shaken when their wife left. A smaller number described themselves as shocked or very shocked and the degree of shock seemed less too. Death is final whereas the wife's leaving is not final at the time of the departure. Events may prove it to have been so but only time can prove this. There is an element of hopeful uncertainty for a period.

In separation or desertion – and most of our fathers were in fact deserted by their wives – there is a strong element of anger. Anger does not prevent grief but it may well lessen it. At or after death it is natural to dwell on the virtues and graces of the deceased so increasing the sense of loss. The opposite is more likely after the wife's desertion. It is bound to lessen the husband's sense of loss for his wife has betrayed her role as mother as well as her duty as wife. This sense of lessened worth must weaken the sense of grief even if only because it means it is not the sole emotion.

What separated and divorced fathers described to us was a very wide range of feelings. There were those who were shattered and overcome. 'I tried to commit suicide three times,' one father recounted. 'I worshipped the ground she walked on. The first time she left I took an overdose of tablets – I thought that would shock her. The second time it was serious. The third time I nearly died. I took 300 codeine and a bottle of whisky.' At the other extreme there were fathers who were prepared for what happened and took it very coolly. 'I expected it really. The marriage had broken up for quite a long while,' said one. 'I'd a fairly good idea she was going,' said another, 'so it didn't hit me as an awful surprise.' 'It had happened before so I just accepted it,' was another response. Between these extremes of desperation and comparative indifference were those fathers who spoke of predictable degrees of shock, distress and apprehension. 'I was very shocked and terribly upset that she could go like that,' said one. 'It was a great blow but I knew I had to carry on,' said another.

Then there were those fathers who had themselves taken the initiative in the situation like the father whose wife had been 'carrying on' while he had been away. 'I gave her a case and told her to go,' he said. A number of fathers emphasized that they felt their wives had failed them and the children. They thought they could do better on their own so they acted accordingly. This did not, however, always mean that they were happy about the situation. 'I couldn't believe it when she went,' one father explained, 'I was lost for a week. I was in a dream. And the funny thing was that I had told her to go if she couldn't change her ways.' Other fathers, too, made the painful discovery when she'd gone that, as one put it, 'However bad she is, it was still companionship.'

It was their wife's action in leaving the children which fathers seemed to find most difficult to understand and most painful. 'I could understand her leaving *me*,' one father said, 'but not how she could leave the children.' 'She must have no feelings for her children. I can't understand how any woman can just walk out and leave her children,' said another. 'I didn't mind her leaving me but I think anyone who leaves her children should be legally punished,' said a third.[17] It seemed to fathers quite unnatural and often unforgivable that their wife should have gone off without any attempt to safeguard the children's welfare. They regarded it as grossly unfair to the children and unfair to themselves in that they were left to bear the sole burden of caring for them.

Marsden describes a third of his mothers as feeling hatred for the father either for what he had done to them or for what he had done to the children. One wife took a knife with her when she went searching for her husband.[18] Few of our fathers displayed feelings as strong as this. It was generally anger rather than hatred which they felt. This suggests it was not only the fact of their husband's leaving them which moved Marsden's sample but its implications. For most of his mothers the implications – poverty and deprivation – were considerably more severe than for our sample.

To explore the reasons for marriage breakdown is very difficult. Ask one party and the result is a one-sided view. Ask both parties and the result is two one-sided views rather than the complete picture. The fundamental problem, says Goode, is that this is one of the areas of behaviour where interviewing is unlikely to elicit the true picture. Only observation could do that.[19] What we gathered was a one-sided view – tempered in some measure by time and thought.

Of the reasons given by the separated and divorced for their wife's leaving, 41·4 per cent were to do with 'another man'. As one of our respondents put it, 'for every motherless family there's nearly always a fatherless one too', by which he meant that the mothers who deserted were nearly always accompanied by other children's fathers.

Underlying the 'another man' reasons was very often the other main group of explanations – 26·4 per cent of the total – which covered the wife's desire for a good time, for freedom from the responsibility of a family. 'She said she wanted to enjoy herself while still young,' one father explained. 'She just didn't want to be tied to a home.' 'I think she married me with the idea of changing me,' said another father. 'She wanted to go out – dancing and mixing with people a lot. She liked a good time. She wanted me to be the same. She wasn't the sort for keeping house. I had my own house and she had everything she wanted. She had to get out of the boredom of an easy house.' 'I reckon she got a bit bored,' another father confessed. 'She said the kids got too much for her. I don't know why because I used to help her a lot but I admit that sometimes I didn't get home from work till eleven o'clock and I used to fall asleep in a chair.' 'She wanted a gay time,' was another father's verdict, 'in my estimation she had security and a good life with me but she wanted a night life.'

The crucial reason in very many cases seemed this desire of the wife's for independence. Home and children became a burden. They could be partially escaped from in work but at work the delights of greater freedom were further emphasized. Working wives were not part of the new free society and some wanted to be. Some felt they had missed out by comparison with their younger unmarried contemporaries and wanted a good time before it was too late. It was not only a different man they wanted but a different sort of life too. This at any rate was how the fathers saw it but it was a less damaging interpretation for them to put on the situation than to admit that they themselves might somehow have failed.

The separated and the divorced seemed rather less prepared for their wife's leaving than were the widowers for her death. 14·5 per cent of the separated and divorced said they 'knew it would happen' – compared, as we have seen, with 41·9 per cent of widowers. On the other hand the separated and the divorced were more likely to suspect that it would happen. Even so more of them found their motherless situation unexpected – 53·7 per cent compared with 41·9 per cent of widowers. Table 53 sets out the differences.

TABLE 53 Whether wife's death or departure was expected or unexpected

	Knew it would happen		Suspected it would happen		Unexpected	
	No.	%	No.	%	No.	%
Widowed	116	41·9	45	16·2	116	41·9
Separated	32	15·0	66	31·0	115	54·0
Divorced	11	13·3	28	33·7	44	53·0
Total	159	27·7	139	24·3	275	48·0

$\chi^2 = 57·210$ $P < 0·001$

For the separated and divorced there was less likely to be certainty about the wife going until she actually left. Her departure would tend to be suspected or unexpected rather than clearly known in advance. The fathers who said her leaving was unexpected were not denying the existence of friction or difficulty in the home. What they did not expect was that their wife would take the ultimate step of going.

'No, no,' said one respondent when asked whether he had any idea that his wife might leave, 'I never thought she'd leave the children although we didn't see eye to eye all the time.' 'I'd got an idea

119

something was going on but I'd never got any proof,' another father told us. 'When she said she was leaving I just laughed especially with the lad being only four months old.' He was wrong and his wife went.

Rather fewer of the separated and the divorced had had practical experience of motherlessness prior to the period we were studying; 50·9 per cent of the wives of the separated and 43 per cent of the wives of the divorced had been away from home before the last absence – compared with 66·6 per cent of widowers' wives. In comparison with the widowers' situation these absences tended to be either shorter – less than a month – or for longer periods – six months or more.

The significance of these facts about the number and length of previous absences is that the wife's absence must have been viewed initially by many fathers as a temporary, emergency situation. Other absences had been temporary. This one can have seemed no more likely to be permanent than the others. This must mark the real difference between the adjustment of widowers on the one hand and the adjustment of the separated and the divorced on the other. For widowers the situation we were studying became clear-cut and final at the wife's death. A definite adjustment had to be made to it. For the separated and the divorced the situation in the immediate period after the wife's departure is quite different. This, perhaps, helps to explain why in some fields the real adjustment to motherlessness comes only after a considerable period. Not only is there more help available in the early period from friends, relatives and the social services but many fathers are likely to see the whole situation as temporary.

The father's subsequent feelings

The father's feelings at the time of his wife's death or leaving are to a large extent predictable. More important for his own future and the family's is how he feels subsequently. We were particularly interested to know how the feelings of the separated and the divorced changed with time. There is a great deal of evidence to show that the passage of time softens grief even though memories remain tender. To what extent does it also soften the feelings of the separated and the divorced about their wife's action in leaving them and the children or do the continuing burdens of motherlessness serve to keep the bitterness alive or even increase it?

TABLE 54 Father's feelings at the time of interview about his wife leaving him (per cent) (n = 287)

Angry/bitter then and now	32·4
Angry then but not now	29·3
Mixed feelings	38·3

Altogether 61·7 per cent of separated and divorced fathers said they felt or had felt anger or bitterness at their wife leaving them and the children, 32·4 per cent still felt this way at the time of interview. 'I will never forgive her,' said one father. 'If I was driving a bus and she happened to be in the road I would put my foot on the gas. Sometimes when I meet her at work I put my hands behind my back to stop myself from swiping her one.' 'I hate her now,' said another father, 'because of the way the children have been upset and because it doesn't seem to worry her at all.' Feelings as extreme as this were rare however.

In contrast to this group who still felt angry and bitter at the time of interview, 29·3 per cent of fathers said they had felt bitter or angry at the start but had ceased to feel like this by the time of interview. 'I don't think I feel bitter now; I feel sorry for the mess she has got herself into,' was how one father put it. Other fathers expressed an absence of feelings: 'Now I don't feel anything. I can pass her in the street and it's just like passing you, someone I know but don't have any feelings for' was how another father explained his feelings to the interviewer. Others were indifferent but aggressive. 'I couldn't give a damn where she is now,' was a common response.

In the early days of the break, anger was an inevitable and possibly a healthy response. It may well bring with it an accession of bitter energy, a refusal to be crushed by the situation, which is what the father needs if he is to overcome the initial difficulties. On the other hand, anger is not a permanently satisfactory basis for living. Goode suggests that the divorced woman has fully adjusted to her situation 'only when she can look at her ex spouse and her former life with *indifference*'.[20] This is perhaps an extreme view but some of our sample seemed to have reached this stage. Though anger does seem to abate, nevertheless, for many it is a strong and lasting reaction. 'To swap your kids for another man is unforgivable,' was the simple explanation one father gave for his continuing bitter feelings and many felt the same. Quite simply their wives had done what they could not forgive.

Fathers' feelings about their wife's action in leaving them and the children was one index of their adjustment to motherlessness. Another index was whether there were occasions when fathers particularly missed their wives. Replies to such a question will say something about the nature of the marriage which has ended and also the degree to which fathers have adapted to their new situation. One might expect that at the beginning of motherlessness the sense of loss will be general. The whole stream of the family's life will recall memories of the past. As time passes new routines and patterns will evolve. Some of the old memories will be overlaid by new ones. The general everyday stream of life will be a less-powerful stimulus to memory. Memories will, however, still be triggered off by occasions, like birthdays, anniversaries or domestic crises when a partner's help or advice are particularly missed.

We therefore tried to explore the extent to which the passage of time and the reasons for motherlessness affected the fathers' feelings. Overall 29·9 per cent of fathers said they did not miss their wives and there was a clear trend for the proportion to increase the longer the family had been motherless. Time did begin to heal the wounds which at first seemed incurable though the process was a slow one.

TABLE 55 Fathers missing their wives or not at the time of interview, analysed by length of motherlessness

| | Did not miss her | | Missed her | |
	No.	%	No.	%
Under 1 year	11	14·1	67	85·9
1–3 years	63	25·8	181	74·2
4 years plus	90	39·6	137	60·4
Total	164	29·9	385	70·1

$\chi^2 = 21 \cdot 526$ P < 0·001

But whereas 46·1 per cent of the separated and 58·5 per cent of the divorced said they did not miss their wives at the time of interview, the percentage of widowers giving this reply was only 8·5 per cent.

'I never miss her. I've been so turned against her by her going,' one deserted father explained, and this was the fundamental explanation of the difference in attitudes. By and large the break-up of the marriages of the separated and the divorced had been preceded by difficulties and differences. Many of the marriages were breaking before they ended. The fathers, therefore, felt they had lost less than the widowers. The fact that they had been left to care for the children was a further blow to their feelings for their wife and so to their feelings about their loss.

When we asked fathers whether there were any occasions on which they particularly missed their wives, we gained an immensely varied range of answers. 23·5 per cent of fathers said they particularly missed their wives at times like birthdays, anniversaries, Christmas or holidays. These were the times when memories were most likely to be quickened, when the past broke through the new routines which had been established, when there was time – often too much – to reflect and when other people were together in families asserting their togetherness. The other large group was the 17·9 per cent of fathers who mentioned the loss of companionship and friendship. This was related to special occasions by some fathers but many more fathers related it to ordinary day-to-day living with replies like:

'When I'm sitting here at night by myself.'

'When I'm on my own sitting and thinking.'

'Someone to talk to at night when the children have gone to bed.'

'It gets a bit lonely at night time.'

'When you've got a bit of time to yourself.'

'When I walk in here from work it's just empty.'

'I miss her intelligent conversation.'

'I miss her especially when I have any problems to discuss.'

A comparatively small number of fathers said they missed their wives sexually, on outside social occasions and domestically. The other answers fell into no obvious groupings. What is interesting in many cases is the particular stimulus which triggered off memories and a sense of loss. Sometimes it was parts of the daily routine, sometimes particular domestic duties, sometimes particular times of day or of the year. When tasks or experiences had been shared the

TABLE 56   Occasions on which fathers said they particularly missed
their wives (per cent)

Sexually	8·9
Birthdays, Christmas, anniversaries, etc.	23·5
Domestically	7·3
Outside social occasions	8·4
Friendship/companionship	17·9

fact that he had to do them on his own was bound to remind fathers
of the past. When he had to undertake unfamiliar tasks not usually
reckoned to be tasks for men or when he had to make decisions on
his own, memory was quickened. These are some of the replies
fathers gave:

'When you come home from work and there's no one to pour you
a cup of tea.'

'I miss her in the morning. I have to get up early when I could
be lying in bed.'

'When I'm going shopping.'

'When the children want something doing that I can't do for
them – sewing in particular.'

'Saturday lunch time – because that was when my wife had a
stroke.'

'When fitting out the children with new clothes.'

'On washdays.'

'Dinner time on Sundays.'

Whether or not fathers felt a particular sense of loss on certain
special occasions was not necessarily a good indication of their
general feelings. We asked fathers, therefore, how they themselves
had felt since they had been left motherless.

As Table 57 shows, only 11·3 per cent of the sample had never felt
lonely or depressed. Widowers were more likely to express feelings
of loneliness or depression than the other groups and their feelings

seemed to be less affected by the passage of time. Fewer had shaken off their initial depression, more said they were depressed frequently or all the time. Widowhood seemed to create a greater and longer lasting sense of loneliness and depression than marital breakdown.

TABLE 57　How fathers had felt since their wife's death or departure (per cent) (n = 564)

	Never lonely or depressed	Lonely and depressed at beginning, not now	Lonely and depressed at beginning/ sometimes/ occasion- ally, now	Lonely and depressed often/ all the time, then and now	Other
Widowed	5·8	8·0	40·4	37·4	8·4
Separated and divorced	16·6	15·9	35·6	22·2	9·7
Total	11·3	12·1	37·9	29·6	9·1

What is striking is the large number of fathers admitting to feelings of loneliness and depression – 37·9 per cent said they felt such feelings occasionally, 29·6 per cent said they felt like that all the time. Although the number of those saying they felt lonely or depressed often or all the time gradually falls the change is slow and the proportion saying they felt lonely or depressed sometimes or occasionally scarcely falls at all. So the feelings of loss are firm and long lasting.

Depression was the product of regret for what had happened and for the way of life which motherlessness had meant – the loss of income, the domestic burdens, the problems of combining work and the care of the children, the undivided responsibilities which could be shared with no one else, the never-ending succession of days filled with work and evenings and week-ends filled with chores.

Loneliness was partly the result of a degree of isolation from other adults particularly in the evenings and week-ends when fathers had to be at home to look after the children. One father explained his loneliness by saying 'I don't get much grown-up talk now'. He was at home all day looking after the children and his world had become completely child-centred. His plight was akin to that of the captive wife on the new housing estate – except that the father could expect no partner to arrive home in the evening to break the monotony.

Townsend suggests that 'the underlying reason for loneliness in old age is desolation rather than isolation'.[21] It is the personal loss of a spouse which makes for loneliness not the absence of other social contacts. This was certainly a factor in the loneliness which our sample felt, particularly the widowers. They missed a particular person not just company. The separated and divorced felt the same though to a lesser extent. There is a period of mourning for the marriage for them but generally it is less intense than what widowers feel. Many separated and divorced fathers did, however, stress the great sense of loss the parting brought, whatever had preceded it. A common comment was that living together meant you were bound to miss the other however much feelings had changed.

Some of the widowers' replies give a vivid picture of their feelings. 'There's no joy in living any more,' said one sadly of his situation. 'No sparkle in life. There's nothing now except for the children. One carries on for them.' 'Often in the evening tears run down my cheeks for no reason at all especially if I'm just sitting watching TV,' another explained. 'The things that would have sent me over the moon don't even cheer me up a little now. I suppose it's self pity,' said another. 'It's a matter of living for the children. It's more or less an existence,' one widower sadly explained. Some tried to escape from their feelings by busyness. 'I get on and do something that *really* needs doing,' was one father's recipe. Others described their hope that 'I might meet someone else. I'm too young to stay on my own.'

Gorer expresses the view that widowhood 'appears to pose 3 alternatives to British men: remarriage, withdrawal into a resigned depression, or removal to a new town and a new job'.[22] The widowers in our sample, however, were rather younger than Gorer's. They were also a biased sample in that they were all men who had managed to preserve their families and the presence of children perhaps prevented retreat into the kind of resigned depression which Gorer describes. Most fathers were determined that the children should suffer as little as possible and this gave them a positive aim and a powerful sense of purpose. Few of our sample pursued the course of seeking a new environment. A number certainly expressed the hope that they would eventually remarry but complained that the restrictions which the children imposed gave them little opportunity to pursue this aim. Marsden similarly found that half his sample said that the pattern of their lives meant that they simply never met any men.[23]

Social life and community attitudes

When we asked our fathers about the effect of motherlessness on their social life the restrictive nature of their situation became abundantly clear. Marris noted that 'widowhood tends to impoverish social life'.[24] Marsden found this same restriction and impoverishment in the social life of his sample. 'At least one in five of the mothers', he writes, 'appeared to have no outside friends whatsoever, and for a further proportion social life was severely restricted.'[25]

In reply to this question about the effect of motherlessness on social life 49·8 per cent of fathers said that it meant that they went out less. This was the third element in their loneliness. There was the personal loss they had suffered in the death or departure of their wife, the loss of day by day adult company which is the lot of the lone parent and finally this loss of social life.

TABLE 58 Effects of motherlessness on father's social life (per cent) (n = 568)

Not affected	26·1
Goes out more	16·2
Goes out less	49·8
Other	7·9

The reasons which fathers gave for going out less fall into two clear groups. First, there were the restrictions imposed by circumstances – domestic duties, children and lack of money. Some 39 per cent of fathers referred to restrictions of this kind. 'Been out three times in five years,' one father reported. 'Before we went out together twice a week – to pictures or to a meal. Now there's no money,' said another. Marsden's conclusion was that 'the lack of money was excluding the families, especially the children from a normal social life'.[26] With our sample this was a factor but it was not as significant as in Marsden's sample. With others the problem was finding someone to look after the children. 'Naturally had to stop in,' said a widower. 'Didn't go out for three years. It was difficult to get someone to look after them.' 'You lose all social life when you have two young children to look after,' explained another father who felt, as others did, that they had a duty not to leave their children in the

127

hands of other people in view of what they had already suffered. Some fathers mentioned the burden of domestic responsibilities which filled the evening after a day's work and left little time or energy for anything else.

Second, there were the restrictions imposed by the fathers' feelings which were mentioned by some 22 per cent of fathers. Some fathers, of course, mentioned restrictions of circumstances and feelings and so they appear in both these groups. About half this group referred to loss of interest in going out and meeting people and half to the feeling that people did not want a man on his own. Several fathers explained how difficulties of getting out and shortage of money meant that eventually they lost the ability to meet people and to mix easily. So they felt less and less desire to move out of the home. 'We used to go into the town a lot,' one widower explained. 'Now I don't go farther than the village. I tend to keep in the village for protection with people I know. It saddens me in town.' 'I lost all wish to move in social circles and you lose touch with friends because you're very busy,' said another father.

Although there were only minor differences between the widowed, the separated and the divorced in the effect which motherlessness had on their social life, there were significant differences between social classes. Fathers in classes I and II were clearly much less restricted by difficulties of circumstances. Problems of child minding, money and domestic burdens made much less impact on their lives than on other fathers. They were more likely to say that they went out more which is in many ways the natural response to the loss of companionship at home if there are no practical difficulties. Fathers in classes I and II were more able to solve the practical problems by paying for domestic help or baby sitters.

What is interesting is that the proportion of replies mentioning a disinclination for company or a feeling of exclusion from mixed gatherings is similar in all classes. All fathers seem to feel the same about their situation. What leads to the differences in this table is clearly the greater ability of fathers in classes I and II to overcome their restrictions. They were able to do what the others would have liked to do.

When Marsden asked his sample of mothers about their relations with the community 'a majority spoke of changes in their relationships with friends and neighbours who seemed to stigmatize the family in some way, tending to isolate it'.[27] Other studies have spoken of the changed relationship which a broken marriage seems

TABLE 59   Effects of motherlessness on father's social life according to social class

Social class	No effect		Goes out more		Goes out less		Other	
	No.	%	No.	%	No.	%	No.	%
I and II	13	20·6	19	30·2	26	41·3	5	7·9
III, IV and V	122	26·3	68	14·6	237	51·1	37	8·0

$\chi^2 = 9\cdot84$ P < 0·01

to create between the family and the community. In part it is the result of the family's retreat into itself – in the case of our sample of the father's disinclination to meet people, his lack of time and money for social activities, his new duties or responsibilities. All these mean a changed relationship which those who do not understand the father's situation may be slow to grasp. Misunderstandings can easily develop on both sides as the father sees diffidence and delicacy as standoffishness, and the community interprets his changed ways as implying a disinclination for further relations. Marsden's sample, too, reported a feeling of being watched by the neighbours to see whether they were grieving enough, to see whether they were getting over their grief too quickly, to see whether the separated or the unmarried were making new relationships or to see whether the children were being cared for adequately.[28]

We, therefore, asked our sample whether they had found that people behaved differently towards them since the family had become motherless; 61·7 per cent of fathers felt that people did behave differently in some ways, the remainder felt that people's behaviour was unaffected. 37·8 per cent of the changes which fathers mentioned were in the direction of greater friendliness or helpfulness though this change did not always last beyond the first few weeks. On the other hand, 38·6 per cent of the changed attitudes which fathers mentioned could be regarded as unsympathetic, unhelpful or rejecting. There were people the father met who made it plain that they did not want any involvement with the family or its problems. 'People shun you when you are a widower – probably they think you are going to ask them to do something for you,' one father complained. Several others made the same point – that as they were talking to someone they could see this fear that they were going to be asked for help, in people's faces. The fact that children were likely to be at home unsupervised after school or in school holidays was apt to make for a certain coolness from neighbours who were more conscious of annoyance to themselves than of the father's problems.

Some fathers sensed a sympathy which they resented. 'People feel sorry for me,' a widower explained, 'but I don't want sympathy. I'd sooner they treated me as they've always treated me.' Others complained of a lack of understanding.

'People regard you as a curiosity,' was how one father put it. Another put it rather more bitterly: 'I find that a lot of people can be very cruel. They don't seem to understand that the children haven't got a mother and they don't realize that it's more difficult for a man to bring up children.'

Some were bitter about how former friends had changed. Friends with whom the father and his wife had exchanged visits in the past ceased to invite them. 'People don't want to know you,' said a widower. 'Married people who had always spoken stopped speaking.' In part this was probably the product of a simple embarrassment at grief and of not knowing what to say. The break-up of a marriage poses difficulties for friends in knowing how or whether they can remain friendly with both parties. 'Your friends don't want to get involved in the break-up,' one separated father complained, feeling that his friends had deserted him just when he most needed them.

There is understandable embarrassment and awkwardness about the new family situation. It may be the product of concern or sympathy or a simple desire to avoid involvement. A number of fathers, however, complained of more than this. A small proportion of fathers described changed attitudes which were the product of sexual jealousy. The separated and the divorced showed that marriage could be less than lifelong. They thus embodied a threat to the fundamental social principle of lifelong marriage. They also represented a more immediate threat to couples held together by nothing stronger than habit or convention. Marsden describes how his mothers from broken marriages were frequently suspected of uncertain standards of morality.[29] Some of our sample made the same direct complaint. 'Former friends never leave me alone with their wives and they keep their daughters away,' one father bluntly explained. This not only meant the end of friendly relations. It was also desperately hurtful to fathers.

What many fathers wanted and needed was reassurance that they were 'doing all right'. Their greatest joy was to be congratulated by teachers or by friends on their children's dress or behaviour.

Frequently they appealed to our interviewers both as mothers and objective judges to pronounce on whether the children were being properly cared for. They were extremely sensitive about their position and extremely sensitive to people's feelings and reactions. No doubt on occasions this made them imagine sidelong glances and muttered comments – 'You have to think they are behaving differently to know they are,' as one father neatly put it. But overall there were a surprisingly large number of mentions of unsympathetic and unfriendly attitudes.

It was interesting that over a third of our sample knew of other motherless families. Some simply knew of them but had no significant contacts. On the other hand, quite a sizeable minority had occasional or frequent contacts and many fathers found such contacts extremely useful. They were able to share problems and pass on ideas to each other. Many spoke of the value of simply being able to meet and talk with those in the same situation. 'It makes you know you're not the only one,' as one father put it.

Changes in the father's habits and attitudes

As part of our attempt to assess the impact of motherlessness on the father we tried to explore whether there had been any changes in a range of his habits and attitudes since his wife had died or left. We looked at areas where grief, stress and pressure of responsibility are known to manifest themselves. What we were seeking was some indication of the psychological burden which the family's motherlessness brings to the father. The problem, of course, is to disentangle the differential effect of changes in economic circumstances, shortage of time, psychological problems and so on. In some cases the pressures will work in opposing ways, in others they will all work in a particular direction. As in other parts of the study, it is the pattern and the general trend which are meaningful rather than individual items.

We started by asking fathers whether their eating habits had been affected in any way since their wife died or left.[30] The emphasis in the question was clearly on habits rather than on cooking problems or adequacy of diet which we discuss elsewhere in the study.

Over half the fathers in the sample said their eating habits had been affected, generally in the direction of eating less. Nearly a quarter of fathers were eating less at the time of interview than they had been before the family became motherless. 'Before I used always

131

to have one hot meal a day,' one father complained. 'Now it's one a week.' 'I only have one meal a day now,' said another father, 'because I'm on my own and I don't bother cooking for myself.' Other fathers were eating the same at the time of interview as before motherlessness but had eaten less immediately after their wife's death or departure. 'For the first fortnight I didn't bother with anything and I ate nothing,' one father recalled. 'For three weeks I had hardly anything – starting to get back to normal now,' said another. Many mentioned loss of weight partly as the result of shock, partly as the result of not eating. 'Didn't eat anything for three days after she died. I lost a stone in a fortnight,' said a widower. 'I've lost two stone,' said another father, 'I work harder and I don't eat so much. I was content before but now I'm worried about everything.' A very small minority of fathers said they ate more. They spoke of their better catering methods and their better housekeeping. 'She used to fry everything for quickness,' said one father with distaste, 'and I had a lot of illness with it. We eat better now.'

To quote overall responses to this kind of question is not wholly satisfactory. The length of motherlessness and the reason for motherlessness are both likely to affect replies. The proportion of fathers saying they ate less at the time of interview than they did before the family became motherless falls over time. As one would expect, too, from what we have seen so far about the impact of motherlessness on the different groups in our sample, the widowed were more likely to report adverse changes in habits than the other groups.

We also asked fathers whether their drinking habits had been affected.[31] Some two-thirds of the sample said that their habits had changed. Some fathers had drunk more initially but were now back to normal. One in ten fathers confessed that he had drunk more initially and was still drinking more. Rather more said that they were now drinking less than they had in normal circumstances.

The percentage of fathers saying they drank more was highest among those who had been motherless for the shortest period and lower among those who had been motherless for several years. 'I used to drink a lot of whisky to drown my sorrows but I got over that,' said one. 'For the first two years I became a habitual drinker,' said one widower. 'When I'd spent all my savings I stopped. Then I only drank at week-ends sometimes.' 'I was drinking a lot at the beginning when I was right down low,' was how another father put it. With some fathers it began before the wife's death or leaving. 'When my wife died I was nearly drinking myself to death – but not now,' one told us.

Drink meant escape from the problems and sorrows. It also meant escape from the house and domestic chores. The pub provided an oasis of normality, a link with the life they seemed to have left, the company of adults.

'I think I drink too often,' one father confessed. 'It started by wanting to get away from the house and be with people I knew. Now I go down to the pub most evenings though I don't drink a lot.' 'I go out every night for a couple of pints from 9.55 p.m. to 10.45 p.m. to have a break and a chat with friends,' said another father. 'I don't drink on my own. I have a couple of pals and I discuss problems with these two friends.'

Drink, of course, is an expensive form of therapy and not all fathers could afford to indulge in it. Only 4·7 per cent of fathers in classes I and II reported that they were drinking less than before the family became motherless compared with 10·7 per cent in class III, 17·3 per cent in classes IV and V and over 20 per cent of the unemployed. This difference is not solely the result of economic constraints. In classes I and II the children were older and the fathers were more likely to have baby sitters so the fathers were less confined to home. The strong class trend, however, suggests the primacy of economic factors.

An increase in smoking is a common response to stress. Over a quarter of our sample said they had started to smoke more immediately after their wife had died or left and still smoked as much.[32] 'I certainly smoke more,' one father reported, 'both because of what happened and also because of the extra responsibility now. Before I used to be able to give it up for 6 months at a stretch. Now I've tried but I can't do without them. I suppose it's because of the tension.' 'Gave it up two years before the wife's death but have to smoke now – about twenty a day,' said another father. The increases reported were often considerable. 'Forty or fifty cigarettes a day now. Previously only twenty a day.' 'I smoke three times as much,' said one father. 'I smoke twice as much. If I've nothing to do for five minutes I smoke,' confessed another.

A very small group of fathers said they had smoked more immediately but had since cut down and were back to normal. 'A few weeks before and just after she died I smoked as many as forty a day. Now I'm back to about ten a day.' A small number, too, said they smoked less since the family became motherless. 'Less now, no funds', as one father explained it. 'I gave up smoking,' said another, moved perhaps by the evidence on smoking and health. 'I thought, I've got to keep fit to look after these children so I gave it up.'

As with changes in eating and drinking habits, changes in smoking were most frequent in the immediate aftermath of motherlessness. The proportion of fathers saying they smoked more fell from 36·4 per cent of those motherless for less than a year to 22·7 per cent of those motherless for four to six years. What is striking is that so many were still smoking more so long afterwards. In effect it was a permanent adaptation.

When we looked at drinking and smoking together just over a third of fathers said that there had been no change in either habit – they drank or smoked the same or still did not drink or smoke. The largest group apart from the non-changers was the third who reported that they either drank more *or* smoked more at some stage after they became motherless. Only a very small proportion of fathers drank *and* smoked more and even fewer drank *and* smoked less. There were a handful who indulged less in one habit and concentrated more singlemindedly on the other. For some it was an antidote to boredom, for some it was a kind of compensation, for some the price of the society of other adults or of a brief escape from the home. For all it was a seeking of a kind of comfort in their need – as Marsden also found.[33]

In his study of widows, Marris found that 79 per cent of his sample had had difficulty in sleeping at least for some months after their husbands died.[34] Gorer found that two-thirds of his female respondents and two-fifths of the male said that they slept less well after their bereavement than they did before. Only 17 per cent of the widowed considered their sleep was not affected by grief.[35] Goode found a similar situation in his study of divorce.[36]

Nearly two-thirds of our sample reported that the death or departure of their wife had affected their ability to sleep.[37] Of those who reported changes, the largest group was the quarter of all fathers who said they had slept less at first but were back to normal by the time of interview.

'I sleep all right now,' said one widower. 'It was hard at first though. I used to get up and go out walking and sometimes I walked most of the night.'

'For six months I could hardly sleep at all – only ten minutes at a time. I never had a good night's sleep. It's better now,' said another father.

One father in ten said he slept less well immediately and still slept less well. 'I still can't sleep at night – only about two hours a night,' said a widower whose wife died fourteen months before. 'I still can't sleep very well,' explained a father whose wife had left him. 'It's been like this since she went. I can't seem to get to sleep. It's worrying about money and the children.'

Roughly the same number of fathers told our interviewers that they slept badly without being more specific about whether their reply related to the time of interview or the period of their wife's death or leaving.

Widowers were more likely to report effects on their sleeping habits than the other groups. Only a quarter of widowers reported 'no effect' compared with nearly half of the separated and the divorced. Larger proportions, too, reported that they were still sleeping less at the time of interview or were sleeping badly. The implication of this is that widowers were more affected than the others and the effects lasted longer. There is a clear fall with time in the numbers of those reporting that their sleep was affected but widowers as a group correspond very closely in their replies to the most exposed group of all – those who have been motherless for less than a year.

Finally we asked fathers whether their concentration at work had been affected. More than half said it had. What comes out quite clearly from the replies to this question is that concentration was affected in two different ways. There were the obvious immediate difficulties of concentrating after a major shock or upset. 'I had two smashes on the bus straight after,' a bus driver told us, 'so I came off the road and worked in the garage for a good year. Then I went back to driving eventually.' 'For the first few weeks I was not there. My mind was somewhere else,' was how one father put it. 'In the first three weeks while I was still at work', said another father, 'I just couldn't stop worrying about the children.' 'I could concentrate so far, then I'd talk about the missus,' said one widower seeking help with his grief.

In many cases, however, it was not only the immediate shock but the continuing additional responsibilities which motherlessness brought which upset fathers' concentration. 'I don't think her leaving bothered me,' one father explained, 'but I do have a lot on my mind now so obviously I don't concentrate so well.' 'I forgot things because of my commitments at home,' said another father. 'This is what's worrying me,' a crane driver confessed, 'and I'm going to see the doctor about it. I work on a crane forty feet up. I think of the men on the ground and what might happen to them.' There was also the loss of interest in work as it came to take second place in the father's mind to all the problems of caring for the children. Several fathers spoke of the continuous worry about whether children had got themselves up and off to school safely in the mornings and again whether they had got home all right in the evenings. Many children were returning to empty houses often alone and this worried fathers. The school holidays could bring even more worries. One father said how whenever a policeman appeared at his place of work he always dreaded that something had happened to the children or that they had got into some kind of trouble.

Altogether we asked fathers about five activities – eating, drinking, smoking, sleeping and concentration at work. Table 60 shows the overall picture. Only 9·9 per cent of the fathers suffered no change in any of these five areas; 48·2 per cent spoke of changes in three or more at some stage during their period of motherlessness. The widowed reported slightly more disturbance in their habits than the separated or divorced.

TABLE 60   Degree of disturbance of father's habits (per cent)
(n = 587)

No disturbance	9·9
One disturbance	19·2
Two	22·7
Three	24·2
Four	19·4
Five	4·6

The most interesting differences in degree of disturbance are those between the social classes. Fathers in social classes I and II suffered less disturbance than the rest. 39·1 per cent of fathers in classes I and II suffered disturbance in three or more habits compared with 50·1 per cent of class III and 52 per cent of classes IV and V. Are fathers in classes I and II inherently more stable or is it that motherlessness provides fewer long-term problems? It seems more likely to be the latter. As we have seen earlier they work shorter hours. They are better able to combine work and the care of children. Because of their better financial position they are able to pay for domestic help and child minding, so reducing their worries and their domestic burdens and the sheer emotional and physical load.

In his study of divorce, Goode drew up a trauma index based on four items – poorer health, great difficulty in sleeping, decline in work efficiency, weaknesses of memory. If respondents reported three or more of these effects they were classified as high trauma cases, if they reported two they were medium trauma cases, if they reported one or no items they were low trauma. 63 per cent of Goode's respondents were high or medium trauma cases, 37 per cent low trauma cases.[38] If we regard disturbances in two or more of our different indices as evidence of medium or high trauma then a very similar proportion of the separated and divorced would be high or medium trauma cases, and a slightly greater proportion of widowers. The disturbance of habits which accompanied motherlessness is an indication both of the mental and physical suffering which widowhood and marriage breakdown bring and of the new responsibilities which our sample had to face. Their situation was doubly stressful.

In addition to the questions about changes in habits and feelings about their loss, we asked widowers a series of questions to try to see whether their bereavement had affected their religious views, whether it had made them think more about life after death and whether it had led to any changes in their religious beliefs.

Table 61 shows that in regard to religion the widowers in the sample fell into two main groups – the interested and the not interested – and that the interested could be further divided into those whose

TABLE 61   Was father a religious person before his wife died? (per cent) (n = 266)

Interested in religion and an occasional or regular churchgoer	29·3
Interested but not a churchgoer	18·5
Not interested and not a churchgoer	44·9
Other	7·3

interest led to some participation in organized religion and those who were not churchgoers.

What was striking about the replies was the difference between social classes. Twice as many fathers in classes I and II as fathers in classes IV and V said they were interested in religion and occasional or regular churchgoers. On the other hand, three times as many fathers in classes IV and V as in classes I and II said they were interested in religion but not churchgoers. Upper-class fathers were much more likely to translate beliefs into practice. In the non-churchgoing of classes IV and V we see the historic working-class alienation from organized religion described by commentators since the mid-nineteenth century.[39]

Although the proportion of fathers saying they were interested in religion did not vary greatly between classes, a larger proportion of fathers in classes IV and V gave a double negative answer – not interested in religion and not a churchgoer. This suggests a sharper alienation from belief and practice in classes IV and V, a greater overall repudiation of religion, than occurred in classes I and II.

When we asked fathers about the impact of their wife's death on their religious views, some 40 per cent said it had made them think more about life after death[40] and just over a quarter said it had led to changes in their beliefs or practices. A small number said both their beliefs and their habits had changed. The remainder fell into two nearly equal groups with some 10 per cent of fathers in each. One group reported changes in beliefs but not habits, the other, changes in habits but not in beliefs. The most interesting point which this suggests is the weakness of the connection between beliefs and practices. Changes in beliefs do not necessarily lead to changes in habits and changes in habits are not necessarily the result of changes in beliefs. This is a good index perhaps of current religious uncertainties.

What we have seen in this chapter is something of what his wife's death or departure means personally to the father, his initial feelings, his feelings in the years which follow, the effect on his social life and his relations with the community. In the changes in habits and attitudes which follow motherlessness we see an indication of the costs for the father and the weight of the burden he assumes. If we concentrate on the family and ignore the father we cannot understand the total situation.

6 The father, the family and the social services

Motherlessness inevitably forces the family to rely more on relatives, friends and the voluntary and statutory social services. If the father gives up work to look after the children he has to rely on the social security service for an income to maintain himself and the children. If he decides to combine full-time work and care of the children then he has to rely on relatives, other individuals or the social services to care for the children for part or for the whole time that he is at work, depending largely on the age of the children. Whether he is at work or not the father will need the emotional and social support of his relatives and friends to help him particularly through the critical period immediately after the loss of his wife. In this chapter we examine the comparative importance of relatives, other individuals and the social services (excluding social security) to the father in his struggle to look after himself and his children alone.

The family

Most of the sociological literature on the family and the kinship system on contemporary society relates to two-parent families. We shall try to present our findings in a way that will, we hope, shed some further light on some of the relevant issues but will also present a clear picture of the father's position. One of the main divisions of opinion among family sociologists and social theorists centres around the two concepts of the isolated nuclear family system and the modified extended family system. The first view maintains that the small nuclear family (husband, wife and dependent children) is better suited than the large extended family to industrial societies which inevitably place a great deal of emphasis on geographical and occupational mobility, on high achievement and on universal values. The nuclear family may have contacts with members of the extended family but these contacts are not basic to the well-being of the nuclear family. Indeed, extensive and intensive contacts with members of the extended family are not conducive to the values of 'achievement' and 'universalism'.[1] The idea of the modified extended family system emerged from empirical research in the United States and in this country which showed that contacts between the nuclear and the extended family were neither limited nor peripheral nor detrimental to the economic well-being of the nuclear family. Quite the contrary. Kin contacts are not a hindrance but an asset to the social, emotional and economic well-being of the nuclear family. 'Major activities of this network are that members give to each other financial aid and good of value, and a wide range of services at specific times and under certain conditions. The aid and service provided within the network supplement rather than displace the basic activities of nuclear family units. Kinship behaviour assists more than negates the achievement of status and occupational advance of component families and their members.'[2] The nuclear family, though physically separate in most but not all cases, is a member of the wider group of kin which extends to its member families social, emotional and economic support in normal times and in crisis periods such as the one we are concerned with. The modified extended family system provides partial aid and is not expected by society to be fully responsible for its members as its predecessor the traditional extended family was. If there has been a reduction in responsibility there has been a corresponding increase in equality among the members of the modified extended family, for as Litwak observes, 'Where the giver is never in a position to provide the entire service, then he is not in a position to ask for complete subservience.'[3]

Our study of motherless families shows clearly that fathers received a great deal of help from their relatives and it is more than likely that without this help many fathers would not have been able to cope. Our study of community attitudes, too, showed that there was strong support for the idea that relatives should help each other when in need. In answer to our question whether relatives should generally be expected to help fathers who have to look after their children alone, 73·7 per cent agreed and 26·3 per cent disagreed mainly because they felt that it should be up to the relatives to decide freely rather than be expected to help. This does not, of course, mean that there will be complete congruence between intent to help and actual behaviour for other factors intervene to modify this relationship. It supports, however, Firth's view that many people 'regard their relatives as a kind of extension of support of themselves in the outer world. Kin represents persons on whom theoretically they may call in need, whether or not in practice they use their kin in this role.'[4] This is one of the very basic differences between relatives and friends.

We distinguished in our main study between help given to the father at the beginning of motherlessness and help given to him later. We felt that the immediate crisis situation brought about by the absence of the mother had strong emotional overtones that were more likely to bring people to the rescue of the father than the less vivid period of motherlessness later on. Besides, help in a crisis is seen to be temporary while help at a later stage may be considered of a more permanent nature and such expectations may deter people from volunteering. This turned out to be the case, for while 17 per cent of fathers said that they did not receive any help from any individual at the beginning, the corresponding proportion for the subsequent period of motherlessness rose to 23·4 per cent. It is most unlikely that this rise is due to the increased ability of fathers to cope alone with all the problems involved in caring for their children and going out to work. This improvement in the situation usually comes about when the children have grown up and in the meantime fathers would need help from others. It should also be borne in mind that the help given at the beginning refers to a period of a few days while help given later refers to a period of a few years and it ought therefore, other things being equal, to have been more likely for fathers to need and receive help.

The crisis situation also makes it easier, more legitimate, for the father to seek help. He is in very unusual circumstances and the help he is seeking is only for a temporary period until he is able to stand on his own two feet again. When the crisis period is over he will be anxious to regain his independence for, as Marris has remarked in the case of widows, 'Any situation where you are continually receiving kindness which you cannot reciprocate tends to become irksome: the sense of being under an obligation is a continual constraint.'[5]

There were significant differences in whether any help was received

TABLE 62   Did father receive help from any individuals?

| | Yes | | No | |
	No.	%	No.	%
At the beginning	488	83·0	100	17·0
Later	445	76·5	136	23·4
The whole period	520	89·5	61	10·5

Comparing help at the beginning and later:
$\chi^2 = 7.039$ $P < 0.01$

according to social class and the reason for motherlessness. One would expect that the widowers would have been more likely to receive help from individuals because, on one hand, death invokes people's sympathy and, on the other, it is not surrounded by any of the moral stigma that is attached to a lesser or greater extent to separation and divorce. What in fact emerged was that there was no difference between widowers and divorced fathers and a greater proportion of both these groups than the separated received help from individuals both at the beginning of the motherless period as well as later on. It appears then that social class must have played a part in this for the widowed and the divorced are very similar in social-class composition and they are different from the separated in this. Indeed, the higher the social class of the father the more likely it was that he received help from individuals both at the beginning and later. The influence of social class on kin relations is well documented though a distinction between mere kin contacts and kin aid is not always made. It is much less demanding to visit than to help a relative especially over a period of time as in the case of motherless families. Not only must the relatives or friends be willing to help, but their financial and occupational circumstances must also be such as to enable them to carry out their intent. In this the middle classes have a strong advantage over the working classes. Their higher economic level and their greater economic security can result in either greater independence from relatives and friends or make it possible to provide more help to them when in need. In the case of motherlessness, the second alternative applied as the figures in Table 63 indicate. It may well be, too, that the help which class I and II fathers needed was more limited and therefore their relatives were less afraid of committing themselves. Our figures were too small to disentangle the influence of the reason for motherlessness and of social class but we feel that though both these factors were relevant, social class was the more important of the two.

Who were the individuals who helped fathers at the initial and later stages of motherlessness? Relatives formed the largest group – only one-third of the fathers received no help from their relatives at the beginning and the others did. Fathers' comments, too, indicated that relatives were, so to speak, the first line of defence and only where

TABLE 63 Did father receive any help from individuals at the beginning of motherlessness?

| | Yes | | No | |
	No.	%	No.	%
Social class				
I and II	60	93·7	4	6·3
III	268	87·9	37	12·1
IV and V	139	79·4	36	20·6
Reason for motherlessness				
Widowed and divorced	327	89·3	39	10·7
Separated	161	73·9	57	26·1

Social class: $\chi^2 = 8\cdot277$ P < 0·05
Reason for motherlessness: $\chi^2 = 22\cdot753$ P < 0·001

help from them was not possible, did fathers turn to other sources. Since only 17 per cent of the fathers received no help from any individual at the beginning of motherlessness it does mean that friends, neighbours and other individuals filled in a substantial gap by helping 16 per cent of the fathers who had no help from relatives. This does not mean that only 16 per cent of the fathers received help from individuals outside their kin network for in many cases help was received from more than one source. There were various reasons why relatives did not help but they were mostly reasons related to age, employment and geographical distance and to a much lesser extent reasons denoting friction, indifference on the relatives' part or independence on the father's side. The father's feeling of independence that led him to decline help which was offered to him and to avoid asking for help was, perhaps, more important than the other two. It features explicitly and implicitly in many cases.

TABLE 64 Reasons why relatives did not help father at the beginning of motherlessness (per cent) (n = 257)

Father did not ask for help	10·5
Father declined help of relatives	4·3
Father does not get on with relatives	5·8
Father lost contact with relatives	4·7
Relatives have their own commitments	14·0
Relatives in full-time employment	4·3
Relatives live at a distance	29·2
Relatives are too old	14·4
Other reasons	12·8

'I didn't want them to help. They offered though. I've only got my sister round here and she offered. If they help you, they come back at you and say "we did this" and "we did that". They can't if I do it all myself.'

'No one helped me. I don't know why unless it was because they wasn't asked. I'm one of those persons who won't ask. If people want to help they should do it without being asked.'

Indifference on the part of relatives was less frequent but it was particularly hurtful to fathers. It runs contrary to societal values and made fathers bitter for they felt that had their relatives been in difficulties they would have gone to their aid.

'I am very bitter about my wife's sister. She used to visit regularly once or twice a week when the wife was alive. She hasn't bothered to come since or to offer to help. It is as if she bears me a grudge.'

Open friction appeared very rarely indeed. What emerged more often was a difference in style of life which kept the families apart or a cooling of relationships in the case of the divorced and the separated between the fathers and their wife's kin.

'Well the trouble is that my wife and I were strong churchgoers. We believed in our religion. All our relatives are drinkers, some pub crawlers. We didn't want our children to be like them. So we kept ourselves to ourselves and when my wife died I just carried on. Never went near any of the relatives.'

There is general agreement among family sociologists that kinship contacts are not only initiated and maintained predominantly by the mother but they are also mostly with her own rather than the husband's kin. In Heraud's words this 'partly reflects women's common functions of child bearing and rearing and the performance of domestic tasks'.[6] It also reflects the fact that with the differentiation of technical skills fathers and sons no longer do the same jobs with the result that a strong link in their relationship has been severed. This does not mean that the father–son link has lost all its value. In the case of middle-class families, Bell reminds us that this link 'is structurally important . . . because through it flows aid to the elementary family'.[7] Most of the literature, however, emphasizes the mother–daughter relationship. Firth's study of middle-class families' kinship contacts found that, 'In general, what appeared in significant though not very marked terms was a maternal bias at various genealogical levels.'[8] Willmott's and Young's study of working-class families found that the mother–married daughter relationship was the one most stressed by the kinship system. Describing this relationship they observed that 'the daughter's labours are in a hundred little ways shared with the older woman whose days of child-bearing (but not of child-rearing) are over. When the time comes for the mother to need assistance, the daughter reciprocates . . . by returning the care which she herself received.'[9] They end their discussion with the conclusion that 'the extended family was her trade union, organized in the main by women and for women, its solidarity her protection against being alone'.[10] Turner's study of a Pennine Parish established that, 'Mother–daughter contacts were not dissimilar from those in Bethnal Green, and the wife's contacts with her mother-in-law were also characteristically close, especially if her own mother was not alive or lived elsewhere.'[11] Rosser and Harris found that the mother was 'at the centre of this web of kinship – the pivot around which the extended family revolves'.[12] Schaffer and Schaffer also found that in the case of families where the mother was admitted into hospital for confinement it was mostly the mother's kin that were approached and who helped the father during the family crisis.[13]

In our study, fathers of necessity had to be the initiators and maintainers of contact with their kin and it is no surprise that they found it easier to receive help from their own relatives rather than from those of their wife. Almost twice as many paternal as maternal relatives helped the father at the beginning of motherlessness and

145

two-and-a-half times as many subsequently. We did not differentiate statistically between male and female relatives because we assumed (and the fathers' replies supported it) that the father's situation necessitated mostly the help of a woman. The reason for motherlessness and the social class of the father affected the father's degree of reliance on his or his wife's relatives. The widowed were more likely than the divorced and they in turn were more likely than the separated fathers to have received any help from their wife's relatives for obvious reasons. The break-up of the marriage through divorce or separation not only divides the marriage partners, it also divides each of them from the other's relatives. The higher the social class the more likely the father was to have received help from his wife's relatives. The differences, however, were not as great as those between the widowed, the divorced and separated which suggests that the important factor is the reason for motherlessness rather than the social class of the father.

Our findings regarding the relationship between the father and his wife's relatives are somewhat different from those of Marsden whose general conclusion was that there was little help coming to the mother from the husband's relatives. He says, 'Very few separated and divorced women now had any contacts with their husband's kin, and there were only three instances of the mother receiving substantial help from them.'[14] The same applied to the widows at the time of the interview and this was in line with Marris's statement that 'in general, widows were reluctant to seek aid outside their own families'.[15] Marris's figures, however, are more in line with ours than with Marsden's, for in spite of his conclusion, he says that 'twenty-four widows did admit, however, that they had received gifts in cash or kind from relatives outside their own household'.[16] In other words one-third of his widows received help from their husband's relatives – a figure very similar to ours. The difference in the findings between Marsden's study and ours may be due first to the fact that most of our fathers were at work whereas none of his mothers were at work, with the result that the need for aid from relatives was less. It may also be that fathers and their wives' kin find it easier to have contacts partly because of the possibility that such contacts existed before motherlessness. Mothers may have little contact with the husband's kin before the break-up of the marriage and find it, therefore, very difficult to approach them for the first time for help when the husband dies or leaves. Finally, there may be an important selective factor in the sense that while most mothers whose husbands die or leave continue caring for their children, this is not so true of the fathers who find themselves in similar situations. Perhaps fathers who have relatives willing to stand by them are more likely to care for their children than those who have not while this may not be such an important factor in the case of mothers. The differences in the findings of these three studies, however, must not be exaggerated for basically they agreed that the caring parent's relatives were much more likely to help than the absent parent's relatives.

TABLE 65   Percentage of fathers who received help from individuals at the beginning of motherlessness and later

	At the beginning	Later
From his parents	34·2	30·6
her parents	19·4	13·9
his other relatives	36·6	30·5
her other relatives	17·9	12·2
grown-up children	10·2	9·1
friends and neighbours	29·1	34·8
employers and workmates	2·6	0·9
other individuals	9·9	5·0

The help from friends and neighbours was quite substantial and its significance increased with the passage of time possibly as the fathers' situation became known and accepted. It may also be due, as we suggested earlier, to the fact that relatives are the first line of defence and only when they fail does one look to other sources for help. Fathers looked to relatives for help at the beginning as expected but some found that help from non-relatives was either more possible or more suitable in their particular circumstances.

The kind of help fathers received from individuals ranged from emotional support to financial aid and above all help with the care of children. As the table below shows child care help in one form or another accounted for at least half of the father's replies. It was the help that was most needed and appreciated by fathers for it enabled them to retain their independence and to carry on as before as much as it was possible under the new circumstances. Marris noted the same feelings when he wrote that the widows 'valued most the help that enabled them to live as far as possible as they had lived before, maintaining their own household and earning their own living. In this way, their marriage seemed less wholly ended.'[17] Perhaps it is not only nostalgia and sentiment that motivates the heads of one-parent families to make up for the lack of the other parent but strong social pressures from a society where the two-parent family is the undisputed reigning institution. Another reason for which this type of help is more valued is that while with more exertion the father can do the various housekeeping tasks, he cannot physically care for his children himself and also go to work. He is much more dependent on others in this as this quotation from a father shows:

'My mother wall-papered the scullery, she did some sewing for us and she brought us food and baking. My boss took me to hospital to see my lad. I had time off when the lad was sick and when I visited the solicitors. My boss's wife sometimes gives me a lift into town. But it is my neighbour that stands out. She gives us food many times. But it's not that. She looks after my son after school and on a few evenings when I am away. You see I need her help most. I couldn't do that myself.'

All in all, then, relatives and friends came to the help of most fathers. Only 10·5 per cent of the fathers said that they received no help at all from any individual at any time either at the beginning of motherlessness or subsequently. Some of these received help from welfare agencies and only twenty-five fathers, 4·2 per cent, received no help from anywhere. It seems that the small number of fathers who received no help from any individual stood no more than an even chance of being helped by the personal social services. Both groups – those that were not helped by any individual and those who received no help from any source – consisted mainly of non-working fathers, two-thirds of each group, and of fathers in working-class occupations. The separated accounted for more than half the total number of each group which is another indication of their comparative alienation from the rest of society. On the whole then it was the separated fathers who drew Supplementary Benefit and looked after their children on a full-time basis who received no help from relatives or from other sources. Again, this is another situation where cause and effect are inextricably bound together with the result that it is impossible to know whether fathers gave up work because they did

TABLE 66 Type of help fathers received from individuals at the beginning of motherlessness and subsequently (per cent) (n = 1,098)

Type of help	
Financial	3·9
Taking children in their homes for overnight stays	9·0
Taking children in their homes for long stays	8·8
Helping with day care of children	28·6
Evening baby sitting	5·2
Helping with domestic work	26·9
Emotional support	6·9
Individual came to live with father	6·1
Other	4·6

not get adequate support from their relatives or whether, having decided to give up employment, they felt they had no need to approach their relatives for any help.

Personal social services

Our general conclusion from all our evidence is that the personal social services are at best peripheral to the problems of most motherless families. That fathers managed to look after their children owed little to the personal social services. It was the result of their devotion, hard work and the help they received from relatives, friends and neighbours. The failure of the personal social services was two-dimensional: they failed to reach most of the fathers, and when they did, they failed, in most cases, to provide any meaningful help.

Almost half the fathers received some 'help' from the personal social services at the beginning of motherlessness, usually with the father making the first approach rather than the social worker. It is significant that the amount of 'help' fathers received fell considerably – it was halved – after the initial period. This was a much sharper fall than the one we discussed in the case of help from relatives and other individuals. The social workers were brought into the picture by the father at the beginning and withdrew to their agencies when

L

TABLE 67 Did father receive any help from the personal social services?*

| | Yes | | No | |
	No.	%	No.	%
At the beginning	263	44·9	323	55·1
Later	121	20·8	460	79·2
The whole period	279	46·6	302	53·4

* These are: Children's Department, Education Department, Health Department, Welfare Department, Probation Department, NSPCC, Medical Social Work Departments, Marriage Guidance Councils, and other voluntary agencies.

the father stopped asking for help. The crisis situation inevitably brought fathers into contact with the personal social services: the divorced and some of the separated would of necessity have seen the Probation Officer, some of the widowed would have seen the Medical Social Worker or their general practitioner, the deserted father may have gone to the Children's Department, etc. Once the crisis passes its peak and the cry for help ceases, the personal social services assume that no help is needed. This can be a good tactful step if the services remain alert to the situation and are ready to offer themselves again without too much trouble. We have no systematic data to back our assertion but the unsolicited comments from the fathers lead us to suggest that this was not the case. A more likely explanation is that the services are either not geared to meet problems of a long-term nature or they are in such short supply that they have to be rationed pretty drastically. The Children's Department, for example, may offer help when asked but once the crisis is over it does not continue keeping an eye on the situation because the Department has traditionally dealt with crises or with families that have openly and unmistakably showed that they cannot cope. A home help may be provided for a few weeks but the demand for the service is such that it has to be withdrawn to meet another crisis. In practice social work services have not yet been able to shed their 'ambulance' image in spite of all the massive recent verbal emphasis on prevention.

Social class proved an important factor in whether fathers received help from the personal social services. Fathers in classes I and II were less likely than other fathers to have received any help both at the beginning of motherlessness and later on. Equally important was the fact that the decline in the numbers receiving help which sets in after the crisis peak, was also related to the father's social class – the higher the class, the sharper the decline. The cumulative result of this selective process is that the personal social services deal predominantly with working-class and particularly with lower working-class families. Thus 72 per cent of fathers in classes I and II, 52 per cent in class III and 48 per cent in classes IV and V received no help from any welfare agency at any time during the whole period of motherlessness. Schaffer and Schaffer also found that all the families where children were received into the care of the local authority during the mother's confinement belonged to social classes III, IV and V.[18] While the middle-class fathers are more likely than working-class fathers to receive help from individuals, the opposite is true for help from the personal social services. All fathers, however, irrespective of social class, receive much more help from individuals than from the personal social services.

This observation extends beyond the one-parent families as other studies have shown. Townsend and Wedderburn in their study of the elderly concluded that 'in illness and infirmity the role of the family in providing personal and household care dwarfs that of the social services'.[19] A study of the disabled reached a similar conclusion: 'By far the most important element in the pattern of care for physically handicapped was in the form of service rendered by members of the family or more distant relatives.'[20] This preference for family help as against social service help is even more marked in the case of social work services. Mayer's and Timms's work with the clients of the Family Welfare Association led them to the conclusion that 'people try to cope with their personal problems by seeking help from their inter-personal environment, particularly friends and relatives',[21] and that 'inadequacies in the clients' informal network generated a readiness to seek help from the Family Welfare Association'.[22] They confirmed the finding of an American study which suggested that a person seeking help from social work services reveals that 'he cannot solve the problem by himself or by the help and advice of family and friends'.[23]

Why did such a large proportion of fathers not receive any help from the personal social services? Briefly this was either because fathers applied but were not helped or because they did not apply for help at all. 20·1 per cent of the total number of fathers in the sample applied for help but were refused and 33·3 per cent did not apply for help at all at any time. The commonest reason for refusing help, second only to giving no reason for the refusal, was that the help the fathers applied for was beyond the powers of the department. At first glance it appears that there was no one department that featured pre-eminently in this – Education, Health and Children's were the three main departments but these were also the three main departments that helped other fathers. If, however, one compares the numbers who received help and the numbers who were refused help by the same department, then the Health Department was more likely to refuse help than the other departments. The explanation for this lies most probably in the fact that the Health Department was responsible for two of the services – home help and day nurseries – which are in short supply, and which were particularly sought after by fathers at work.

Those who did not apply for help gave various reasons but the one that stands out well above all others is the father's desire to manage his own affairs without getting involved with local authority departments. This was expressed in two forms: some of those who said they could manage really meant that they would rather fight it out themselves than ask for help; and those who saw a stigma attached to help received from local authority services. Self-reliance and independence are strong social values that affect people's conduct in many aspects of life and under diverse circumstances.

'I'm proud. I wouldn't ask nobody for help. I could have done with some help though but I never asked.'

'Didn't think I needed it. I wasn't going to have charity from anyone. If there was trouble I'd meet it at the time.'

The second group of fathers who did not ask for help were those who would rather rely on help from relatives and friends than from local authority departments. Apart from those who verbalized this feeling clearly, some of those who said they did not need any help implied it. Bearing in mind also the greater proportion of fathers getting help from relatives than from the personal social services, the claim of two American sociologists that 'turning to kin when in trouble before using other agencies established for such purposes is the mode rather than the exception',[24] is fully justified.

Two-thirds of the descriptions given by fathers of their contacts with officers of the personal social services at the beginning of motherlessness were favourable and the other one-third unfavourable without any differences according to social class or reason for motherlessness. There were warm expressions of appreciation and gratitude

TABLE 68 Reasons why father did not apply to personal social services for help (per cent) (n = 351)

He felt he could manage/ Didn't need help	60·4
Stigma	10·5
He preferred help from relatives and friends	12·3
He knew there was nothing 'they' could do	4·3
He was afraid the children would be taken away	3·4
He was not aware of the services	9·1

even in some cases where no help was given but where the application for help had been handled with sympathy and understanding. There were officers who were considered as 'friend of the family', 'real toff', 'a good bloke, one of the best', 'very helpful, kind and efficient', etc. On the other hand, there were descriptions of other officers being 'nosey', 'correct, cool, distant, sometimes unpleasant', 'bossy types', or 'off-hand, officious, bureaucratic, unfeeling – we were just another number on the record'. There were two main themes of dissatisfaction – lack of resources and therefore inability to help the father with his problem and a feeling by the father that when help was given it was of little value. Home helps and day care facilities for children were the scarcest resource that caused the worst disappointment. Inability to help was openly and instantly frustrating to the father for he had to look elsewhere for help and since the social services were often the last resort, it meant he had nowhere else to turn to. Equally damaging was the line followed by some officers of giving vague promises and not fulfilling them. They may have felt that a vague promise was less disappointing than a downright statement that they were unable to help but some fathers were more hurt by this because they felt they were not treated as persons of any worth. A father who had approached the Children's Department for day care facilities for the children had this to say: 'I have never been so disgusted in my life. It finished me. I was given two names and addresses of possible foster parents by the lady welfare officer who said "Don't go to the first one – she's getting on a bit and hasn't a deal of patience". I was there about two hours asking about fostering and all the head man was interested in was how much I could pay.'

Another father who went to the Children's Department for help said: 'They sent me to the home helps. But although they saw me, I never heard anything from them. They said they would write to me. I am still waiting' (two years later).

We saw that the personal social services were more likely to help fathers at the beginning of motherlessness than later on. It was, therefore, not unexpected that the proportion of fathers who described their contacts with social workers as helpful declined during the later stages of motherlessness. Social workers had to ration scarce resources and however tactful they may have been in their dealings with the fathers they were considered responsible for their inability to offer any help. Social workers are forced to act as protectors and guardians of inadequate social services. Their professional skills that enable them to handle dissatisfied clients with tact and understanding may reduce public pressure for the improvement of social services. In this respect they unwittingly act against the improvement of the very social services they administer. An overstrained service cannot deal with cases till they become acute and in this way it produces more work for itself for it acts as an ambulance service.

The contemporary role set for social workers has become not only more complex than it was in the past but it has also incorporated conflicting expectations. The social worker's role requires him, among other things, to provide help to people in need, to act as a guardian of society's cherished social values and to be actively critical of his employing local authority when the services provided are inadequate. There have been various examples recently of direct conflict between these components of the role set and there will be many more in the future if social workers involve themselves more in community action. This greater involvement in community work and social action is the inevitable result of the increasing influence of sociology on social work thinking. So long as psychoanalysis was the dominant influence on social work, the root of social problems was sought in the client's personality and family system. Sociological theories of social problems on the other hand look for the explanation of social problems in the institutional structure of society. Social workers are, therefore, called upon to act not only as counsellors to their clients but to become social activists on their behalf.[25]

Several fathers felt bitter about the lack of help especially when they knew that if only they neglected the children and 'proved' to the authorities that they couldn't cope they would have received help. It seemed a senseless line of policy to them and, apart from the fact that rationing of services inevitably meant help to the most critical cases, there is nothing to commend it. There were isolated cases where this was admitted to the father by officials and even where it was recommended. A headmistress, for example, 'asked if I was getting any help. She said I was looking after them too well. She said I should let them look dirty and ragged so that people would take notice of the fact and say I needed help, and then I could ask for help. Yes, she meant I should do that.'

The differences of opinion as to what constituted useful help or advice was between fathers wanting practical help and the social workers offering them 'casework support'. One father wrote to us that he approached Children's and Welfare Departments but, 'None was of any use, from a practical standpoint. I did better by living on my wits and avoiding officialdom. They are hidebound by rules, and theory, and are unimaginative as to how to get the best from an existing situation. The job needs more lateral thinkers.'

Another father who approached the Children's Department said: 'All they did was listen. They couldn't actually do anything. It was useless in the end. The situation was the same, the facts were not altered. The only good thing was that you had a sense of being able to tell someone your troubles. I would recommend it to others whose problems are not so serious.'

This gap between clients' and social workers' expectations is a well-known problem in social work services. It is particularly wide in the case of people seeking material help from social work agencies. There is a tendency among trained social workers to view the request for material help as the 'presenting problem' and to delve more deeply in their interviews with the clients for the 'underlying problem'. Undoubtedly there are instances when there is a presenting and an underlying problem but it would be as damaging for social workers and clients to maintain that for all presenting problems there are underlying problems as to reject the whole notion of the two-tier structure of the problem situation. This is not the place to explore the controversy whether social workers should meet the 'presenting problem' before being able to reach the 'underlying problem'.[26] What we want to emphasize is the frustration of some of our fathers who asked for material help and received only 'casework treatment'. As Mayer and Timms rather picturesquely put it, this is 'to offer a suit of clothes to a drowning man'.[27] More plainly expressed such a policy offends the intelligence of ordinary people who need help. Moreover, excessive emphasis on the 'underlying problem' can increase the stigma that is attached to the receipt of social work help for the concept of the 'underlying problem' is in some ways a remnant of the nineteenth-century opinion of the moral defect of the poor that marked the work of the Charity Organization Society.

TABLE 69 Fathers' descriptions of their contacts with officials of the personal social services at the beginning of motherlessness (per cent) (n= 311)

Helpful, sympathetic	62·7
It all depends who comes	1·9
No real interest – just another case	4·5
Useless	10·3
Not very helpful	20·6

The dissatisfaction shown by some fathers towards verbal social work help must be seen in the general context of the total type of help offered to them by the personal social services. The descriptions of the help offered were equally divided between non-material and material type. In view of this high proportion of non-material help it was not surprising that some fathers reacted against this but we feel certain that had we asked a more specific question, the proportion of fathers who would have expressed dissatisfaction would have been higher. Indeed, this was the case with regard to the advice which fathers sought from the personal social services before the wife left or died. Only 43·6 per cent of the descriptions considered such advice useful and the remaining 56·4 per cent classified it as not useful. A great deal of the advice sought at this stage, however, concerned marital problems, advice which is notoriously difficult to give and to receive. With this in mind, the proportion of fathers who would have found advice on other problems not useful would not be expected to be so high.

The home help service is predominantly concerned with the problems of the elderly: 90 per cent of the cases of the service are elderly persons, 7 per cent are chronic sick and the remaining 3 per cent include various population groups of which motherless families is one.[28] The shortage of this type of service was often remarked upon by our fathers and various harrowing accounts were given of futile attempts to obtain such help. Other fathers felt there was no point

TABLE 70   Type of help which father received from personal
social services throughout the period of motherlessness
(per cent) (n = 386)

Advice, information, support	42·7
Material help – in kind	21·2
– in cash	3·6
Day nursery, nursery school	7·0
Home help	11·7
Other	13·7

in applying as their chances of getting help were minimal. It was a
good illustration of the well-known social administration thesis that
shortage of supply restricts the demand for a particular service. When
asked in what ways social services should be improved, the largest
single group of fathers, 27·2 per cent, referred to the home help
service. This is not peculiar to motherless families, however, and the
need for expanding the service has often been stated by official and
unofficial reports. A recent government study of the service concluded that 'it is reasonable to say that, in order to satisfy the unmet
needs of present recipients and to provide home help for those who
are eligible by present standards but are not currently receiving it the
size of the home help service would need to be increased to between
two and three times its present size'.[29]
    Day care facilities for children under school age was another
service which was in very short supply in some areas and non-
existent in others. The shortage of this service may lead fathers to
leave their children with unsatisfactory private foster parents. It
can lead to children being received into the care of local authorities
or to the father giving up work. Again this is a problem for other
population groups such as working mothers, fatherless families, etc.
It is, however, of special significance to the motherless families for
though society stresses both child upbringing in a family setting and
that men should go out to work, it does very little to help those
fathers attempting to fulfil both these roles. The shortage of nursery
facilities for children whose parents are at work is generally acknowledged. A government survey in 1968 found that only 6 per cent of
children aged two years and under whose mothers were at work were

cared for in day nurseries while the proportion of children aged three to four cared for in day nurseries, nursery schools or nursery classes was 12·3 per cent. The majority of the remaining children were cared for by the father or by relatives and a minority by private minders.[30] The reliance on relatives for this service was no less extensive in our group of working fathers with young children, as Table 71 shows. It is a re-affirmation of our previous conclusion that the modified extended family system and not the personal social services is the father's greatest source of help and support for himself and his children. It is also a prelude to the discussion in the section that follows where we put to the test the fathers' expressed reliance on the modified extended family by examining the care of children during critical periods.

TABLE 71   Arrangements for care of children under the age of five while father is at work (per cent) (n = 58)

Day nursery	6·9
Nursery school or class	13·7
Private daily minder	19·0
Relatives	44·9
Other	15·5

A count of the sources and types of help, though useful, does not constitute an adequate measure of the value of help the father receives. One would like to know how reliable different sources of help are, how long they last, under what conditions they are made available and how useful the father considers them to be. The length of our questionnaire precluded us from going into all these aspects of the question and we confined ourselves to asking the father which of the various sources of help he considered the most useful. When the father received help from various sources this was not always an easy question to answer and indeed some fathers could not decide on any one source only. In spite of these qualifications, the insignificance of the personal social services, statutory and voluntary, is abundantly clear again. Relatives, particularly the husband's relatives, are the source of help considered most useful by the majority of fathers. Interestingly enough a greater proportion of fathers considered the help from their friends and neighbours more useful than the help from their wife's relatives. There was also clear evidence to support our previous conclusion that widowers were more likely to rely on their wife's relatives than the divorced and the separated were. Thus while 20·6 per cent of the widowers considered help from their wife's relatives the most useful, the corresponding proportion for the separated and the divorced was 6·3 per cent and 9·8 per cent respectively. For reasons we explained earlier, widowers are more likely than the other two groups of fathers to be in the comparatively advantageous position of being able to choose between the two sets of relatives and to rely more on the set that is better placed to help them. As one father said: 'There is that bit of "air", their daughter was to blame, so there's that bit of resentment between us. Difficult for them and me not to think that way.'

TABLE 72 Which source of help father found the most useful at the time of interview (per cent) (n = 331)

His parents	29·0
Her parents	8·5
His relatives	17·2
Her relatives	5·4
Children	11·4
Friends and neighbours	18·4
Personal social services (statutory)	4·2
Personal social services (voluntary)	2·7
Other (clergy, solicitors, etc.)	3·2

Where the father was living with a relative or where he had a housekeeper, he had no difficulty in deciding which source of help he found the most useful. Many fathers commented not only on the in-built stability and reliability of such situations which reduce the worry about the physical care of the children and of the house considerably, but also provide social and emotional support for the father himself. Also where the father was living on his own but received help primarily from one source, he had no difficulty in reaching his decision. Where, however, he lived on his own and had similar help from various sources, it was not easy for him to decide on priorities. The stability and reliability as well as the value of the help in terms of scarcity were the criteria most used to decide on priorities. The first two qualities tended to be associated with help from kin, particularly parents, but the value of the help did not always run on kin lines. Where such conflict occurred there did not seem to be any consistent pattern on the rating of the importance of the various sources of help. The few fathers who rated help from the personal social services as the most important fell into this group. Most of these fathers had received help from relatives but thought more highly of the help from personal social services mostly because they received day nursery and home help facilities or because they had formed close attachments to one individual social worker.

The Seebohm Report stressed the contribution of the personal social services to secondary prevention, i.e. help given at an early stage of an individual or family problem and suggested that they should make special efforts to give 'more help during periods when an individual or family passes through transitional epochs and has to make *radical changes* in roles, adjustments and attitudes' – when a young person leaves school for work, when married people are widowed, divorced or separated, when a working person retires from work, etc.[31] Apart from the practical problems involved in implementing this suggestion to the full on a planned basis, ethical objections have also been raised involving the individual's right to privacy. We asked our respondents in the community attitudes study and those of our fathers who had lost their wife in the year prior to our study whether a social worker should visit a motherless family automatically or only when requested by the father. Just over three-quarters of both groups felt that the social worker should visit automatically mainly in order to advise the father what social service help is available and to see that everything is all right. This should be encouraging news to the social work profession for it shows wide community support for its work. It is a logical extension of existing community services. If society requires health visitors to visit mothers with children under five years of age, it is not unreasonable to do the same with social workers in relation to one-parent families. It may well be that after the first visit there will be no need to maintain further contact but at least the visit can lay the foundations for future help if needed.

Care of children during critical periods

Fathers who gave up work to look after the children on a full-time basis may have experienced a drop in income and in their standard of living but they did not have to make hurried arrangements for the care of their children during the critical periods in the morning before school, in the afternoon after school, during school holidays or when the children were sick. It is an unenviable position to be in – a choice between a drop in the standard of living or a constant worry about the care of the children. The lack of any statutory or voluntary services for these critical periods is as clear as it is alarming. As Hunt has said not only is there 'evidence of a large demand for accommodation for children of pre school age' whose mothers go out to work but, 'A still greater demand exists for facilities for after-school and school holiday care for children between the ages of 5–15.'[32]

TABLE 73   Ways in which fathers arrange for the care of their children (per cent)

	Who gets children's breakfast	Who cares for children during: Latch-key period	Holidays	Sickness
Father	39·3	14·5		22·0
Relative	17·8	28·4	38·4	34·0
Neighbour/Friend	1·9	14·3	16·7	8·7
Siblings stay off work/school	3·2	3·3		8·1
Housekeeper	3·2	3·3	4·1	3·6
Home Help	0·6			
Children themselves	31·4	33·2	32·7	
Other	2·6	3·0	8·1	23·5*
Total	100·0	100·0	100·0	100·0
	(n = 471)	(n = 461)	(n = 510)	(n = 468)

* Includes 18·4 per cent who said they had no special arrangements.

With the exception of school holidays, the father himself cared for his children in a substantial proportion of the families. There would be few, if any, firms which would be willing to allow fathers time off

161

for the summer, Easter and Christmas holidays, a total period of three months. Even if this were possible there would be financial difficulties for in most cases the father would have to rely on Supplementary Benefit and there is no guarantee that such benefit would be paid easily without too much questioning and delay. By far the most important source of help for all four critical periods are the relatives. This is achieved often at a great inconvenience to the relatives and to the children themselves. Relatives often have to look after their own family as well and children often have to get accustomed to having two homes – one at their relative's who gives them their meals, or just looks after them, and their own home when their father is back from work. Cold statistics do not tell the whole story of what is involved even under the best possible arrangements where the relatives or friends help out. Inevitably the father feels obliged to his relatives or friends and since he can hardly reciprocate the help this feeling of obligation must be hard to bear for most and unbearable for some.

It was impossible to read the fathers' accounts of the breakfast and latch-key arrangements for their children without being struck by their makeshift, insecure and unsatisfactory nature. The father's nerves must be tested to the limit though as one father wrote to us, one has to get used to this type of life. There were fathers who had to arrange the children's life in the morning by the alarm clock and hope for the best. There were others who entrusted their children with the key to the house and hoped that the children would be sensible enough to come home from school and look after themselves until they arrived home from work. Some fathers' hours of work meant that they were either able to see their children off to school in the morning or to be home when the children returned from school but not both. There were even cases when fathers could do neither. The responsibility placed on the children is tremendous and some rise to the occasion but others fail.

'I'm off early in the morning so the children have to be up early so they will have a good breakfast but trust must be placed in them to go to school. What about when they come home? Will they have to have a fire to keep warm? Will they try to use the kettle? Will they try to start a meal? One's heart is in one's mouth until their faces are seen at the door or window at night. As I said all this was in the first two years by then one's more or less used to it.'

162

'I used to go to work at 6.20 a.m. and leave him in bed with nobody in the house; he got up and went to school and was never late and was a good scholar and never in trouble.'

'I leave for work at 6.30 a.m. and I put the alarm clocks on to wake them (ages nine and six) at 8. They get up, have something to eat then go to school. When they leave school they come home and wait for me. I come home at 5 p.m. When I am at work, I can't help worrying if they got to school all right. I just live day by day until they grow up.'

The school holidays was the period dreaded most by fathers without a willing relative near by. A multitude of improvisations were made to suit each particular set of family circumstances. The father may have reduced his hours of work or tried to come home for lunch; the children may have been parcelled off together or separately to one or more relatives for the whole or part of the holidays; the older children may have been put in charge of the younger ones; the father may have taken his son to work with him to potter around the workplace; the children may have visited their relatives to kill time, etc. Many of these arrangements are 'chancey' as one father said and the father's mind while at work is never at rest. One father wrote:

'School holidays are the one thing I dread for although I have two sensible and responsible children, the sight of a policeman appearing at my place of employment is enough to set my heart beating at a rapid rate whilst I try to compose myself for the bad news I am always sure that he is going to bring me regarding my children.'

One-fifth of the fathers said that when their children are sick they took time off work sometimes with the firm's approval, sometimes risking their employment opportunities with the firm and sometimes suffering financial hardship as one father found.

'Another problem I have come up against is when either of my children are ill and I have time off work to look after them. I don't get any benefit from social security. I was off work for two weeks some time ago when my son was ill. I contacted the local Social Security Office and explained that I had been unable to work on account of my son's illness, and I was told that as a *single man* I should put a bit of money away to help out in such emergencies.'

These experiences during the four critical periods showed few variations according to reason for motherlessness, length of motherlessness or social class of the father. A greater proportion of the divorced, though the difference was not statistically significant, tended to get help from their relatives possibly due to the fact that a greater proportion of them than the other two groups had moved house to be near their relatives. Length of motherlessness was only important in the sense that as the children got older, they tended to be trusted with the care of younger siblings or expected to look after themselves. Social class was not always relevant though in the case of school holidays and latch-key period a smaller proportion, though not a statistically significant one, of classes I and II than the other classes left the children to care for themselves. In general these problems affected all fathers very much alike.

Data on two-parent families where both parents are at work show that the position of the children is not as bad as in the case of motherless families. We have already seen that this was true for the care of children under the age of five mainly because in a large number of cases the father cares for the children. For the same reason the same data show that the children did not experience the same difficulties as children of motherless families during the morning or latch-key period or during the school holidays. Almost half the mothers worked part-time anyhow and during term-time one or other of the two parents was likely to cover completely or partly the latch-key period in most cases. It was the school holidays that caused the greatest worry but two parents with two sets of relatives are more likely than one parent with an impaired kinship system to deal with the problem satisfactorily. The various studies on this question confirm the conclusion reached by Yudkin and Holme that 'an alarming number of school children of all ages are apparently left to manage on their own not only after school but also during the holidays'.[33] Parents, however, do not always share, or they appear not to, the researchers' worries about ill-effects on the children. Hunt found that 84·4 per cent of working mothers with children under sixteen felt that the children benefited by their going out to work and only 7·1 per cent thought they did not.[34]

It may at first appear surprising that 90 per cent of our fathers said they were satisfied with the care which their children were receiving and only 10 per cent were dissatisfied. Many fathers saw in the question a potential censure for the care they were providing for their children. They did their best for their children and no one could ask more from them. Occasionally fathers called the children to tell the interviewer whether they were satisfied with the way they were being looked after. Another reason was that for many fathers the worst period was over since their children were now older and were less dependent on others. There was a slight but clear tendency for satisfaction to increase with increased length of motherlessness. A third possible factor influencing the father's replies was that, as the quotation from a father on page 162 showed, when you have lived with a situation over a long period of time you tend to get used to it and to accept it as normal and satisfactory. Finally, many of the divorced and the separated had been dissatisfied with the care which their wife had been providing for the children before she left and comparatively speaking they therefore felt satisfied with the care they provided for their children. The mere fact that they had been dissatisfied with their marriage may have also led a few to rationalize and assert that life for the children did not suffer, in fact they benefited from the mother's departure, a feeling which we observed when discussing the effects of motherlessness on the children.

The father

It is possible to read through the tables quantifying the type and source of help reaching the fathers and draw the conclusion that their relatives, friends, neighbours or the social services have relieved them of most of their troubles and worries. This would be a gross misinterpretation of the fathers' role in caring for their children. Whatever help they may receive and from whatever source it may come, they remain responsible for their children's daily care and future welfare. At one end of the continuum there were the one hundred fathers who had a related and less often a non-related woman living with them at the time of interview. They had the least worries about the daily care of their children but many were worried about the future. After all, they had suffered before and the possibility of having to take on again the whole responsibility for the daily care of their children must have been a daunting proposition. Fathers were worried in case their mother died, in case she became infirm or in the case of lodgers whether the woman decided to leave. At the other end of the continuum were the few fathers who went out to work and cared for their children as well without receiving any help from anywhere. They were not a homogeneous group with regard to the number and ages of their children or their occupation. Hence their problems were not exactly the same but they all had to work long hours and under heavy pressure to achieve their goal. Perhaps there is no better way of discussing their problem than by citing the diary of two such fathers. They were two of many fathers who agreed to keep a diary for us for a period of a week. For reasons of space we reproduce here their accounts of a day's schedule only. We have selected these two accounts because they are typical of many others rather than because they present an unusual picture.

The first father was employed and had two children of school age.

5.45 a.m.	Up, wash, dress, make bed, make a quick breakfast, i.e. – tea, bread, butter and peanut butter.
6.25 a.m.	Took Janet cup of tea and woke her. She then has to cope with her own breakfast and Stephen's and see they both get off to school OK. Note: I don't find this a very happy arrangement but what else can I do?
6.30 a.m.	Off to work.
6.57 a.m.	Clock in.
11.45 a.m. 12.30 p.m.	Lunch break, meal at works canteen.
3.45 p.m.	Clocked out.
4.25 p.m.	Arrived home, having done shopping on way for foodstuffs, etc.
4.30 p.m.	Out again, more shopping locally. (Janet and Stephen at home waiting for me on first arrival home. Janet washing up their breakfast things. As Janet is the first home (her school being nearest) she has the front door key and so they do not have to wait in the street for my arrival); anyway I am fortunate enough to have working hours whereby I am not too late getting home. By the same token, however, I do have the extra worry in the mornings as to whether they cope OK (during my absence) as regards having a good enough breakfast, and dressing properly according to the weather. I sent Stephen to get a haircut prior to writing this so will have to wait before we can have tea. I'm off.
4.50 p.m.	Home again, during this 'out' period Janet has laid the table for tea.
5.20 p.m.	Stephen not home yet, Janet impatient, so we decide to commence tea; choice of cold ham, cheese, peanut

butter, jam with bread and butter and tea, choc-marshmallows after.

5.45 p.m.	Stephen has arrived, so I now fix him up.
6.10 p.m.	Janet and I wash up and clear away. Stephen gets ready for Cubs.
6.20 p.m.	Janet off out to visit a school friend. Stephen off to Cubs. I now get cracking and have a bash at cutting the back lawns.
8.10 p.m.	I can't take any more, have not managed to complete the job very satisfactorily, I must stop. Talk about mixed emotions! there are times without number that I would give anything to get a little peace and quiet, and yet when they are both away somewhere, such as now, I miss the kids terribly.
8.40 p.m.	Stephen has come home, gosh but it's good to see him. Now to fix him up with a drink and snack, before popping him off to bed.
9.15 p.m.	Have seen Stephen up to wash and clean teeth and go to bed. Janet has just come in, thank goodness, I'm like a 'cat on hot bricks' when either of them is not under my watchful eye. Now to do a little more clothes washing. Stephen's underwear (changed at bath time last evening) and their pyjamas.
9.40 p.m.	Finished washing, now to make tomorrow's sandwiches. Then my Ovaltine.
11.00 p.m.	I'm whacked so off to bed. It's been a miserable day all day today and I am in a grim state of depression, but then that's nothing new.

The second father was unemployed, with four children all of school age:

7.15 a.m.	Got up. Washed and dressed. Raining heavy. Lit fire, prepared table.
7.30 a.m.	Got children up. Betty and Jean much the same, still off school.
8.00 a.m.	Breakfast. Tinned tomatoes and fried bread, tea. Cathy made beds.
8.30 a.m.	Cathy to school.
8.45 a.m.	Paul to school
9.00 a.m.	Started to clean up. About 10.15 went to make a cup of tea.

10.45 a.m.	Leave for Labour Exchange.
11.20 a.m.	Arrive home with social security of £9.8.0d. (£9.40).
11.30 a.m.	After seeing Betty and Jean are OK go to shops.
12.15 p.m.	Arrive home, spent over £2 on food, soap powders, etc. Dinner of pie, chips and peas.
12.45 p.m.	Washed up and pressed my suit (only one I have).
1.30 p.m.	Left home for launderette, feel out of place in these places, all women in them.
2.45 p.m.	Arrived home, washing not quite dry, put out on clothes line. Made a cup of tea.
3.30 p.m.	Vicar of church called, calls about once a month. Talks for about 20 minutes, but I have lost much of my faith (C. of E.).
4.15 p.m.	Paul home from school. Tells me Betty has failed her 11 plus. I thought she would have passed, very upset, so is she. May have something to do with her mother leaving her, she took it very badly at the time and was doing very well at school at one time.
4.30 p.m.	Cathy home from school. Tells me they are off school next Thursday for election day.
4.45 p.m.	Prepare tea.
5.00 p.m.	Have tea of fish and chips. 1 fish between 2 children.
5.30 p.m.	Clear table, Cathy washing up, Paul drying pots. I take in washing.
6.00 p.m.	Another calamity – TV sound gone, can't very well send for them when I owe them money.
6.15 p.m.	Read paper, children upset because no TV. No music either, radio gone.
6.30 p.m.	Tidy up and play games with children, little homework. Cathy seems 'edgy' tonight, something wrong. Cathy goes to friend's house near by.
8.30 p.m.	Cathy home, seems OK now. Put all children to bed.
9.00 p.m.	Relax, or try to, but start ironing. Get out all my debts, total £137, excluding about £38 in County Court.
11.30 p.m.	Bed, but can't sleep, too much on my mind. A tiring day, laid in bed feeling very depressed.

One day of overwork and excessive worry is a common occurrence in the lives of most people. It is the cumulative effect of many such days with few prospects of any substantial ease up that makes life hard to bear. This was the lot of many of our fathers. In spite of all their burdens, however, 92·2 per cent said they had no regrets about their decision to care for their children on their own. They felt they had done what they ought to have done to do their best for the children. They asserted fiercely and instinctively their objections to parting with their children. Though the majority felt that they could not provide for all their children's needs they nevertheless felt they could do better than any other available solution.

7   Social policy and social problems

In this last chapter we attempt two things: first a theoretical discussion of social problems and social policy which we hope will be of interest and of value to students of social policy and administration. Social policy is to a large extent concerned with the amelioration and possible solution of social problems and we feel that an exploration of the relationship between problems and policy can act as a framework for the discussion of social problem situations courting social action. We are not in any way suggesting that social policy is concerned solely with social problems for as Kahn has said, 'Plans are meant to implement aspirations and not merely to solve problems.'[1]

Having discussed the nature of social problems and social policy and their relationship to each other, we move to our second task of examining the nature of motherlessness as a social problem and the relevance of social policy measures to motherlessness. We put forward the suggestion that if society wishes to reduce the trend towards the reception of increasingly larger numbers of children from motherless families into the care of the local authorities and also to ensure that motherless families have a socially acceptable standard of living, an insurance benefit for all one-parent families is necessary. We realize that we are not suggesting anything new, for Beveridge suggested the possibility of such a programme almost thirty years ago. What we are claiming is that we are stating the case for such a benefit with greater conviction and we hope with some clearer understanding of the issues involved than was possible then.

The definition of a social problem

One of the most interesting questions for the student of society and social policy is how some social conditions come to be defined as problems about which society as such ought to take some action, whereas others are regarded simply as facts or as problems merely for individuals, not for society as a whole. In the mid-nineteenth century, writes Marshall, 'Poverty one might venture to say, was regarded more as a social fact than a social problem.'[2] Within a generation this had changed. Poverty had ceased to be regarded simply as a social fact and had come to be regarded increasingly as a problem which was rooted in the contemporary social structure and which only social action could ameliorate.

Another example more relevant to motherlessness is how over the past century and a half society has more and more concerned itself with the condition and welfare of children. First of all society came to concern itself with child employment, then with neglect and cruelty, and in the early years of this century with children's diet and health. What happened to children was no longer seen as of concern only to parents but came gradually to be viewed as a matter of importance to society as a whole. Child neglect and cruelty, malnutrition and ill health came to be regarded as social problems.

'No social problem,' Becker writes, 'is solely a matter of objective conditions but is instead the product of a process of definition.'[3] For anyone concerned with the formation of social policy the process of definition which lies behind these different approaches to often seemingly similar situations is crucially important. To understand a social problem fully, to quote Becker again, 'we must know how it came to be defined as a social problem'.[4]

The process of definition is complex. Each problem will have its own 'natural history'.[5] In each, the growth of awareness and the process of definition will be different depending on the political, economic and cultural context. Nevertheless, it is possible to make certain generalizations about conditions which come to be defined as social problems. They share certain common constituent elements and the presence of one or more of these is usually necessary for a condition to be defined as a social problem. For the purpose of analysis it is possible to list six elements which seem to be vital.

For a condition or situation to be seen as problematic it has first of all to be visible and measurable. Visibility must, however, be accompanied by some sense, however vague and uncertain, that the situation is problematic or likely to become so. It is the feeling that a situation is or may be problematic which leads to definition, research, and measurement. For concern to become at all widespread

171

there must be agreement about the origin and nature of the phenomenon and, almost as important, there needs to be information about its extent. Lack of precise information about the nature and size of a problem does not preclude social concern but it is an obstacle to rational discussion and debate and militates against discussion of policy to combat the problem. Absence of knowledge is a dangerous weakness for those trying to create concern. The acquisition of such knowledge is an essential stage in the evolution of the sense of a social problem coming between the period when the matter is the concern of a small minority and the stage of wider public concern which is the aim of the protagonists of the problem.

One of the great advances in the understanding of the problem of poverty in the nineteenth century was the result of the detailed attempts by Booth and Rowntree to estimate the extent of poverty in London and York.[6] Prior to their research basic information about the numbers of people who might be considered to be in poverty was simply not available. This did not prevent discussion – Booth's work was the product of a sense of a problem generated by this debate – but it prevented understanding and effective action. 'It was the sense of helplessness,' writes Simey, 'caused by the almost total lack of factual information which baffled and depressed all those who attempted to deal with the chronic poverty of their time.'[7]

Booth and Rowntree established that a third of the population of London and York were in poverty. In the face of this finding the conventional wisdom of Victorian England, that poverty was the result of a lack of moral fibre, collapsed. Their findings put discussion about poverty on a new footing. It could no longer be explained in the individualistic terms so satisfying to Victorian moral and social principles. A whole view of society was challenged. A social condition which had previously been definable as an individual problem gradually came to be viewed as a social problem.

The same was true of the rediscovery of poverty in the 1960s. The analysis carried out by Townsend and Abel-Smith enabled estimates to be made of the numbers of people living below certain defined income levels.[8] This measurement of the problem, and analysis of the reasons for it, generated a new social concern which furthered the work of pressure groups and led to more study and research which in turn further quickened the sense of a problem.

Second, to be defined as a social problem the conditions at issue must challenge society's values. Rose defines a social problem as 'some pervasive condition in society which is in conflict with, or at least out of harmony with, some significant social value'.[9] Social progress means that society gets more sensitive to such discrepancies. Each generation is always amazed by the blindness and hypocrisy of the one before. What this means is that there is a strong tendency for society to involve itself in a wider range of action to ensure that value conflict is kept within bounds. Action may be a positive attempt to improve on a situation or the aim may be simply to conceal it. The value conflicts involved, for example, in the way society treats the mentally ill or the subnormal in long-stay institutions are kept to a minimum as long as conditions are decently concealed. Unfortunately truth will occasionally out.

In our society, to look at a more immediately relevant example, there are certain strongly held convictions about children, about their rights and about how they should be treated. When standards of child care are seen to be significantly below generally accepted standards, we see this as a problem with which society as such ought to be concerned. Every child, we believe, has a right to good parenthood. Society therefore lays down conditions of intervention in an effort to secure this. The Children and Young Persons Act (1963) says that a child may be brought before a court as in need of care, protection or control if he or she is not receiving the care, protection and guidance which a good parent may reasonably be expected to give. Society's intervention is based on this challenge to its values.

Another slightly different example of this type of definitional process is when generally accepted values are strongly or persistently challenged or contradicted by the realities of the situation. Society pays lip service to the ideal of equality of opportunity in education. All children, we believe, should have a fair and equal chance. Research has shown that this ideal is very far from being realized in practice. The Plowden Committee was so concerned about this gap between ideal and reality that it called for a more than equal chance for the most deprived children to give them a better chance of being equal.[10]

Not only, however, was the Plowden Committee wrestling with this particular discrepancy between values and reality. It was also having to struggle with society's inconsistency about equality. Public policy is concerned with achieving equality of educational opportunity but not for social equality. The Plowden Committee's aim, therefore, was to achieve equality of opportunity in education, because inequality offended society's values, while of necessity

173

ignoring the underlying problem of social inequality – apart from the hope that equality in education might lead to greater social equality. Values are a crucial element in the definition of problems. They are also, as we shall see later on, a crucial factor in the formation of policy.

Third, to be defined as a social problem a situation must pose or promise difficulties for society, not just for those immediately involved in the situation. Raab and Selznick's view[11] is that

A social problem exists when organized society's ability to order relationships among people seems to be failing; when its institutions are faltering, its laws are being flouted, the transmission of its values from one generation to the next is breaking down, the framework of expectations is being shaken.

* To be a social problem a condition must threaten society's smooth functioning, its stability or its survival, or the self-perpetuation which is the central aim of every society. As examples of this kind of concern one might quote nineteenth-century concern with public health services or the concern which every society has about those who break its laws. In an advanced industrial society an example of this kind of situation is the failure of the educational system to produce the trained manpower society needs. The Plowden Committee was not only concerned about the gap between the ideal of equality of opportunity in education and the reality. It was also concerned about the loss to the community which results from such inequality. The same kind of concern about waste was a factor in the development of personal health services at the beginning of this century. The personal health of individuals came to be seen as a matter of concern to society for military and other reasons. Ill health was dysfunctional for society as well as the sufferer and was therefore a social problem.

Crucial to the preservation of social order and to the smooth functioning of society is its success in socializing the next generation, of turning its children into sober, honest, hardworking citizens who believe in prosperity, democracy, the family and the other crucial constituents of civilized life. Society has grown increasingly aware of the social importance of the socialization process. The task is now more and more one which is shared by the family and society in and through the education system of social services of one sort or another. When the processes are interrupted through family break-up, or seem likely to be ineffective for any reason, the matter is of concern to society as a whole because of the implications and repercussions.

Fourth, to be defined as a social problem a condition has to be one which can be changed, which is soluble or at any rate capable of improvement. Implicit in the definition of a condition as a problem is an idea of its solution. We only define issues or situations as problems when we feel solutions can be found. 'It is not really worthwhile defining a condition as a problem,' Timms points out, 'if the only possible response is that of endurance.'[12] The problem itself may be insoluble – for example some medical conditions – but the social problems it poses can be eased. When there is no possibility of a solution, a condition is a fact not a problem. Poverty only becomes a problem when there are resources available which *could* be used to reduce it. A society has to attain a certain degree of prosperity before it has any sense of a problem of poverty. Similarly it is only in recent years that there has been any recognition of the problem of world poverty – partly because of the increasingly sharp contrast between the West and the Third World, partly because this contrast, as Miller argues, has been made more visible by the mass media,[13] partly because the West is now in a position, if it so wished, to do something about the situation.

The Plowden Committee provide a neat illustration of this point. Inequality of opportunity, the Committee said, is avoidable and in consequence intolerable.[14] It was intolerable not simply because it existed but because it existed when it could be avoided. Inequality of educational opportunity was not just an unfortunate fact. It was a problem to which some of the answers were known.

The final elements in the process of definition are that to be seen as a social problem the conditions must be seen as, in part at least, socially caused and, in part too, as capable of being changed only by social action.

In the 1840s conditions in the new industrial cities came slowly and painfully to be regarded as problems for government because they were the product of a particular form of social life demanded by the contemporary economic system. The age of great cities, Bagehot wrote, requires strong government. It required strong government because urban life by its very nature produces problems which are only soluble by collective action. The much-heralded collapse of urban life in the US is the product of the fact that changes in political philosophy have not matched economic and social changes.

Prior to the 1890s there was no sense of unemployment as a social problem. The very word does not appear in use until 1888. Before that there were simply the unemployed, a collection of individuals with individual problems for which they were considered personally responsible. Gradually unemployment has come to be regarded not as the result of the inherited idleness of the working classes but rather as the product of inefficiencies in the economic system. Beveridge called his first study of the problem *Unemployment: A Problem of Industry*,[15] showing clearly where he thought the root of the problem lay. In his second study he saw the preservation of full employment as a clear duty of government.[16] Gradually society accepted a responsibility, first for helping men to find work, then for providing them with a minimum income when there was no work. Finally society accepted responsibility for pursuing a policy of full employment.[17] Because unemployment was viewed as a social problem, to maintain full employment became a responsibility of government.

It is important to emphasize the point that social problems are not simply problems which have their roots in a particular form of social structure or particular pattern of social life. A condition may be defined as a social problem not because of its origins but because of the demands it imposes on society. In our society, for example, mental illness and old age are social problems primarily because of the necessity for social action which they produce. In part, too, of course, they are problems with social causes. They have assumed the size they have in large measure because of the way in which traditional patterns of family and community care have been weakened by the demands of the economic system. But whatever the origins of the problems there is a clear need for public action and because of the size of the problems they can only be effectively tackled by such action.

Case defines a social problem as 'one which can best be solved by measures applied to the problem as a whole, rather than by dealing with each individual as an isolated case'.[18] This need for problem-centred rather than individual-centred action is an important element in a social problem but problem-centred action does not necessarily imply social action. Social action on the other hand does mean that problems are considered as a whole rather than from the point of view of particular individuals.

To be defined as a social problem a condition must normally contain one or more of these six elements – it must be visible and measurable, social values must be challenged, there must be problems posed to and for society, the situation must be one that can be changed, it must be in some measure socially caused and only amenable to action by society. The situation must be seen in these terms either by large numbers of people who may or may not be personally involved in the situation, by a powerful minority in government, or by a few very vocal people who can create a wider concern. Some problems come to be defined in one of these ways, some in others. Crime, for example, is defined as a social problem by the whole community. On the other hand it was a small group of key civil servants – 'the greatest range of masterful talent ever assembled in the public service', McGregor calls them[19] – who helped define the urban problems of the 1830s and 1840s as social problems. A good example of a vocal minority which has helped to mould public opinion on a specific issue is the Disablement Income Group. It has worked hard to persuade society to see the disabled as a social problem and a public responsibility, rather than to look upon them as a collection of individuals with individual problems.

The definition, causation and solution of social problems are all affected by the sociological standpoint of the writer. There are two basic approaches to the study of society – the functional approach which tends to see social problems as examples of social pathology and the conflict approach which tends to see social problems as the result of the conflicting interests inevitable in society. This is outside the terms of our present discussion but we hope to explore this question in a future publication.

As regards social policy, the crucial step is the recognition and definition of the problem rather than the process by which recognition is achieved. It is necessary then to consider whether motherlessness is a social problem.

Is motherlessness a social problem?

We saw in the last section how social facts become social problems. It is a process affected by a multiplicity of socio-economic, moral and political factors. The end result of this process is the recognition by society and by the state that a certain social condition is problematic enough to demand social action. Clearly, social problems vary in their dimensions – in the number of people they affect, in the threat they pose to society and in the ease with which they can be tackled by social action.

Crucial to our discussion is the question of whether family disorganization is a social problem or simply a problem for the

177

individuals immediately involved. Is it, to use Wright Mills's distinction, a personal trouble or a public issue? Troubles, he says, 'occur within the character of the individual and within the range of his immediate relations with others; they have to do with his self and with those limited areas of social life of which he is directly and personally aware'. Issues, on the other hand, 'have to do with matters that transcend these local environments of the individual . . . They have to do with the organization of many such milieux into the institutions of a historical society as a whole, with the ways in which various milieux overlap and interpenetrate to form the larger structure of social and historical life. An issue is a public matter.'[20]

The thesis of this section is that family disorganization in general, and motherlessness in particular, are not simply personal troubles but are public issues, or to use the language of the previous section, social problems because of their origins, nature and implications. The origins of motherlessness are to be found in social and economic changes, it has repercussions for the rest of society and it calls for social action.

It was Durkheim who first showed that the private and personal act of suicide seemed in large measure to be socially determined. His researches showed that suicide rates varied from time to time and place to place in a way which was explicable only in terms of social causation.[21] Similarly family break-up cannot be understood if regarded simply as the fruit of the incompatibility of two individuals. 'Conflicting norms and values,' in the larger world, Elliott and Merrill point out, 'are reflected in how marriage partners evaluate each other, hence are important factors in determining the number of marriages that fail.'[22] They go on to point out that the interplay of social, economic, political, technological and philosophical factors has given rise to new attitudes, values and norms that have affected the family as well as every other institution. Changes in patterns of marriage and in rates of marriage break-up are indices of these wider changes.

Motherlessness is one aspect of family disorganization. It is a social problem in itself though, like all other social problems, it is part of a wider problem. The crucial factor in the creation of motherless families is the changed position of women in society. The large-scale employment of married women has lessened their economic dependence on their husbands. Greater economic independence has given them a new status in the family. It has also given them new aspirations and perhaps lessened their tolerance of what in the past had to be tolerated. Women today are in a position when it is increasingly possible for them to leave their husbands. In this they have gained equality.

Changes in the role of women inevitably mean changes in the role of men. These changes have made it more possible for fathers to care for their children on their own. This is the product of a pattern of shared conjugal roles rather than the traditional pattern of role segregation. It is also a product of a more family-centred life which characterizes the greater separateness of the nuclear family from its kin.

Geographical mobility means, too, that the extended family is less real and so less likely to absorb the motherless as it did in the past. Not only does social change seem to have made motherlessness more likely, it has also made it less likely that the motherless family will be absorbed by the wider family.

So while motherlessness is clearly a private trouble it is also a product of social change, changes in family patterns, changes in men's and women's position and expectations. On the whole, society does not see it in this way. It sees family break-up as essentially the product of the incompatibility of two individuals. The social scientist must make clear that society is often responsible for what seem to be the acts of individuals. His task, as Wright Mills puts it, is 'continually to translate personal troubles into public issues, and public issues into the terms of their human meaning for a variety of individuals'.[23]

Society then cannot regard motherlessness purely as a private trouble because it is in part the product of social change. There are also more practical grounds for social concern. Family break-up of any kind is a matter of importance to society because the family has a number of important social functions. An incomplete family is likely to find it more difficult than a complete family to carry out these functions so society is bound to be concerned.

The family has four obvious social functions in our society. First, it has the main responsibility for socializing the next generation and so it becomes the central mechanism in the transmission of culture. Second, it provides a unique opportunity for the child to learn the basic social roles of mother and father, of male and female, of husband and wife, of worker and homemaker. 'The folkways, mores and institutional controls that regulate courtship, marriage and the public and private roles of husband and wife,' say Elliott and Merrill, 'are largely learned in the family.'[24]

Thirdly, the family gives an opportunity for the satisfaction of the emotional needs of children and parents which seem necessary to personal fulfilment. Finally, the family is an important agent of social control. The opinion of those closest to us is one of the strongest influences on behaviour and for most people the opinions of the intimate family group are a powerful guiding force.[25]

Because of the importance of these functions to its stability and well-being society is bound to be concerned with the family. In recent years one of the supposed guiding aims of social policy has been to support the family in the performance of its social functions.

No longer [says Titmuss[26]] is the family taken for granted as it was, like progress, in Victorian England . . . In discovering the family, we have simultaneously discovered that the quality of its internal life is also a matter of public concern. In this sense *the family of today is a social institution.*

Society today aids and supports the family in its socialization function through the education system and the social services. It provides family advice centres, family casework, family allowances, a Family Incomes Supplement and family planning. Public money and resources are spent in trying to forestall and prevent family break-up. It is true that this effort is neither sustained nor substantial enough. Wynn, for example, concludes her survey of government policies for the family by saying that 'the great majority of families with dependent children do not achieve a modest-but-adequate standard of living'.[27] Nevertheless, this activity is evidence of society's interest in the stability and well-being of the family.

In general society is ambivalent and uncertain about the nature and degree of its responsibility for children. Two sets of values are in conflict – values about the rights and responsibilities of parents and values about the rights of children. Society believes in the primacy of parental rights and responsibilities in the rearing of children but accepts too, that 'the doctrine of parental rights should not be allowed any longer to be a doctrine of children's wrongs'.[28]

While it asserts its right to intervene in the relationship between parents and children as an ultimate prerogative, society is reluctant to exercise the right. Nevertheless, when the way in which children are being brought up conflicts too sharply with social values and is clearly dysfunctional, society will act to try to reduce the conflict. Society finds it easier to act in a negative than in a positive, preventive manner.

180

The crucial question with regard to the one-parent family, including the motherless family, is whether it is less able than the two-parent
family to perform its social functions. As we have shown in previous
chapters, this is inevitable in a number of areas of family life. There
is a limit to the time and energies of a lone parent. The tasks normally
undertaken by two parents will necessarily be performed rather less
efficiently by one parent. Whether one parent, however devoted, can
as effectively socialize children as two parents seems unlikely. A
one-parent family certainly does not provide the same opportunities
for role learning as a normal family. If there is no mother substitute,
girls will lack a role model. The absence of a mother – and the prob-
ability of a busy father – is likely, too, to make the family less able to
meet the emotional needs of its members. There are therefore grounds
for concern about the ability of the motherless or the fatherless
family adequately to perform the social functions which our society
expects of the family. This must make motherlessness or fatherlessness into issues of public concern.

Motherlessness also challenges certain social values. It is generally
accepted that a child needs two parents – partly because earning a
living and caring for children make up jobs for two, and partly
because two parents are thought to be necessary for a child's satisfactory emotional development. Because of these beliefs, society
is likely to feel concern about families where there is only one
parent. The belief, too, that every child has a right to good parenthood and that children should not suffer for the 'sins' of their parents
is likely to make society feel some responsibility for the situation.
What finally forces society to involve itself in the problem is the fact
that a man left to bring up children on his own cannot always combine this with full-time employment. Society is here trapped with two
values at stake – values which assert the necessity of the family unit
to the child's full development and values which assert that men
should work. Whatever its values society will have to provide some
kind of care for the children when, and if, the father is unable to
cope. Values are significant in that they will make for a concern
for the situation before the family breaks up. Society's values are
such that if consistent it will seek in some way to support the lone
parent and to enable him or her to care rather than simply provide a
long-stop solution. So the values which our society holds are likely
to make for concern about motherless children *per se* not simply
because there is a high and statistically measurable risk of them

becoming a public responsibility and money will be saved if this can be prevented.

In the previous section it was argued that one of the characteristics of social problems was that they could most effectively be tackled by social action. This is true of motherlessness. Society cannot alter a family's motherless situation but it can take steps to reduce the risk of the children having to be received into the care of local authorities and it can also mitigate certain of the problems and so better enable the family to undertake the functions which society requires of it.

The problems are such that a family cannot always solve them for itself in a mobile industrial society. Only social action can provide the father with an adequate income if he decides that it is his duty to stay at home to look after his children. Equally, social action is necessary to provide the range of services – day nurseries, nursery schools, domestic help and so on – which will be required by a father who feels able to continue at work. Only society can compensate a family for the increased expenditure which seems an inescapable part of motherlessness. If a father decides that he is unable adequately to care for his children on his own, only society can provide adequate substitute care – as it does for all children 'deprived of a normal home life'. The kind of benefits and services provided, however, can influence the father's decision whether to care for the children himself or whether to allow them to be received into care.

At the moment motherlessness is a new and almost unstudied issue but it has many of the classic constituents of a social problem. It is a product of the uneasy action of social change which contributes to family break-up. The continued existence of such families rather than their absorption into the extended family is equally the product of social change. Motherlessness, too, poses problems for society in the way it weakens the family in the performance of its various social functions. To mitigate the ill effects for itself and for the children society is compelled to be concerned. Given its public implications, motherlessness cannot be construed as a private issue. The appointment by the government of a committee to look into the problems of one-parent, including motherless, families and the financing of research by the Department of Health and Social Security to investigate the conditions of motherless families are indications that society is gradually recognizing motherlessness as a social problem.

Social action and social problems

Government recognition of the existence of a social problem does not necessarily lead to social action. In the first place there are degrees of government awareness and acceptance of the existence of a problem. References to government recognition cover a variety of parliamentary steps – the raising of questions on a specific social problem by Members of Parliament; the attempt by a Member of Parliament to introduce a Private Member's Bill; a statement by a Minister that the government is concerned about a specific issue or problem; the commissioning of government research; the establishment of a committee to look into a problem and so on. Such stages represent varying degrees of awareness and concern.

Even if a government recognizes the existence of a social problem it may still feel that it is not a matter for government action. The official view may be that at the time of consideration the problem is not sufficiently serious or widespread. An example of this kind of issue is the problem of the lack of suitable sites for gipsies. This has been a recognized problem for decades and had been discussed several times by government before it was finally accepted in 1968 as an issue which was sufficiently serious to demand real government action.[29] A government's assessment of seriousness is, of course, essentially a value judgment. Problems do not have to be large to be regarded as serious. The problem of sites for gipsies is of immediate concern to only a tiny minority. Widows are an example of a relatively small group who have long had special treatment in the social security system. Widowers, on the other hand, have had no such special consideration.

On the other hand, while accepting the existence and seriousness of a particular problem, a government may feel it is not the kind of issue which a government could or should tackle. Race relations had been a problem in certain areas for many years before government accepted this as a matter where government intervention was right and necessary. Refusal to act was based partly on the assumption that the problem was not widespread enough but also on the belief that this was an area where it was not ethically right for the state to intervene. Relationships between immigrants and natives were considered to be an individual affair and state intervention was considered undesirable.[30]

A government may also accept that although a particular issue is ultimately a matter for social action the time is not ripe. Reasons commonly adduced for delay are lack of information about the precise extent or nature of the problem and so about what needs to be done and the costs involved. In such situations government cannot easily completely refuse to act; it can easily, however, defer action until the required information is available through government or other research. The Labour Government, for example, refused to introduce any new social security benefits for the disabled until a government survey was completed although it recognized that poverty among the disabled constituted a social problem. This may be a charitable interpretation of the government's intentions. An equally likely interpretation is that the government, faced with economic difficulties, needed breathing space and was using the lack of adequate information as its excuse for postponing action.[31]

Lack of resources, whether in terms of finance, buildings or staff, is the other reason or excuse used by governments to defer or decline action on a social problem. In the last analysis this indicates that the government is either not committed enough or that it considers other problems more pressing. The ability of an industrial society to provide the resources for new or expanded services is not such a major problem as it is often made out to be, for as Schlakman has said, 'what a country can afford to spend on social welfare is a function of its productive capacity. What it is willing to commit to social welfare depends on its values'.[32] The problem of economic resources is crucial in developing societies but it is not of the same dimension in developed societies where the wealth to meet society's public and private needs exists, and the question becomes one of allocation between the private and the public sector as well as between services in the public sector.

A further complication is that it is not always possible to provide accurate estimates of the costs involved in a particular policy. This may be a help or a hindrance to action depending on the government's commitment. If the government is disinclined to act, uncertainty about costs can be an acceptable justification for caution and delay. On the other hand, ignorance can be a valuable weapon for a committed body. Policies may be adopted in the enthusiasm of ignorance when, if the facts were known, advance would be far more cautious. Underestimates of the likely cost of the National Health Service certainly reduced opposition and uncertainty at the time of its creation. Had the truth been known about future costs it could only have been discouraging. The Rent Act (1957), is another good example of a measure based on ignorance and misconception. Had the government been in possession of the facts it would have seen the irrelevance of the sweeping solutions which ignorance suggested.[33] Ignorance can be a reason for inaction or action and knowledge is the same. It can be a basis for action or a reason for prolonged contemplation. 'There is nothing a government hates more than to be well informed,' Keynes recorded, 'for it makes the process of arriving at decisions much more complicated and difficult.'

There is the problem, too, of calculating the unanticipated costs of action as well as the direct costs. The direct cost of providing an insurance benefit for all one-parent families where the father or mother cannot work is not very great simply because the majority of such families receive Supplementary Benefit. The unanticipated cost, however, will be greater if the alleged fears that the introduction of an insurance benefit will lead to more families breaking-up do in fact materialize. Unanticipated costs represent value judgments and are impossible to estimate. In the case of one-parent families one can argue that an insurance benefit will help to combat the ill-effects of economic deprivation on children and in this way it can promote the country's economic well-being. There is a tendency to translate value judgments into economic considerations that give the impression of mathematical exactitude. Perhaps this is a characteristic of industrial societies where secular rather than ethical or moral values are held in greater esteem. In the words of Marris and Rein, in such societies 'morality is an uneasy ground from which to argue any specific proposal'. They advise reformers to remember that 'Even though some moral commitment must lie at the foundation of any social policy, it is wiser to pursue, as long as possible, a more dispassionate line of argument', one that appears 'scientifically rational'.[34]

In the particular field of insurance benefits for one-parent families it is fear of the possible social costs rather than the direct or indirect economic costs which prevents social action. Implicit in inaction is the fear that action might remove some of the existing deterrents to family break-up and so increase the number of broken homes. A social insurance benefit could go against the general trend of social policy which is to support and buttress the family. The general aim of social policy is the fostering of social integration.[35] A social insurance benefit for one-parent families could be regarded as likely to have the opposite effect. In general, developments in social policy follow social change at a safe distance. The provision of insurance benefits for one-parent families might be regarded as likely to induce social change rather than follow it and seek to mitigate the resulting diswelfares.

Finally, a government may accept the existence of a social problem but refuse to act because it feels that such action will contravene social values in some other area of life. The solution of one social problem by legislation may sometimes help to create a new problem or help to exacerbate an existing one. As Rose has said, 'it is somewhat redundant to say that law creates social problems. Laws are attempts to deal with social problems; they usually transform the social problems in some unanticipated way; in so doing they often create new social problems.'[36] The attitude of successive governments towards the wages stop rule is a case in point. It is generally recognized that the question of the wages stop rule results in a number of families receiving Supplementary Benefit allowances which are below the official levels of subsistence.[37] In other words, the government accepts that a number of families will live in poverty and refuses to deal with the problem because it feels that such action may have undesirable effects on the people's willingness to work. Society considers both poverty and voluntary unemployment as social problems and in the ensuing clash of values, the value placed on work is considered supreme by the government.

For a variety of reasons, therefore, government recognition of a social problem does not necessarily lead to action to deal with it. Recognition is an essential preliminary to action but action does not always follow recognition. In this section we have looked at some of the more immediate and practical reasons which governments give for non-action. There are, however, more fundamental factors which need to be considered.

Social values, social class and social policy

Anyone concerned with the practical development of social policies or their extension into new fields needs to be aware of the kind of factors which affect the development of social policy. The policy maker must take account of these for they are important elements in the situation with which he is trying to deal.

Much has been written about the multiplicity of factors which affect the development of social policy. While not ignoring the relevance of other factors we believe that the two main determinants of the nature of social policy are the interrelated systems of social values and social class which prevail in a particular society. As we have already suggested, we see economics as subsidiary to these two factors since an advanced society can in large measure afford what it wants to in this field.

There is general agreement in the social administration literature in this country of the influence of social values on the formation of social policy. Warham's dictum that 'any development in the field of social policy involves value-conflict'[38] is generally accepted. She goes on to elaborate, that 'Any piece of social legislation, therefore, is the outcome of attempts to reconcile complexes of values which are differently weighted, and differently interpreted, by different individuals and groups within the society in which that legislation is formulated and has to operate.'[39] In a similar vein, Eyden suggests that, 'Social policy is essentially concerned with value judgements.'[40] Slack speaks of 'the values and value judgements that are an intrinsic part of social administration.'[41]

What is lacking from the literature regarding the impact of social values on social policy is an appreciation of the relationship between social values and social stratification. It is clearly stated that different social values are held by different population groups but it is nowhere stated that values are related to social class. Our own study provided a number of examples of the varying emphasis given to certain values by different classes. Classes I and II, for example, believed much more strongly than classes IV or V that a father left with children under school age should nevertheless go out to work. In a different area classes I and II were much less confident than classes IV and V that a lone parent could provide adequately for children. Little attempt has been made in the past by social administrators, however, to demonstrate that the society's value system and social-class system are related and that they both affect social policy. Therefore, when we discuss the influence of social values on social policy we may in fact be discussing the impact of middle-class values and not the values of the entire society on social policy. Social values and economic and political power are related, and Marx's view that 'the ideas of the ruling class are in every age, the ruling ideas' is generally accepted today.

Social values are distributed differently in the social-class system whichever of the following two schools of thought on this subject one accepts. The first school maintains that the values of the working class are so different from those of the middle class that it is more correct to speak of two separate value systems than a unitary value system for the whole society.[42] The other school of thought, while not denying the existence of differences between working-class and middle-class values, considers the overlap of values substantial enough to claim one unitary value system for the whole of society.[43] Parkin, elaborating on Marx's thesis, argues that 'Values are much more likely to flow in a "downward" than "upward" direction' in the social structure.[44] This is because 'the social and political definitions of those in dominant positions tend to become objectified and enshrined in the major institutional order, so providing the moral framework of the entire value system'.[45] This legitimization of middle-class values through institutional means, means that middle-class values are accepted and are aspired to by the working class even if they benefit the middle class.

The insurance principle in the field of social security stemming from the Victorian middle-class value of self-help[46] is an example of a middle-class value becoming part of social policy and supported strongly by the working class as well, in spite of the fact that it is to the financial advantage of the middle class. When Beveridge declared so resoundingly, that 'Benefit in return for contributions, rather than free allowances from the State, is what the people of Britain desire,'[47] he was stating his own personal conviction about the value of insurance rather than the considered and informed judgment of the British people. But what he said was probably correct. The middle-class value had become the dominant one.

The general condemnation of the 'scroungers' in social security compared with the general admiration of tax dodgers are other examples where middle-class social values which benefit the middle class most have received widespread acceptance in the community. To abuse the social security system is indicative of lack of self-reliance while to cheat the Inland Revenue shows personal initiative.[48] Self-reliance and personal initiative are both values that form part of the 'great idea' of individualism that Wilensky and Lebeaux refer to in their discussion of the relationship between industrialization and welfare provision.[49] In the case of motherless families a similar process has taken place with the result that many fathers who draw Supplementary Benefit in order to care for their children feel guilty of their behaviour and would rather be at work.

A number of studies have shown how dominant social values affect attitudes to the social services. Land, for example, found that many of the large families she studied did not always obtain the benefits to which they were entitled. One of the important reasons was the ambivalent attitude society has to those who need support from the state particularly financial support. Society offers help but dominant social values make it personally costly for those who need help to apply. 'Those who have to ask for assistance in feeding and clothing their families,' Land writes, 'feel a loss of self-respect because it means admitting to themselves as well as to others that they have failed.'[50] 'Most applicants for social services remain paupers at heart,' says Pinker,[51] discussing the problem of stigma involved in social service organization. There is bound to be stigma and so discouragement from using services as long as society's value system is fundamentally hostile to the partial and half-hearted attempts it makes to reduce intolerable inequalities.

The dominance of middle-class values in social policy making is plain if one examines the fields where social policy has supposedly been most concerned with equality. In fact, the concern has been with equality of access to a very limited range of limited services. It has not been concerned with the major inequalities of wealth, status and power. Equality of access to services has only been granted, too, where continuing inequality would be manifestly dysfunctional economically, militarily or socially – in education and health services, for example. The dominant values, however radical social policy proposals have sometimes seemed to less perceptive contemporaries, have always been fundamentally middle class, a compromise between *laissez-faire* and collectivism.

How is this discussion on the relationship between social values and social policy relevant to our central theme of motherlessness? Social policy provision for the motherless is part of the wider question of social security provision for those in need. So long as the values of individualism, self-reliance and hard work reign supreme and as long as we look at social contingencies from the point of view of their causes rather than their social meaning, it will be impossible to provide an adequate income for fathers caring for their children. We shall continue to provide a minimum and means tested, rather than an adequate and universal income for, as Miller and Riessman have argued for social security benefits in the United States, 'we are still fearful of sapping morale and incentive to work'.[52] The only radical solution is to reconsider our social values and examine their implications for, as Wedderburn has argued, 'a Socialist cannot be simply concerned to perpetuate and to emphasize in state legislation the values of the market; he must be involved with the ideological

189

struggle against these very values'.[53] It needs, of course, to be borne in mind that the relationship between social values and social policy is a two-way process. Social values affect the formation of social policy; equally social policy affects the pattern of social values.[54]

The neglect of the influence of social-class conflict on social policy is very marked in the social administration literature of this country even among those writers who support the 'institutional' view of the welfare state. The concept of social class conflict-free social policy may not have been explicitly stated but implied. A selection of the definitions of social policy will illustrate this point: Eyden's definition of social policy is government action 'which is deliberately designed and taken to improve the welfare of its citizens, either collectively or as individuals'.[55] Warham also states that 'social policy may be identified as positive action to rectify a negative situation'.[56] Rodgers also regards 'as social a policy which is aimed at the removal of elements in society which are upsetting the equilibrium of that society'.[57] This is what may be called the 'literature of welfarism' viewing society as made up of groups who have common social needs or who face common social problems and who act together to provide welfare services to deal with these problems.

This is not to suggest that this school of thought considers social policy as a smooth process. It accepts the existence of conflict among competing groups and individuals but it over-emphasizes the unity of society's response to social problems and the common nature of the benefits accruing to all sections of the community from social policy. It perhaps tends to see social policy and the welfare state as the fruit of high-minded social principles, as a neighbourly response to human need, rather than in broader and more functional terms as a greasing of the wheels of industrial society. It has its roots on one hand in the 'order' or functionalist sociological theories of society and in the 'pluralist' political theories of the state on the other. Consensus and stability are considered eufunctional to society while conflict is seen as dysfunctional. The various groups that unite to make up society do come into conflict, but this is intermittent and stability is soon restored to the benefit of all in society. The state acts as an impartial arbiter between the conflicting groups and sees that measures are taken which, by and large, benefit all groups more or less equally in the long term. There is no one group or class in society which dominates the formulation of social policy and whose long-term economic interests are primarily served.

The 'welfarist' view of the nature of social policy has been a dominant one – indeed the only one until very recently. It is only during the last few years that a new school of thought seems to be emerging centring on the 'conflict' sociological theories of society and the 'élite' political theories of the state. It looks upon society as the arena where a continuous struggle between the major social classes takes place over power and wealth. Conflict is a normal everyday phenomenon in society and consensus is rare. The state does not act as an impartial umpire resolving social conflicts to the equal benefit of all groups in society but on the whole it serves the interests of the ruling class or the 'power élite' under whose dominating influence it constantly functions.

Wedderburn's contribution was the first major attempt to classify the various views of the Welfare State and to put forward the view that if we are to understand the development of social policy 'we have to examine political forces. We have to focus attention upon the demands of the working class for social justice and upon an analysis of the political strength of the working class; and its success in winning allies from particular pressure and interest groups then becomes an essential part of the story.'[58] At various points in her excellent review, Wedderburn implies that class conflict as a force in shaping social policy has been ignored. At one point she is explicit and this is when she discusses Titmuss's analysis of the development of social services. She writes:[59]

> In his study of the development of individual services in the
> welfare state (for instance the health service) Professor Titmuss
> has produced a revealing model of the way in which the conflict
> of different interest groups can shape and mould the final form
> of legislation which emerges. What is missing, however, is any
> notion of class conflict as crucial in creating the overall balance
> of political forces which determines whether or not social
> legislation is enacted, or as an influence upon the final form of
> that legislation. At times it is as though classes, shaped by the
> overall distribution of economic power and authority in
> industrial society, did not exist.

Coates and Silburn share Wedderburn's concern about the advance of the values of the market in recent years. They suggest in their discussion that social-class interests have been paramount in the formulation of the character of social services. If society is dominated by 'market principles', i.e. distribution of resources according to individual means, then the upper classes will benefit most; if it is dominated by 'welfare principles', i.e. the distribution of resources according to some objective measurement of individual needs, then the working classes will benefit most. They present a picture of constant conflict between market and welfare principles and they conclude:[60]

> The truth is that welfare and market principles are irreconcilably in conflict with one another, and at no point in time is there a declared truce; there is no gentleman's agreement as to the proper province of each, no honourable observation of agreed demarcation boundaries. On the contrary, the two methods of distribution remain in a perpetual and dynamic state of opposition.

It appears to us that on the whole it is more profitable to view social policy in terms of the conflict model than the 'welfarist' model. Social policy is not a unified national effort to meet social needs or to eradicate social problems in an impartial way to the benefit of all in society. It is rather an accommodating process resolving the conflict of social values and interests along social-class lines. Social class may not be the dominating factor in all social-policy issues but it is certainly clear in the major issues – those of housing, health, education and income distribution. The social-class conflict is on two levels – first, whether social-policy measures should be introduced or whether provision should be made by private enterprise; and second, when social policy is decided upon, what form it should take and who it should cover. This conflict is continual on both levels and, to use Coates's and Silburn's analogy, the character of social policy shifts between 'welfare' and 'market' principles in this unceasing struggle. Up to now social and economic policies have not changed significantly the distribution of power and wealth in society though they have helped to mitigate the more glaring inequalities and suffering inherent in the capitalist system. The ruling class or élite has accepted some restrictions to its power and wealth in its conflict with the working class but it has managed to retain its superior position. In the words of Gouldner, 'On the principle that it is better to be wealthy and secure than very wealthy and insecure, the rich have compromised with progressive taxation and with universalist and achievement values. They bend and compromise, but they do not compromise themselves out of existence.'[61]

Planning and social policy

The need for planning is part of the contemporary conventional wisdom. It is a central concern of the student of social policy, of governments and local authorities. In this section we attempt to explore the extent to which planning is possible in social policy in order to provide a background against which we can consider the planning of policies to meet the needs of motherless families.

Comprehensive planning is an elusive term and it is difficult to define. Numerous definitions have been put forward and we offer here one by Webber. He sees comprehensive planning as a 'process of making rational decisions about the future goals and future courses of action, which relies upon explicit tracings of the repercussions and the value implications associated with alternative courses of action and, in turn, requires explicit evaluation and choice among the alternative matching goal action sets'.[62] The process he defines is a complex one and it involves the collection of data on facts and values, the evaluation of such data in the light of existing theories and the formulation of alternative policies designed to achieve the desired goals.

To appreciate the implications of this definition of comprehensive social planning it is worth discussing the main stages through which the planning of a specific social policy will go. The first stage is what Kahn calls the formulation of 'the planning task'. A social problem can be viewed from different perspectives and the perspective chosen decides the goal of social policy. Is poverty, for example, a problem of lack of basic necessities, of income inequality, of lack of social mobility or of social disorganization? Depending on the perspective chosen 'the planning task' can be the provision of social security benefits, measures of income redistribution, educational reforms or social-work measures. In the case of motherlessness, if the problem is seen as emotional, the planner stresses the provision of psychiatric and social-work services; if it is seen as one of ill-effects on the education of children, 'the planning task' is the establishment of special educational policies; if the problem is economic, then the emphasis must be on adequate social security measures. If the various aspects of the problem are related and compatible 'the planning task' will be composite and will aim at them all. If they are incompatible, however, 'the planning task' becomes much more complex. Without the definition of the planning task, the planner lacks 'a beacon' to quote Kahn again.[63]

Having decided the nature of the social problem and defined the planning task, the next step perhaps is to examine the ways in which the problem in question is affected by and the way it affects the social and economic sub-systems in society. In what ways, for example, do the socio-economic conditions of the country affect motherless families and vice versa, what effect does the existence of such families have on the social and economic sub-systems of society? This is a complex question and one may not be able to provide detailed and definite answers. It is nevertheless important to explore this relationship at least in broad and tentative terms in order to avoid the mistake of formulating policies which consider the particular problem in isolation from its socio-economic context. Very much related to this point is the added complication that each problem is part of a wider problem. Motherless families are part of the problem of one-parent families which in turn is part of the problem of family disorganization. That in turn forms an aspect of the wider problem of social and economic change. This interconnectedness of problems creates questions about boundaries which the planner has to decide endeavouring not to be so narrow that he attempts to deal with the problem in a vacuum and, on the other hand, not so broad as to render planning an impossibility.

The third step in the formulation of social policy is for the social-policy analyst to put forward alternative policies through which the desired goals can be achieved. Ideally one would expect these proposals to be free of the social values of the analyst. If, for example, he has to make policy proposals to ensure that motherless families have an adequate income he can suggest an insurance benefit for such families, a special family allowance for every child in this group of families, a system of special tax concessions, and so on. He will document his proposals impartially so that the policy makers, i.e. politicians, can make what they consider to be the more rational decisions or those which are more politically viable. In this way the social policy analyst does not usurp the role of the politician who is the real policy maker but he provides the reasoned alternatives which can make rational decisions possible. This line of thought presents the social-policy analyst as a value-free person who can arise above and beyond his own value system. This, of course, is an impossible requirement and it is more realistic to accept the fact that he cannot be free of his own values and that he will be more honest to himself and to society if he makes his value premises clearly explicit.

This stage of policy making is as difficult as the preceding ones. In putting forward proposals, the analyst is faced with the fundamental obstacle that for many problems we do not know the solutions. As Hansen and Carter have said, 'One of our most serious problems is that the consequences of certain actions are presumed to be known when in fact they are not . . . This situation makes for a difficult environment in which to examine alternatives.'[64] This can be true for both major as well as minor policy questions. We do not know which measures, for example, might have the effect of reducing family break-up nor do we know whether such a simple policy measure as the wages stop has the effects it is designed for.

In devising a policy covering the three stages we have mentioned, the analyst has to rely on research data and theories appertaining to the problem under consideration. Research data will cover facts as well as values. Factual information can never be 100 per cent complete even with the best of surveys. Data on motherlessness, for example, are both scarce and unreliable. We have no accurate estimates of the total number of motherless families in the community, or how many families are left motherless every year, or how many motherless families are in time reconstituted. We do not know what proportion of families left motherless survive as independent units, how many are absorbed by relatives or how many children come into the care of the local authorities because of motherlessness. We lack the factual data which are the essential basis for sound policy making.

Nevertheless, given the will and the resources it would be possible to acquire this information so that the size and precise nature of the problem would be known. But as well as knowing the facts the social planner needs to analyse the values surrounding any social problem. As Simey has said, 'it is the understanding of the dynamic force of values that is so often a necessary prerequisite to the understanding of social facts'.[65] What social values are challenged or threatened by motherlessness? Does public opinion feel that motherless families should be helped and if so how? How does public opinion define the problem – in financial, caring or emotional terms? How do the motherless themselves see their situation? The relevant social values will vary by age, sex and class and possibly by region. In the end the government has to balance conflicting opinions. It has to decide whether to seek to follow or to form public opinion. It has to decide whether to give more weight to the informed views of a minority of experts or to bow to ignorance and tenaciously held misconceptions. It has to decide, too, whether children ought to be helped rather than old people, whether physically or mentally handicapped children should be helped rather than the motherless or fatherless. It has to seek a rationale for decisions about priorities when there is no possible method of assessing the relative urgency of many competing claims for resources.

Apart from the manifold difficulties involved in collecting information on facts and values, there is the additional problem of how to integrate facts and values into a theoretical framework that can be useful for social-policy making. This has been achieved to some extent in the field of economic policy but we are nowhere near the same stage in social policy. For example, industrial societies have developed economic theories which have enabled them to deal to a lesser or greater extent with such problems as unemployment, inflation, etc., but they have not devised theories to influence social policies with regard to, let us say, preventing family disorganization. This is due partly to lack of theoretical knowledge but it is also due to social values regarding individual freedom, responsibility, etc. Social planning is in some ways more difficult than economic planning because, 'Social problems and policies seem to involve individual responsibilities and individual initiatives in ways and degrees more complex and more pervasive than do most economic policies.'[66]

This brief review of the issues involved in comprehensive social planning shows clearly that such planning has not been the practice of governments so far. The Seebohm Report, for example, which led to the radical reorganization of the local authority personal social services had no research evidence on which to base its proposals. There was, however, general consensus of opinion regarding the inadequacy of the existing organizational structure and a general demand for its reform. Similarly the reorganization of secondary education was preceded by no adequate programme of research. Change was the product of dissatisfaction with the *status quo* rather than the proven superiority of the new system. Marsh's view, harsh and cynical though it may seem, is not an incorrect reflection of the situation in this country. He writes,[67]

Despite some encouraging signs it seems that we are still at the stage where the natural inclination of British politicians, administrators and businessmen and trade union leaders is to despise facts and mistrust theories, with the result that the actual as distinct from the assumed situation in governmental and industrial fields is rarely closely examined, and theoretical concepts of possible courses of action are hardly considered.

Lindblom, Dahl, Braybrooke and others have argued that not only does comprehensive planning not take place in practice but that it is an impossible ideal since we do not know enough about many social problems, we do not agree enough about the values underlying social policies or their goals and objectives and society does not possess enough resources to deal with all problems simultaneously. We should abandon the concept of comprehensive planning, they argue, and adopt instead the idea of 'incrementalism' or 'disjointed incrementalism' or the 'branch method' of planning or, to use Popper's phrase, 'piecemeal social engineering'.[68] These terms mean similar ideas and broadly incrementalism is[69]

a method of social action that takes existing reality as one alternative and compares the probable gains and losses of closely related alternatives by making relatively small adjustments in existing reality, or making larger adjustments about whose consequences approximately as much is known as about the consequences of existing reality, or both. Where small increments will clearly not achieve desired goals, the consequences of large increments are not fully known, and existing reality is clearly undesirable, incrementalism may have to give way to a calculated risk. Thus scientific methods, incrementalism, and calculated risks are on a continuum of policy methods.

This kind of incrementalism does not deny the value of research and planning. It merely asserts that planning can be more effective when the changes contemplated are incremental rather than radical and that such changes are more likely to be acceptable than major changes in policy. It also takes into account the influence of political factors and pressure groups on social policy sometimes to the extent that the rational plan is abandoned for the sake of the acceptable plan. It accepts that radical changes may be the answer when there is general agreement in the community or when it is known that incremental changes cannot achieve the desired goals. In fact incrementalism can mean different things to different people, but its basic idea is that social policy builds out 'from the current situation, step-by-step and by small degrees' compared with the rational-comprehensive method where policy starts 'from fundamentals anew each time, building on the past only as experience is embodied in a theory, and always prepared to start completely from the ground up'.[70]

o

197

There is no reason to think of incrementalism and comprehensive social planning as two mutually exclusive alternatives. They are rather ends of a continuum each with its advantages and disadvantages. We have already mentioned the weaknesses of comprehensive planning stemming from its ambitious, almost ideal, standards. Incrementalism though practically more possible suffers from two disadvantages as a result of the fragmented nature of the planning it aims at. It can lead to a waste of resources since its piecemeal planning can involve overlaps, patched-up methods of approach and in fact many of the organizational weaknesses of the local authority personal social services which the Seebohm Report proposals attempted to rectify. Second, it treats problems and issues in isolation and in this way it fails to bring about planning that makes provision for the interdependence of social phenomena.[71] The fact that a great deal of social planning has been of incremental nature so far does not in the least mean that we must accept it as our ideal. As Kahn has said, 'Efficient action is not advanced by enshrining an ideology about the limitations of rationality.'[72] Social progress can best be served in the long term by social policy planning that aims for perfection.

Social policy and motherlessness

Before we set out the social policy measures we envisage for motherless families, it is imperative to state clearly the objectives of social policy in this field. The same objectives may well be achievable through different policy measures but unless they are stated clearly, social policy will be chasing its tail in the dark. Without a destination, a route can become a meaningless maze. The objectives of social policy for motherless families as we see them are twofold: first, to encourage more fathers to look after their children when their wife dies or leaves and thus, hopefully, to halt the trend towards larger numbers of such children being received into the care of local authorities and voluntary organizations. Second, to ensure that motherless families have an income which not only reaches the official level of poverty but goes beyond it to compensate in some measure for the economic loss that these families suffer as a result of the mother's absence.

These two interrelated social policy objectives are based on the two interrelated premises that children are the nation's most precious resource and that their potentialities can best be promoted within the family system. Thus the principles underlying our policy objectives are both economic and humanitarian in an individual and a collective sense. Achievement of these policy objectives will benefit both society as a whole and the children as individuals. We may well have placed the interest of the children above those of their parents but this is, we feel, how it should be. We hope, however, that the social policy measures we shall propose to achieve these objectives will make it easier for the caring parent to serve the interests of his children.

What policy measures, then, can best achieve these objectives? All our evidence leads us to the conclusion that the existing social security measures are not geared towards the preservation of the one-parent family unit. In the first place there is no clear and explicit policy to encourage fathers to care for their children. What policy there is is in the form of departmental circulars which are not categorical and which are not open public policy. It is a situation which places a heavy burden on the judgment of individual Supplementary Benefit officers. A policy measure which is ambivalent and which is left to the individual interpretation of the officers that have to administer it may lead to friction, inconsistency and muddle and it therefore needs replacing.

The existing social security measures for one-parent families are inadequate on another count – they give preferential treatment to one group of one-parent families, widows and their children. What is at fault is not the preferential treatment which this group of one-parent families receives but rather that much inferior treatment meted out to the other groups of one-parent families. It is a case where social policy measures need levelling up and definitely not levelling down. The present system is based on the two-fold value judgment that men should be at work (hence no insurance benefits for widowers) and that only 'respectable' forms of marriage break-up should merit generous financial aid from the state (hence insurance benefits for widows but only supplementary benefits for other fatherless families). It lays too much emphasis on the reason responsible for one-parent status and not enough on the needs of one-parent families. It is a parallel situation to the provision of benefits for disability where industrial disability is catered for more generously than civil disability. In the same way that recent discussion on disability has emphasized the need for parity of treatment, we also feel that the time has come for the same aim in the field of one-parent families.

Finally, the existing system provides no special financial help to those heads of one-parent families who are at work, with the exception of widows. The state assumes that, apart from widows, other caring parents who go out to work can combine work and caring for their children without any state aid. Clearly such a policy does not encourage lone fathers or mothers to care for their children and in this way is an accomplice to the reception of children into the care of lcoal authorities and voluntary organizations. In all these ways the existing social policy measures not only do not achieve the policy objectives we set out but they also run counter to them. It is perhaps more correct to speak of the absence of any coherent set of policy measures than the existence of mistaken measures for they were developed piecemeal and with other objectives in mind.

We feel that the type of social policy measures that will best achieve our two policy objectives is an insurance benefit on similar lines to the benefits provided for widows. Improved provision of pre-school and other related facilities for children will make our objectives more possible but we consider these provisions beyond our scope of reference for they are facilities needed by two-parent families as well. We are reviving Beveridge's idea of an End of Marriage Allowance with one important qualification: the allowance for motherless families should be subject to an earnings rule, similar to that operating for retirement pensioners. Our reason for limiting this to motherless families is the higher wages which men earn compared with women. An earnings rule for fatherless families will be largely ineffective for women's wages are low especially since the earnings rule we have in mind would take into account the size of the family. But why an earnings rule at all? Our view is that to achieve our two objectives a father must first have an income as of right and second, if he is at work, the income should be higher than his income out of work to compensate him for the extra expenditure that is involved in trying to combine two roles. This combined income for working fathers, however, need not include the full insurance benefit where the father's wages are above a certain weekly amount.

An important question raised by the suggestion for an insurance benefit for all one-parent families is whether marriage break-up is an insurable risk. There are no generally accepted criteria distinguishing risks which are insurable by the state from those which are not. Three implicit assumptions can, however, be traced in the social security literature: a risk must be widespread enough in society, it must affect all citizens more or less equally and it must be involuntary. A risk must satisfy one or more of these criteria before it can be considered worthy of state action. These are ambiguous criteria and inevitably one can find as many examples supporting as refuting them. Widowhood, for example, is neither a widespread risk nor does it affect all population groups alike nor is the benefit denied when the death is not involuntary. Maternity benefits are paid though childbirth is more planned than involuntary; industrial injury benefits are paid irrespective of whose fault it was that the accident occurred, and so on.

In spite of the basic weaknesses of these three criteria, it is worth trying to apply them to the break-up of marriage. It is widespread enough in the sense that there are social security benefits – widow's benefits, guardian's allowance, child's special allowance – covering risks which are even less prevalent in society. In spite of the extensive prevalence of marriage break-up society does not want to believe that this is a risk as common as disability or widowhood. It likes to feel that marriage lasts for the whole of the partners' life and not for part of it. Social policy makers, however, cannot continue indefinitely ignoring the existence of the problem and wishing it would go away. Marriage break-up also affects all people in society alike with the qualification that it affects younger people more than older people but this is not a relevant disqualification since all old people were younger once. To what extent, however, is marriage break-up an involuntary phenomenon? It is involuntary in the sense that no person who gets married wants it or pursues it deliberately. It is also seen to be involuntary in the cases where one spouse through no fault of their own is deserted or divorced by the other. Vice versa, it is seen as a voluntary course of action in those cases where one spouse decides to leave the matrimonial home. These, however, are legalistic categorization and in real life marriage break-up is not such a simple one-way process. Married life inevitably creates strains and stresses and it is usually impossible to decide to what extent each spouse contributed to the strained relationship that led to the break-up of the marriage. Beveridge's recommendations for an End of Marriage Allowance were of necessity based on these legalistic views of marriage break-up. He felt that the principle for such an allowance was clear in the case of 'a married woman who without fault of her own loses the maintenance to which she is entitled from her husband'.[73] He had doubts about such an allowance in cases where it was the wife's fault that the husband left and, reflecting the spirit of his period, he did not even discuss the possibility for such an allowance for fathers who were left to care for their children through the wife's death or desertion. On the whole, he was not in principle against such an allowance for fatherless families. He saw practical difficulties, however, and in view of the numerous other risks he had to consider, he merely suggested that 'the point to which the principle of compensating a housewife for the loss of her maintenance otherwise than by widowhood can be carried in practice calls for further examination'.[74] Thirty years later, the Finer Committee has examined the same question but extended to cover motherless families. The practical difficulties are not insurmountable and we make some suggestions later on.

Our analysis of social problems and social policy showed that the formulation of any new policy measures activates conflicts in the prevailing values and interests. We acknowledge the fact that our suggestion for an End of Marriage Allowance runs counter to certain social values and interests. We feel, however, that the force of this conflict is not so powerful when each conflict situation is analysed coolly. We attempt to do this below, but we want to state first our belief in rational planning which, though it attempts to accommodate conflicting values and interests, does not allow itself to be blown off course to the extent that what it achieves at the end is significantly different from what it set out to achieve in the beginning.

Perhaps the strongest objection to an End of Marriage Allowance stems from the fear that such a benefit will undermine the stability of marriage and in this respect it will have the opposite results from those intended in the first place. Married life inevitably involves conflict between the two partners for it is difficult to believe that two people living together for years agree on everything at all times. This has been true of married life at all times in all cultures. As Goode says, what differs from one culture to another is the 'bearable level or degree of conflict' and the 'appropriate solution for conflict'.[75] In contemporary industrial societies the trend towards equality between men and women, between husbands and wives has meant that the acceptable level of forbearance has diminished and the likelihood of marriage break-up has, therefore, increased. The state has accepted the truth of this trend as evidenced by the easier divorce laws.[76] An insurance benefit clearly has no influence on the degree of marital conflict but it is feared that it may have a downward effect on the forbearance level. In other words, husbands or wives may be more willing to leave each other when they know that whoever is left to care for the children will not face impossible financial hardships. This argument overestimates considerably the likely effects of meagre financial assistance on human behaviour. It assumes that the existing policy of paying a Supplementary Benefit to fatherless and motherless families acts as a deterrent to family break-up. Deterrent policies, unless they are savage in character, do not have their intended effects. Our society has reached a stage of ethical development when it disapproves of savage deterrent policies in this field and it does not, therefore, refuse financial assistance to fatherless and motherless families. It frowns upon marriage break-up, however, and it shows its disapproval by providing such families with Supplementary Benefit which is stigmatized for, as Beveridge said, assistance benefit 'must be felt to be something less desirable than insurance benefit'.[77] The failure to provide an insurance benefit for fatherless and motherless families is based on the outdated fear that it will undermine marriage stability when all the evidence shows that social and economic changes account for the changing marriage patterns in contemporary society.

The second objection to an End of Marriage Allowance is based on the belief that it is the parents' responsibility to maintain each other and their children. We agree fully with this view and we envisage the state requiring the non-caring parents to contribute to the social security fund according to their means up to a maximum equivalent to the amount of the benefit paid to the caring parent. This should be the responsibility of one of the government departments and not the responsibility of the caring parent as is the case at present. Several studies have shown that the existing system of maintenance allowances lays too much burden on the wife and it provides little return. This is partly due to the refusal of the state to assume responsibility for this problem but it is also due to the fact that often the non-caring parent has an income which is inadequate to maintain himself, possibly a new family and his old family as well.[78] There should be nothing in these arrangements barring the caring parent from taking court action against the non-caring parent for a maintenance allowance over and above that contributed to the state fund even though such cases will be few. Our suggestion then will strengthen rather than weaken the emphasis placed on the responsibility of parents to maintain each other and their children.

The third objection is that it will make the caring parent financially better off than he or she was before the break-up of the marriage. Anyone who has read through our previous chapters can only reply that those mothers or fathers who care for their children alone deserve to be better off for it is only a slight recompense for the sacrifices they make for their children. Nevertheless, we are aware of public feelings on this matter and we therefore suggested an earnings rule in the case of motherless families. This will not eliminate completely the possibility of a small number of families being slightly better off but there will be even more families which even with an insurance benefit will be worse off so that on balance an insurance benefit will have no detrimental effect on either the parental responsibility, willingness to work or any other cherished social values. Insurance benefits are based on presumed needs and they never meet fully the needs of all individuals.

The fourth objection is that an insurance benefit for one-parent families will be costly for the country and for the government. We said earlier that if industrial societies can afford the social services they will, and such an insurance benefit is not beyond the economic resources of this country. The argument can be modified in the sense that though the country has the wealth to provide such a benefit, it will mean a rise in the burden which social security imposes on government expenditure. This argument comes mainly from those who feel that government expenditure is either not productive or even a waste of national resources – an argument with which most social scientists disagree. To take up the point of the burden imposed on government expenditure, an insurance benefit will be less of a burden on government revenue for it will be financed mainly through contributions, unlike the present Supplementary Benefit allowances to motherless and fatherless families which are paid for out of government revenue. We accept the charge that an insurance benefit will be less redistributive vertically than Supplementary Benefit but this is a price that has to be paid to achieve the objectives we set out earlier on. In the absence of detailed statistics it is not possible to estimate accurately the annual cost of such a benefit. Any such estimates, however, must take into account the savings that may be made from the reduction of children in the care of local authorities. Moreover, the governing principle regarding the relationship between economic and social policy must be that the economic wealth of a nation should be the servant of the nation's social welfare and not the other way round.

The fifth objection to an insurance benefit is that it will give preferential treatment to one-parent families as against some other groups of social security beneficiaries since the benefit will be paid in whole or in part even when the caring parent is at work and earning wages. This is clearly not a new principle because widows' benefits and industrial disability pensions are paid in full to wage earners while retirement pensions are paid to old people at work but subject to the earnings rule. Our evidence showed clearly that the loss of a mother makes life more expensive for the family and in the long run it can also affect the father's career prospects. Our suggestion for an earnings rule for motherless families is designed to ensure that the benefit paid to fathers at work is roughly equivalent to the economic loss they and their children suffered through the mother's loss.

The final objection is that such a scheme will be administratively complex. The administrative difficulties have not, to our knowledge, been stated in detail though again a gleaning of the literature shows two problems have been raised. In the case of non-legal separations it will be difficult to establish whether the father or the mother actually left. This is not a problem for widowed, legally separated and divorced persons for presentation of the relevant document can establish the loss of one parent. Non-legally separated parents will clearly have to provide satisfactory evidence of the loss of their spouse. We suggest that the procedure used today for the payment of Supplementary Benefit to this group should be adopted for the payment of the insurance benefit. In other words the caring parent should contact the local office of the Department of Health and Social Security, a visit should be paid by an officer of the Department and if he is satisfied, arrangements will be made for the payment of the benefit. This system is obviously open to criticism because it depends on the judgment of the individual visitor whether he is employed by the Department of Health and Social Security, the Probation and After-Care Committee or the local authority. This is a necessary evil for society cannot pay out benefits without some form of evidence that the beneficiary suffers from the risk for which the benefit is paid. The non-legally separated parents will, of course, have the right of appeal against the officer's decision.

The second administrative problem is that non-legal separation is not permanent and the risk of abuse of the social-security system is thus greater since the return of the non-caring parent may not be notified to the department. Again we suggest that the present system used for the supervision of fatherless and motherless families in receipt of Supplementary Benefit be retained. In other words, periodic visits should be made to such families by an officer of the Department of Health and Social Security though obviously in a flexible way for there will be a number of cases where the department is satisfied that the caring parent will report the return of the other parent. The risk of abuse exists in all social security benefits and though the state should do all in its power to safeguard itself against it, it would be completely unjustifiable if it were used as an excuse to reject a plan that is otherwise viable.

There are two obvious alternatives to an insurance benefit for one-parent families. There could be some kind of special addition to Family Allowances for the children – a motherless or fatherless child's allowance. Alternatively there could be a simpler flat rate allowance for all one-parent families irrespective of the number of children. These would be payable whether the parent was at work or not. For a working parent such an allowance would help compensate for the extra expenses incurred by working – child minding, domestic help and so on. For a non-working parent the allowance would help compensate for the fact that a single-parent family on Supplementary Benefit is rather worse off than a two-parent family taking into account the comparatively small reduction in expenditure which one less adult will mean and the considerable proportional loss of income. On balance we believe that neither of these methods of dealing with the problem is as satisfactory as an insurance benefit.

The introduction of either scheme would signify the triumph of incrementation over planning. Any worth-while scheme must, we believe, look at the needs of one-parent families as a whole. It is no longer right or justifiable to discriminate in favour of one group on the grounds of the reason for one-parent status. If this principle of looking at needs rather than reasons for needs is accepted then either all groups have to be treated in the same way as widows or widows have to be treated like all the others. At present widows have an income as of right. To replace that with a system of allowance to supplement earnings or Supplementary Benefit is scarcely possible. So the present position of widows in the social security system is both an argument for an insurance benefit for all one-parent families and a major obstacle to any system of allowances. As we said earlier, the proper policy is for a levelling-up in the position of other families rather than a levelling-down in the position of widows.

Another argument in favour of a system of insurance rather than a system of *ad hoc* allowances is that it can better take account of the long-term financial implications of one-parent status. The existing social security scheme accepts the problems which widows will face in getting jobs in middle age when children have grown up. The same problems will face other single parents. A father who has been off work for several years looking after his children may find it very difficult to get a job of any kind, let alone one commensurate with his previous qualifications and experience. By staying at home to care for his children a man – or woman – is likely permanently to have reduced his or her earning capacity. This problem is likely to become even more acute in the future with the increased pace of technical change. We believe that any parent who has done this has earned the right to have their reduced earning capacity made good by society. An insurance benefit with an earnings rule for men can better take account of this point than a system of allowances which almost inevitably is a less sensitive type of help.

There are other practical points which contribute to the case against a system of allowances. Such a scheme would not guarantee the lone parent an income as of right. It does not, therefore, avoid the necessity for recourse to Supplementary Benefit for those who feel they should stay at home to care for their children. Because of the stigma which people feel in receiving Supplementary Benefit there is, therefore, a disincentive to the lone parent to apply for benefit when it may be the best course for the children. The only way to give the parent a genuine choice in this is to provide an adequate income as of right. We believe that such a choice is important for the sake of the children and the parent – and so for society.

A motherless or fatherless child's addition to Family Allowances may sound administratively simple. This would not, however, be the case if such an addition was paid to one-child families who are not at present eligible for Family Allowances. If this was done it would also be increasingly difficult for governments to resist the case for Family Allowances for the first child. On the other hand, if the allowance was paid only for children at present receiving Family Allowances many families would be excluded from all help.

Another difficulty in basing any scheme of help on an addition to Family Allowances is that the loss of income and the extra expenditure which a single-parent family suffers is not really proportional to the number of children in the family. Age is an important factor. The Family Allowance scheme is based on the principle of flat rate benefits. The tradition of insurance is much more flexible.

What we have attempted to do in this last chapter is to set the scene for a consideration of the role of social policy in relation to one-parent families, in particular motherless families. Our recommendations are inevitably general rather than specific because we believe it is important to be clear about the principles before proceeding to detailed practicalities. Society needs to be clear about whether this is an issue for public action, about the value conflicts involved, about the implications of action for other areas of social policy.

We hope that our findings in the rest of the study have provided issues for further research as well as material relevant to policy making. We are very conscious of the need for more specific studies to test our findings on particular points.

'One sometimes wonders,' Schorr writes, 'whether the outcome of research is significant – or is research the shadow cast before itself by social change?'[79] The concern about the plight of the motherless which led to our study is an example of society's increasing sensitivity to avoidable human suffering. We hope our study will further that concern.

Notes

1 The study of motherlessness

1 S. Butler, *The Way of All Flesh*, p. 121.
2 Ministry of Health, *Report on an Investigation into Maternal Mortality*, Cmd 5422, p. 2.
3 The future Mrs Gaskell, for example, was sent to an aunt in Knutsford when her mother died soon after she was born, while her father continued in his pastoral duties in Manchester. *Cranford*, Dent, 1908, p. 10.
4 See, for example, E. Gaskell, *Wives and Daughters*.
5 *On the State of the Public Health*, Annual Report of the Chief Medical Officer, Department of Health and Social Security, p. 9. In 1934 the maternal mortality rate was still as high as 4·41 per 1,000 births. Cf. *Twentieth Annual Report of the Ministry of Health*, Cmd 6089, 1939, p. 35.
6 On 31 December 1969, 4,800 guardian's allowances were being paid by the Department of Health and Social Security to people bringing up children totally deprived of parental support, normally following the death of both parents, but in certain circumstances following the death of the only effective parent. Some of these would have been relatives, some not. *Annual Report*, 1969, Department of Health and Social Security, p. 302.
7 The Home Office Research Unit Report, *Workloads in Children's Departments*, studied a sample of nine departments. The total working time spent on preventive work varied from 6 to 29 per cent.
8 In 1967–8 expenditure under this heading varied from £8,199 in Lewisham to £6 in Burton-upon-Trent. Cf. *New Society*, 8 January 1970.
9 M. Wynn, *Family Policy*.
10 H. Gavron, *The Captive Wife*, ch. 9.
11 J. and E. Newson, *Patterns of Infant Care in an Urban Community*, p. 226.
12 E. Dahlström (ed.), *The Changing Roles of Men and Women*.

13 Lord Simon was addressing an all-day conference of High Court and County Court judges on the problems of deciding the custody of children – the first conference of its kind ever to take place. *Guardian*, 1 May 1971.

14 The Commission's policy is that when a man has given up work because of domestic responsibilities, following the death or desertion of his wife, and there is no reasonable alternative to his remaining at home, a supplementary allowance is payable to meet the family's requirements. Communication from the Department of Health and Social Security.

15 In his study, *Mothers in Poverty* (p. 186), L. Kriesberg noted that since the beginning of this century there seems to have been a trend for children of broken families to remain with one of their parents. Kriesberg suggests that, 'Perhaps the general rise of the standard of living, urbanization and to some extent welfare measures have played major roles in the change.'

16 Home Office, *Children in Care in England and Wales*, Cmnd 1237, 1960, p. 5.

17 Home Office, *Children in Care in England and Wales*, Cmnd 4559, 1970, p. 5.

18 Ibid.

19 J. Packman, *Child Care: Needs and Numbers*, p. 37.

20 Ibid.

21 This information was the result of special tabulations from the Census which were made available to us by the Department of Health and Social Security.

22 J. W. B. Douglas and J. W. Blomfield, *Children Under Five*, tables 67 and 68, pp. 114–15; cf. also G. Rowntree, 'Early Childhood in Broken Families', *Population Studies*, vol. 8, 1954–5.

23 M. Rutter, *Children of Sick Parents*, p. 50.

24 *Children and their Primary Schools*, Report of the Central Advisory Council for Education, vol. 2, p. 105.

25 B. Schlesinger (ed.), *The One-parent Family*, p. 3.

26 P. Glasser and E. Navarre, 'Structural Problems of the One-parent Family', *Journal of Social Issues*, vol. 21, 1965, p. 102.

27 J. Bowlby, *Maternal Care and Mental Health*, p. 12.

28 D. Marsden, *Mothers Alone*, p. 113.

29 B. Schlesinger (ed.), op. cit., p. 10.

30 D. Marsden, op. cit., p. 104.

31 Ibid., p. 100.

32 W. J. Goode, *Women in Divorce*, p. 12.

33 G. Beltram, 'Methods of Surveying Categories of People Presenting Special Problems or Needs', *International Social Security Review*, vol. 23, no. 2, 1970.

34 W. J. Goode, op. cit., p. iv.

35 D. Marsden, op. cit., p. 10.

36 P. Marris, *Widows and Their Families*, p. 4.

37 M. A. La Sorte, 'The Caseworker as Research Interviewer', *American Sociologist*, vol. 3, no. 3, August 1968.

38 W. J. Goode, op. cit., p. 24.
39 '"Felt" deprivations do not match the "objective" distribution of poverty at all closely: misery, militancy and poverty (like happiness, complacency and wealth) are not very closely correlated with each other.' *Research on Poverty*, p, 5.
40 W. G. Runciman, *Relative Deprivation and Social Justice*, Ch. 2.
41 W. J. Goode, op. cit., p. 25. Cf. also D. Marsden, op. cit., p. 10.
42 The classification of the replies and their translation into numerical terms ready for putting on punch cards.
43 Committee on One-Parent Families, Chairman Mr Morris Finer, Q.C.
44 P. Marris, op. cit., p. 2.
45 Sir William Armstrong, 'Research and Government, The View from the Government', *Social Science Research Council Newsletter*, no. 7, December 1969, p. 3.
46 The Department of Health and Social Security agreed to put the research team directly in touch with beneficiaries, subject to the following conditions:
   1 Each member of the research team was required to sign a declaration under the Official Secrets Act.
   2 An initial letter was to be sent by the Department to each person, making it clear that the rescarch was being carried out under the Department's auspices and that all information supplied by the person for the purposes of the research would continue to be treated as strictly confidential. Thus the person interviewed could be given an undertaking that his identity would not be disclosed to any person outside the Department and the research team. It was also to be explained that the person was perfectly free to withhold co-operation if he so wished and that in such cases no further information would be passed to the researchers beyond the name and address already given.
47 D. Matza, *Becoming Deviant*, p. 1.

2 General characteristics of motherless families

1 D. C. Marsh, *The Changing Social Structure of England and Wales*, p. 37.
2 Ibid., p. 44.
3 M. A. Elliott and F. E. Merrill, *Social Disorganization*, p. 435.
4 J. Dominian, *Marital Breakdown*, p. 119. He concludes that 'evidence from the United Kingdom and the USA indicates that between 70 and 80 per cent of the divorcees remarry'.
5 P. Marris, op. cit., p. 57.
6 Central Statistical Office, *Social Trends*, no. 1, HMSO, 1970, table 12, p. 55.
7 D. C. Marsh, op cit., p. 44.
8 A. Harris and R. Clausen, *Labour Mobility in Great Britain, 1953–1963*, table 6, p. 8.
9 Social class is one of the three main factors – the other two being

reason for motherlessness and length of motherlessness – we use to analyse a great deal of our data in subsequent chapters. Since the social-class distribution of our fathers at the time of motherlessness and at the time of interview was not the same, it was not useful to analyse all our data according to one of the two social-class distributions but rather to use that social-class distribution that was more relevant to different sets of data. For reasons of simplicity of style we do not specify in the text to which social class our analysis refers.

10 Ministry of Social Security, *Circumstances of Families*, p. 129.

3 The children

1 M. Wynn, *Fatherless Families*, p. 14.

2 S. Andreski in *The Protestant Ethic and Modernization*, S. N. Eisenstadt (ed.), p. 53.

3 E. Wight Bakke, *The Unemployed Man: A Social Study*, p, 72; quoted in P. Worsley (ed.), *Modern Sociology: Introductory Readings*, p. 227.

4 N. S. Morse and R. S. Weiss, 'The Function and Meaning of Work and the Job', *American Sociological Review*, vol. 20, 1955.

5 T. Parsons, quoted in *The Sociology of Child Development*, J. Bossard and E. Boll, p. 215.

6 D. Wedderburn, 'Workplace Inequality', *New Society*, 9 April 1970, p. 593.

7 W. G. Runciman, *Relative Deprivation and Social Justice*, p. 224.

8 A. Oakley, 'The Myth of Motherhood', *New Society*, 27 February 1970, p. 348.

9 *The Times*, 10 May 1971.

10 L. Taconis, 'The Role of the Contemporary Father in Rearing Young Children', *Educational Research*, vol. 2, no. 2, February 1969; J. and E. Newson, *Patterns of Infant Care in an Urban Community*, chapter 12.

11 A. Hunt, *A Survey of Women's Employment*, vol. 1, p. 120.

12 J. and E. Newson, op. cit., p. 226, table 28.

13 P. Glasser and E. Navarre, 'Structural Problems of the One-parent Family', *Journal of Social Issues*, vol. 21, no. 1, January 1965.

14 Office of Health Economics, *Malnutrition in the 1960's?* p. 29.

15 J. McKenzie in *The Concept of Poverty*, P. Townsend (ed.), p. 85.

16 D. Marsden, op. cit., p. 44.

17 H. Land, *Large Families in London*, p. 45.

18 D. Marsden, op. cit., p. 46.

19 H. Land, op. cit., p. 49.

20 D. Marsden, op. cit., p. 45.

21 Ibid., p. 44.

22 H. Land, op. cit., p. 49.

23 G. Lynch, 'Food Intake and the Education of Children', *Medical Officer*, vol. 121, no. 4, 24 January 1969.

24 Education Statistics, 1969–70, p. 39.

25 D. Marsden, op. cit., p. 46.

26 H. Land, op. cit., p. 49.
27 G. Lynch, op. cit.
28 D. Marsden, op. cit., p. 44. ·
29 G. Lynch, 'The Feeding Habits of School Children', *Catering and Hotel Management*, December 1970.
30 G. Gorer, *Death, Grief and Mourning*, p. 93.
31 Ibid., p. 23.
32 P. Marris, op. cit., p. 37.
33 P. Morris, *Prisoners and Their Families*, p. 91.
34 D. Marsden, op. cit., p. 122.
35 Differences were significant at the 0·01 level.
36 S. Anthony, *The Child's Discovery of Death*; A. Gessel and F. Ilg, *The Children from Five to Ten*; M. Nagy, 'The Child's Theories Concerning Death', *Journal of Genetic Psychology*, 1948; J. Hinton, *Dying*.
37 M. Rutter, *Children of Sick Parents*, p. 43.
38 D. Marsden, op. cit., p. 121.
39 W. J. Goode, op. cit., p. 316.
40 Ibid., p. 323.
41 D. Marsden, op. cit., pp. 121–2.
42 E. Leach, quoted in M. Farmer, *The Family*, p. 2.
43 P. Marris, op. cit., p. 37.
44 W. J. Goode, op. cit., p. 318.
45 L. Kriesberg, *Mothers in Poverty*, pp. 201–2.
46 M. Rutter, op. cit., p. 39.
47 J. Bowlby, op. cit., p. 12.
48 WHO, *Deprivation of Maternal Care*, p. 98.
49 S. Wolff, *Children Under Stress*, pp. 19–20.
50 D. Marsden, op. cit., p. 123.
51 Central Advisory Council for Education, *Children and Their Primary Schools*, vol. 1, p. 59.
52 M. L. K. Pringle, *et al.*, *11,000 Seven-Year-Olds*, pp. 133–4.
53 D. Marsden, op. cit., p. 124.
54 P. Marris, op. cit., p. 119.
55 S. Wolff, op. cit., p. 87.
56 E. Bott, *Family and Social Network*.
57 P. Marris, op. cit., p. 67.
58 P. Glasser and E. Navarre, op. cit.
59 N. Bell and E. Vogel, *A Modern Introduction to the Family*, p. 583.

4 Occupation and income

1 D. Marsden, op. cit., p. 183.
2 D. Wedderburn and C. Craig, 'Relative Deprivation in Work', Paper presented at the British Association for the Advancement of Science, Exeter, 1969; quoted in F. Parkin, *Class, Inequality and Political Order*, p. 25.
3 D. Wedderburn, 'Workplace Inequality', *New Society*, 9 April 1970, p. 593.

4 A. Hunt, op. cit., p. 132.
5 Ibid. p. 86. Of the sample who were responsible for children under sixteen, 37·3 per cent were working full or part time.
6 Cf. *Hours of Work, Overtime and Shift Working*, National Board for Prices and Incomes, Cmnd 4554.
7 *Employment and Productivity Gazette*, vol. 78, no. 12, December 1970, p. 1139.
8 *Department of Employment Gazette*, vol. 79, no. 2, February 1971.
9 Attempts to compare this data with other published information on income and expenditure in the East Midlands are not very profitable. Median gross weekly earnings for manual workers in the area were £25 in April 1970. For non-manual workers the median was £29 16s per week and for all full-time men the figure was £26 2s (*Department of Employment Gazette*, vol. 79, no. 1, January 1971, p. 24). Interesting as these figures are it is difficult to come to any firm conclusions about how our fathers compare with the general population – partly because of the nature of our samples and partly because of the difficulties of translating gross pay into take-home pay and vice versa. It looks, however, as though the take-home pay of our sample is below rather than above average.

Another possible basis of comparison is with household expenditure figures from the *Family Expenditure Survey*. In the two-year period 1968–9, average household expenditure in the East Midlands was running at £24 8s. This was for an average household of 2·96 persons (*Family Expenditure Survey*, 1969, HMSO, 1970, p. 90). If one adds an assumed sum for family allowances for the average size of the families in our sample the total available for expenditure in 1970 was some £23 6s. So the families in our sample – a larger if different type of household – had less money available to spend than the average expenditure of the average household one to two years earlier. Given the rapid general increase in wages in this period our families seemed to be lagging behind in the race for affluence.

5 The father's emotional and social adjustment

1 P. Marris, op. cit., p. 2.
2 Marsden, on the other hand, says that 'for something like half' his sample of widows the death had not been a major upheaval. Several had found it a release. Op. cit., p. 118.
3 C. M. Parkes, 'Grief as an Illness', *New Society*, 9 April 1964, p. 11.
4 E. Lindemann, 'Symptomatology and Management of Acute Grief' in *Crisis Intervention: Selective Readings*, Howard J. Parad (ed.).
5 E. Lindemann, op. cit., pp. 9–10.
6 P. Marris, op. cit., p. 21.
7 C. M. Parkes, 'Bereavement and Mental Illness', *British Journal of Medical Psychology*, vol. 38, no. 1, 1965, p. 1.
8 C. M. Parkes, 'The Effects of Bereavement on Physical and Mental Health: A Study of the Medical Records of Widows', *British Medical Journal*, ii, 1964, p. 274.

9 P. Marris, op. cit., p. 14.
10 M. Young, B. Benjamin and C. Wallis, 'The Mortality of Widowers', *Lancet*, ii, 1963, p. 455.
11 Ibid., p. 456.
12 C. M. Parkes, 'Grief as an Illness', p. 12.
13 C. M. Parkes, 'Bereavement and Mental Illness', p. 2.
14 M. Young, B. Benjamin and C. Wallis, op. cit., p. 454.
15 M. Klein, 'Mourning and its Relation to Manic Depressive States' in *Contributions to Psycho-Analysis*, pp. 329–30.
16 E. Lindemann, op. cit., p. 18.
17 Several of Marsden's sample suggested forced labour camps for husbands who left their wives and children in a situation of shame and financial insecurity. Op. cit., p. 118.
18 Ibid., p. 117.
19 W. J. Goode, op. cit., p. 27.
20 Ibid., p. 200.
21 P. Townsend, *The Family Life of Old People*, p. 205.
22 G. Gorer, *Death, Grief and Mourning,* p. 99.
23 D. Marsden, op. cit., p. 129.
24 P. Marris, op. cit., p. 127.
25 D. Marsden, op. cit., p. 111.
26 Ibid., p. 60.
27 Ibid., p. 106.
28 Ibid., p. 107.
29 Ibid., pp. 109–10.

30 TABLE 59A   Effect of motherlessness on father's eating habits (per cent) (n = 575)

Eats more	7·1
Eats less	22·5
Eats the same	43·1
Less immediately/now the same	14·1
Other	13·2

31 TABLE 59B   Effect of motherlessness on father's drinking habits (per cent) (n = 578)

No change	64·9
More initially/now back to normal	6·6
More initially/and still more	10·9
Less	12·8
Other	4·8

32 TABLE 59C Effect of motherlessness on father's smoking habits (per cent) (n = 580)

No change	56·9
More initially/and still more	26·2
More initially/now back to normal	5·7
Less	6·4
Other	4·8

33 D. Marsden, op. cit., p. 52.
34 P. Marris, op. cit., p. 14.
35 G. Gorer, op. cit., p. 53.
36 W. J. Goode, op. cit., p. 186.

37 TABLE 59D Effect of motherlessness on father's sleeping habits (per cent) (n = 583)

No effect	36·9
Less at first/now back to normal	26·6
Less at first/and still less	11·3
Sleeping badly	13·6
Other	11·6

38 W. J. Goode, op. cit., p. 186.
39 'It is the upper and middle classes who form the churchgoers throughout this country and a vast mass of the population are estranged not only from the Church of England, but from the Gospel itself . . . in our crowded cities and in our remote country districts, there is a numerous body of the poor who cannot, and another who will not enter the churches.' Randall T. Davidson, *Life of Archbishop Tait*, 1891; quoted in E. R. Wickham, *Church and People in an Industrial City*, p. 113. For an interesting and up-to-date discussion of these issues cf. J. Brothers, *Religious Institutions* chapter 6.
40 In his study *Exploring English Character*, Gorer found that 47 per cent of his volunteer sample believed in an after-life. In *Death, Grief and Mourning*, the proportion was 49 per cent. Op. cit., p. 166.

6 The father, the family and the social services

1 T. Parsons and R. Bales, *Family, Socialization and Interaction Process*, also T. Parsons, *Essays in Sociological Theory*.

2 M. Sussman and L. Burchinal, 'Kin Family Network' in *Kinship and Family Organization*, B. Farber (ed.), p. 131.
3 E. Litwak, 'Extended Kin Relations in a Democratic Industrial Society' in E. Shanas and G. Streib (eds), *Social Structure and the Family: Generational Relations*, p. 310.
4 R. Firth, J. Hubert and A. Forge, *Families and Their Relatives*, p. 386.
5 P. Marris, op. cit., p. 49.
6 B. J. Heraud, *Sociology and Social Work*, p. 63.
7 C. Bell, *Middle Class Families*, p. 92.
8 R. Firth, op. cit., p. 200.
9 M. Young and P. Willmott, *Family and Kinship in East London*, p. 56.
10 Ibid., p. 189.
11 C. Turner, *Family and Kinship in Modern Britain*, p. 31.
12 C. Rosser and C. Harris, *The Family and Social Change*, p. 13.
13 H. Schaffer and E. Schaffer, *Child Care and the Family*, Occasional Papers in Social Administration, p. 30.
14 D. Marsden, op. cit., p. 104.
15 P. Marris, op. cit., p. 45.
16 Ibid.
17 Ibid., p. 54.
18 H. Schaffer and E. Schaffer, op. cit., p. 21.
19 P. Townsend and D. Wedderburn, *The Aged in the Welfare State*, Occasional Papers in Social Administration, p. 42.
20 F. Skinner (ed.), *Physical Disability and Community Care*, National Council of Social Service, p. 98.
21 J. Mayer and N. Timms, *The Client Speaks*, p. 38.
22 Ibid., p. 100.
23 G. Gurin, J. Veroff and J. Feld, *Americans View Their Mental Health*, p. 305.
24 M. Sussman and L. Burchinal in *Kinship and Family Organization*, B. Farber (ed.), p. 130.
25 K. Coates and R. Silburn, *Poverty: The Forgotten Englishmen*, chapter 11.
26 G. Parkinson, 'I Give Them Money', *New Society*, 5 February 1970, pp. 220–1.
27 J. Mayer and N. Timms, op. cit., p. 140.
28 A. Hunt and J. Fox, *The Home Help Service in England and Wales*, Government Social Survey, p. 6.
29 Ibid., p. 25.
30 A. Hunt, *A Survey of Women's Employment*, Government Social Survey, vol. I, p. 87.
31 *Report of the Committee on Local Authority and Allied Personal Social Services*, Cmnd 3703, p. 141.
32 A. Hunt, op. cit., p. 88.
33 S. Yudkin and A. Holme, *Working Mothers and Their Children*, p. 67.
34 A. Hunt, op. cit., p. 99.

7 Social policy and social problems

1 A. J. Kahn, *Studies in Social Policy and Planning*, p. 299.
2 T. H. Marshall, *Social Policy*, p. 15.
3 H. S. Becker (ed.), *Social Problems: A Modern Approach*, p. 14.
4 Ibid., p. 11.
5 R. C. Fuller and R. R. Myers, 'The Natural History of a Social Problem', *American Sociological Review*, vol. 6, 1941, pp. 320–8.
6 C. Booth, *Life and Labour of the People in London*; B. S. Rowntree, *Poverty. A Study of Town Life*.
7 T. S. and M. B. Simey, *Charles Booth, Social Scientist*, p. 92.
8 B. Abel-Smith and P. Townsend in *The Poor and the Poorest*, Occasional Papers on Social Administration.
9 A. M. Rose, 'Law and the Causation of Social Problems', *Social Problems*, vol. 16, 1968–9, p. 33.
10 *Children and their Primary Schools*, vol. 1, para. 151 et seq.
11 E. Raab and G. J. Selznick, *Major Social Problems*, p. 6.
12 N. Timms, *A Sociological Approach to Social Problems*, p. 13.
13 S. M. Miller, 'Poverty', *Transactions of the Sixth World Congress of Sociology*, London, 1967; quoted in A. J. Kahn, *Studies in Social Policy and Planning*, pp. 173–85.
14 *Children and Their Primary Schools*, para. 1235.
15 W. H. Beveridge, *Unemployment: A Problem of Industry*.
16 W. H. Beveridge, *Full Employment in a Free Society*.
17 *Employment Policy*, Cmd 6527.
18 Quoted in J. Warham, *Social Policy in Context*, p. 61.
19 O. R. McGregor, 'Social Research and Social Policy in the 19th Century', *British Journal of Sociology*, vol. 8, no. 2, 1957.
20 C. Wright Mills, *The Sociological Imagination*, pp. 14–15.
21 E. Durkheim, *Suicide*.
22 M. A. Elliott and F. E. Merrill, op. cit., p. 339.
23 C. Wright Mills, op. cit., p. 207.
24 M. A. Elliott and F. E. Merrill, op. cit., p. 340.
25 H. D. Willcock and J. Stokes, *Deterrents to Crime Among Youths Aged 15–21 Years*, S.S. 356, Part 2, 1968.
26 Quoted in R. Fletcher, *The Family and Marriage in Britain*, p. 198.
27 M. Wynn, *Family Policy*, p. 267.
28 Quoted in D. C. Marsh (ed.), *An Introduction to the Study of Social Administration*, p. 191.
29 The Caravan Sites Act, 1968.
30 For a review of the development of race relations in this country see E. J. B. Rose, *Colour and Citizenship*.
31 P. Townsend, 'The Disabled Need Help', *New Society*, 28 September 1967, pp. 432–3.
32 V. Schlakman in *Social Security in International Perspective*, S. Jenkins (ed.), p. 12.
33 M. J. Barnett, *The Politics of Legislation, The Rent Act: 1957*.
34 P. Marris and M. Rein, *Dilemmas of Social Reform*, p. 9.

35 K. Boulding, 'The Boundaries of Social Policy', *Social Work*, vol. 12, no. 1, 1967.
36 A. Rose, 'Law and the Causation of Social Problems', *Social Problems*, vol. 16, 1968–9, p. 35.
37 In February 1970 the number of persons receiving Supplementary Benefit who were wage stopped was 26,700. These were heads of families and the number of people affected can be estimated to at least 140,000 – *Annual Report of the Department of Health and Social Security for the Year 1969*, table 128, p. 336.
38 J. Warham, op. cit., p. 122.
39 Ibid.
40 J. L. M. Eyden, *Social Policy in Action*, p. 1.
41 K. M. Slack, *Social Administration and the Citizen*, p. 68.
42 W. Miller, 'Lower Class Culture as a Generating Milieu of Gang Delinquency', *Journal of Social Issues*, vol. 14, no. 3, 1958.
43 R. K. Merton, *Social Theory and Social Structure*.
44 F. Parkin, *Class, Inequality and Political Order*, p. 81.
45 Ibid., p. 83.
46 Sir William Beveridge, *Social Insurance and Allied Services*, Cmd 6404, para. 21.
47 Ibid.
48 Each year both the Inland Revenue and the Department of Health and Social Security attempt to recover revenue lost through fraud, wilful default or neglect. The sum lost by the Inland Revenue through tax evasion is considerably greater than the sum lost by the Department of Health and Social Security and the same applies to the amount recovered every year. Thus in 1969 the Inland Revenue recovered £14,430,100 from persons who underpaid their taxes while the Department of Health and Social Security raised £816,000 from persons who were overpaid in social security benefits. *House of Commons Hansard*, Written Answer, vol. 799, col. 168 and vol. 799, col. 162. Reprinted in *Poverty*, no. 14, Spring 1970, pp. 24–5.
49 H. Wilensky and C. Lebeaux, *Industrial Society and Social Welfare*, p. 34.
50 H. Land, op. cit., p. 147.
51 R. A. Pinker, *Social Theory and Social Policy*, p. 142.
52 S. M. Miller and F. Riessman, *Social Class and Social Policy*, p. 52.
53 D. Wedderburn, 'Facts and Theories of the Welfare State' in R. Miliband and J. Saville (eds), *The Socialist Register*, p. 144.
54 R. M. Titmuss, *The Gift Relationship*: D. Howard, *Social Welfare: Values, Means and Ends*.
55 J. L. M. Eyden, op. cit., p. 5.
56 J. Warham, op. cit., p. 71.
57 B. Rodgers, *Making Social Policy*, vol. 107 of *Memoirs and Proceedings of the Manchester Literary and Philosophical Society Session 1964–65*, reprinted as a pamphlet, p. 1.
58 D. Wedderburn, 'Facts and Theories of the Welfare State', pp. 142–3.
59 Ibid., p. 138.

60 K. Coates and R. Silburn, op. cit., p. 185.
61 A. W. Gouldner, *The Coming Crisis of Western Sociology*, p. 302.
62 M. Webber in *The Urban Condition*, L. Duhl (ed.), p. 320.
63 A. J. Kahn, *Theory and Practice of Social Planning*, p. 69.
64 M. Hansen and C. Carter in *Economic Progress and Social Welfare*, L. Goodman (ed.), p. 98.
65 T. S. Simey, *Social Science and Social Purpose*, p. 199.
66 R. Nathan in *Economic Progress and Social Welfare*, L. Goodman (ed.), p. 223.
67 D. Marsh, *The Welfare State*, p. 100.
68 K. Popper, *The Open Society and Its Enemies*, vol. I, pp. 139-44.
69 R. A. Dahl and C. E. Lindblom, *Politics, Economics and Welfare*, p. 82.
70 C. E. Lindblom, 'The Science of "Muddling Through"', *Public Administration Review*, vol. 29, no. 2, Spring 1959.
71 Cf. P. Townsend, 'The Reorganisation of Social Policy', *New Society*, 22 October 1970.
72 A. J. Kahn, *Studies in Social Policy and Planning*, p. 295.
73 *Social Insurance and Allied Services*, Cmd 6404, para. 347.
74 Ibid.
75 W. J. Goode, op. cit., p. 8.
76 Divorce Reform Act, 1969.
77 *Social Insurance and Allied Services*, para. 369.
78 *Report of the Committee on Statutory Maintenance Limits*, Cmnd 3587; also O. R. McGregor, L. Blom-Cooper and C. Gibson, *Separated Spouses*.
79 A. L. Schorr, *Explorations in Social Policy*, p. 9.

Bibliography

ABEL-SMITH, B. and TOWNSEND, P., *The Poor and the Poorest*, Bell 1965.

ANTHONY, S., *The Child's Discovery of Death*, George Routledge, 1940.

ARMSTRONG, SIR WILLIAM, 'Research and Government', *Social Science Research Council Newsletter*, no. 7, December 1969, p. 3.

BARNETT, M. J., *The Politics of Legislation: The Rent Act 1957*, Weidenfeld & Nicolson, 1969.

BECKER, H. S. (ed.), *Social Problems: A Modern Approach*, Wiley, 1966.

BELL, C., *Middle Class Families*, Routledge & Kegan Paul, 1969.

BELL, N. W. and VOGEL, E. S., *A Modern Introduction to the Family*, Collier-Macmillan, 1968.

BELTRAM, G., 'Methods of Surveying Categories of People Presenting Special Problems and Needs', *International Social Security Review*, vol. 23, no. 2, 1970.

BEVERIDGE, W. H., *Unemployment: A Problem of Industry*, Longmans, 1909.

BEVERIDGE, W. H., *Full Employment in a Free Society*, Allen & Unwin, 1944.

BEVERIDGE, W. H., *Social Insurance and Allied Services*, HMSO, Cmd 6404, 1942.

BOOTH, C., *Life and Labour of the People in London*, Macmillan, 1902–4.

BOSSARD, J. H. S. and BOLL, E. S., *The Sociology of Child Development*, Harper & Row, 1966.

BOTT, E., *Family and Social Network*, Tavistock, 1957.

BOULDING, K., 'The Boundaries of Social Policy', *Social Work*, vol. 12, no. 1, 1967.

BOWLBY, J., *Maternal Care and Mental Health*, World Health Organization, 1952.

BROTHERS, J., *Religious Institutions*, Longmans, 1971.

BUTLER, S., *The Way of All Flesh*, Jonathan Cape, 1948.

221

BIBLIOGRAPHY

Central Advisory Council for Education, *Children and Their Primary Schools* (Plowden Report), HMSO, 1967.
COATES, K. and SILBURN, R., *Poverty: The Forgotten Englishmen*, Penguin, 1970.
DAHL, R. A., and LINDBLOM, C. E., *Politics, Economics and Welfare*, Harper & Row, 1953.
DAHLSTRÖM, E. (ed.), *The Changing Roles of Men and Women*, Duckworth, 1967.
Department of Employment Gazette, vol. 79, no. 2, February 1971.
Department of Health and Social Security, Annual Report of the Chief Medical Officer for 1969, *On the State of the Public Health*, HMSO, 1970.
DOMINIAN, J., *Marital Breakdown*, Penguin, 1968.
DOUGLAS, J. W. B. and BLOMFIELD, J. W., *Children Under Five*, Allen & Unwin, 1958.
DUHL, L. (ed.), *The Urban Condition*, Basic Books, 1963.
DURKHEIM, E., *Suicide*, Routledge & Kegan Paul, 1952.

EISENSTADT, S. (ed.), *The Protestant Ethic and Modernization: A Comparative View*, Basic Books, 1968.
ELLIOTT, M. A. and MERRILL, F. E., *Social Disorganization*, Harper & Row, 1961.
Employment and Productivity Gazette, vol. 78, no. 12, December 1970.
Employment Policy, Government Policy Statement, HMSO, Cmd 6527, 1944.
EYDEN, J. L. M., *Social Policy in Action*, Routledge & Kegan Paul, 1969

FARBER, B. (ed.), *Kinship and Family Organization*, Wiley, 1966.
FARMER, M., *The Family*, Longmans, 1970.
FIRTH, R., HUBERT, J. and FORGE, A., *Families and Their Relatives*, Routledge & Kegan Paul, 1970.
FLETCHER, R., *The Family and Marriage in Britain*, Penguin, 1966.
FULLER, R. C. and MYERS, R. R., 'The Natural History of a Social Problem', *American Sociological Review*, vol. 6, 1941, pp. 320–8.

GAVRON, H., *The Captive Wife: Conflicts of Housebound Mothers*, Penguin, 1968.
GEORGE, V., *Social Security: Beveridge and After*, Routledge & Kegan Paul, 1968.
GESEL, A. and ILG, F., *The Children from Five to Ten*, Harper & Row, 1946.
GLASSER, P. and NAVARRE, E., 'Structural Problems of the One-parent Family', *Journal of Social Issues*, vol. 21, no. 1, 1965.
GOODE, W. J., *Women in Divorce,* Collier-Macmillan, 1965.
GOODMAN, L. H. (ed.), *Economic Progress and Social Welfare*, Columbia University Press, 1966.
GORER, G., *Exploring English Character*, Cresset Press, 1955.
GORER, G., *Death, Grief and Mourning*, Cresset Press, 1965.
GOULDNER, A. W., *The Coming Crisis of Western Sociology,* Heinemann, 1971.

GURIN, G., VEROFF, J. and FELD, J., *Americans View Their Mental Health*, Basic Books, 1960.

HARRIS, A. and CLAUSEN, R., *Labour Mobility in Great Britain, 1953–1963*, Government Social Survey Report, HMSO, 1966.

HERAUD, B. J., *Sociology and Social Work*, Pergamon Press, 1970.

HINTON, J., *Dying*, Penguin, 1967.

Home Office, *Children in Care in England and Wales*, Cmnd 1237, HMSO, 1960.

Home Office, *Children in Care in England and Wales*, Cmnd 4559, HMSO, 1970.

Home Office Research Studies, no. 1, *Workloads in Children's Departments*, 1969.

HOWARD, D., *Social Welfare: Values, Means and Ends*, Random House, 1968.

HUNT, A., *A Survey of Women's Employment*, HMSO, 1968.

HUNT, A. and FOX, J., *The Home Help Service in England and Wales*, HMSO, 1970.

JENKINS, S. (ed.), *Social Security in International Perspective*, Columbia University Press, 1969.

KAHN, A. J., *Studies in Social Policy and Planning*, Russel Sage Foundation, 1969.

KAHN, A. J., *Theory and Practice of Social Planning*, Russel Sage Foundation, 1969.

KLEIN, M., 'Mourning and its Relation to Manic Depressive States', in *Contributions to Psycho-Analysis*, Hogarth, 1950.

KRIESBERG, L., *Mothers in Poverty*, Aldine, 1970.

LAND, H., *Large Families in London*, Bell, 1970.

LA SORTE, M. A., 'The Caseworker as Research Interviewer', *American Sociologist*, vol. 3, no. 3, August 1968.

LINDBLOM, C. E., 'The Science of "Muddling Through"', *Public Administration Review*, Vol. 29, no. 2, Spring 1959.

LYNCH, G., 'Food Intake and the Education of Children', *Medical Officer*, vol. 121, no. 4, 24 January 1969.

LYNCH, G., 'The Feeding Habits of School Children', *Catering and Hotel Management*, December 1970.

MCGREGOR, O. R., 'Social Research and Social Policy in the 19th Century', *British Journal of Sociology*, vol. 8, no. 2, 1957.

MCGREGOR, O. R., BLOM-COOPER, L. and GIBSON, C., *Separated Spouses*, Duckworth, 1970.

MARRIS, P., *Widows and Their Families*, Routledge & Kegan Paul, 1958.

MARRIS, P. and REIN, M., *Dilemmas of Social Reform*, Routledge & Kegan Paul, 1967.

MARSDEN, D., *Mothers Alone: Poverty and the Fatherless Family*, Allen Lane, 1969.

MARSH, D. (ed.), *An Introduction to the Study of Social Administration*, Routledge & Kegan Paul, 1965.

223

MARSH, D., *The Changing Social Structure of England and Wales*, Routledge & Kegan Paul, 1965.

MARSH, D., *The Welfare State*, Longmans, 1970.

MARSHALL, T. H., *Social Policy*, Hutchinson, 1967.

MATZA, D., *Becoming Deviant*, Prentice-Hall, 1969.

MAYER, J. and TIMMS, N., *The Client Speaks*, Routledge & Kegan Paul, 1970.

MERTON, R. K., *Social Theory and Social Structure*, Free Press, 1956.

MILLER, S. M. and RIESSMAN, F., *Social Class and Social Policy*, Basic Books, 1968.

MILLER, W., 'Lower Class Culture as a Generating Milieu of Gang Delinquency', *Journal of Social Issues*, vol. 14, no. 3, 1958.

MILLS, C. WRIGHT, *The Sociological Imagination*, Penguin, 1970.

Ministry of Health, *Report on an Investigation into Maternal Morality*, HMSO, Cmd 5422, 1937.

Ministry of Social Security Report, *Circumstances of Families*, HMSO, 1967.

MORRIS, P., *Prisoners and Their Families*, Allen & Unwin, 1965.

MORSE, N. and WEISS, R., 'The Function and Meaning of Work and the Job', *American Sociological Review*, vol. 20, 1955.

MYERS, R. and FULLER, R., 'The Natural History of a Social Problem', *American Sociological Review*, vol. 6, 1941.

NAGY, M., 'The Child's Theories Concerning Death', *Journal of Genetic Psychology*, 1948.

National Board for Prices and Incomes, Report no. 161, *Hours of Work, Overtime and Shift Working*, HMSO, Cmnd 4554, 1970.

NEWSON, J. and E., *Patterns of Infant Care in an Urban Community*, Penguin, 1965.

OAKLEY, A., 'The Myth of Motherhood', *New Society*, 27 February 1970, pp. 348–51.

Office of Health Economics, *Malnutrition in the 1960's?* London, 1967.

PACKMAN, J., *Child Care: Needs and Numbers*, Allen & Unwin, 1969.

PARAD, HOWARD J. (ed.), *Crisis Intervention: Selective Readings*, Family Service Association of America, 1965.

PARKES, C. M., 'Grief as an Illness', *New Society*, 9 April 1964, pp. 11–12.

PARKES, C. M., 'The Effects of Bereavement on Physical and Mental Health', *British Medical Journal*, vol. ii, 1964, p. 274.

PARKES, C. M., 'Bereavement and Mental Illness', *British Journal of Medical Psychology*, vol. 38, no. 1, 1965, p. 1.

PARKIN, F., *Class Inequality and Political Order*, MacGibbon & Kee, 1971.

PARKINSON, G., 'I Give Them Money', *New Society*, 5 February 1970, pp. 220–1.

PARSONS, T., *Essays in Sociological Theory*, Free Press, 1964.

PARSONS, T. and BALES, R., *Family, Socialization and Interaction Process*, Routledge & Kegan Paul, 1970.

PINKER, R. A., *Social Theory and Social Policy*, Heinemann, 1971.

POPPER, K., *The Open Society and Its Enemies*, Routledge, 1945.

PRINGLE, M. L. K., *et al.*, *11,000 Seven-Year-Olds*, Longmans, 1967.

RAAB, E. and SELZNICK, G., *Major Social Problems*, Harper & Row, 1964.

Report of the Committee on Local Authority and Allied Personal Social Services (Seebohm Report), HMSO, Cmnd 3703, 1968.

Report of the Committee on Statutory Maintenance Limits (Chairman, Jean Graham Hall), HMSO, Cmnd 3587, 1968.

RODGERS, B., 'Making Social Policy', vol. 107, *Memoirs and Proceedings of the Manchester Literary and Philosophical Society*, 1964–65, reprinted as pamphlet, p. 1.

ROSE, A., 'Law and the Causation of Social Problems', *Social Problems*, vol. 16, 1968, p. 33.

ROSE, E. J. B., *Colour and Citizenship, A Report on British Race Relations*, Oxford University Press, 1969.

ROSSER, C. and HARRIS, C., *The Family and Social Change*, Routledge & Kegan Paul, 1965.

ROWNTREE, B. S., *Poverty. A Study of Town Life*, Macmillan, 1902.

ROWNTREE, G., 'Early Childhood in Broken Families', *Population Studies*, vol. 8, 1954–5.

RUNCIMAN, W. G., *Relative Deprivation and Social Justice*, Routledge & Kegan Paul, 1966.

RUTTER, M., *Children of Sick Parents, An Environmental and Psychiatric Study*, Oxford University Press, 1966.

SCHAFFER, H. R. and SCHAFFER, E. B., *Child Care and the Family*, Bell, 1968.

SCHLESINGER, B. (ed.), *The One-parent Family*, University of Toronto Press, 1969.

SCHORR, A. L., *Explorations in Social Policy*, Basic Books, 1968.

SHANNAS, E. and STREIB, G.F. (eds), *Social Structure and the Family: Generational Relations*, Prentice-Hall, 1965.

SIMEY, T. S., *Social Science and Social Purpose*, Constable, 1968.

SIMEY, T. S. and M. B., *Charles Booth, Social Scientist*, Oxford, 1960.

SKINNER, F. (ed.), *Physical Disability and Community Care*, National Council of Social Service, 1969.

SLACK, K. M., *Social Administration and the Citizen*, Michael Joseph, 1966.

TACONIS, L., 'The Role of the Contemporary Father in Rearing Young Children', *Educational Research*, vol. 2, no. 2, February 1969.

TIMMS, N., *A Sociological Approach to Social Problems*, Routledge & Kegan Paul, 1967.

TITMUSS, R. M., *The Gift Relationship*, Allen & Unwin, 1970.

TOWNSEND, P., *The Family Life of Old People*, Penguin, 1963.

TOWNSEND, P., 'The Disabled Need Help', *New Society*, 28 September 1967.

TOWNSEND, P. (ed.) *The Concept of Poverty*, Heinemann, 1970.

TOWNSEND, P. and WEDDERBURN, D., *The Aged in the Welfare State*, Bell, 1965.

TURNER, C., *Family and Kinship in Modern Britain*, Routledge & Kegan Paul, 1969.

WARHAM, J., *Social Policy in Context*, Batsford, 1971.

WEDDERBURN, D., 'Facts and Theories of the Welfare State' in *The Socialist Register*, Miliband R. and Saville, J. (eds), Merlin Press, 1965.

WEDDERBURN, D., 'Workplace Inequality', *New Society*, 9 April 1970.

WICKHAM, E. R., *Church and People in an Industrial City*, Lutterworth, 1957.

WILENSKY, H. L. and LEBEAUX, C. N., *Industrial Society and Social Welfare*, Collier-Macmillan, 1965.

WILLCOCK, H., and STOKES, J., *Deterrents to Crime Among Youths Aged 15–21 Years*, Government Social Survey, S.S. 356, 1968.

WOLFF, S., *Children Under Stress*, Allen Lane, 1969.

World Health Organization, *Deprivation of Maternal Care*, Geneva, 1962.

WORSLEY, P. (ed.), *Modern Sociology: Introductory Readings*, Penguin, 1970.

WYNN, M., *Fatherless Families*, Michael Joseph, 1964.

WYNN, M., *Family Policy*, Michael Joseph, 1970.

YOUNG, M., BENJAMIN B. and WALLIS, C., 'The Mortality of Widowers', *Lancet*, ii, 1963.

YOUNG, M. and WILLMOTT, P., *Family and Kinship in East London*, Routledge & Kegan Paul, 1957. Also Penguin.

YUDKIN, S. and HOLME, A., *Working Mothers and Their Children*, Michael Joseph, 1962.

Name index

Abel-Smith, B., 172
Ainsworth, M. D., 67
Allen, A., 19
Andreski, S., 38
Anthony, S., 58
Armstrong, Sir W., 21

Bagehot, W., 175
Bakke E. Wight, 38
Bales, R. F., 140
Barnett, M. J., 185
Becker, H. S., 171
Bell, C., 145
Bell, N. W., 75
Beltram, G., 9
Benjamin, B., 114
Beveridge, W. H., 170, 176, 188,
    200, 201–2, 203
Blom-Cooper, L., 203
Blomfield, J. W., 6
Booth, C., 172
Bott, E., 74
Boulding, K., 185
Bowlby, J., 8, 43, 67
Burchinal, L., 140, 152
Butler, S., 1

Camus, A., 38
Carter, C., 195
Case, C. M., 176
Clausen, R., 28
Coates, K., 154, 191–2

Craig, C., 87

Dahl, R. A., 198
Dahlstrom, E., 3
Davidson, R. T., 138
Dominian, J., 25
Douglas, J. W. B., 6
Durkheim, E., 178

Elliott, M. A., 24, 178, 179
Eyden, J. L. M., 187, 190

Firth, R., 141, 145
Forge, A., 141, 145
Fox, J., 156–7
Fuller, R. C., 171

Gavron, H., 3
Gessel, A., 58
Gibson, C., 203
Glaisdale, Lord S., 3
Glasser, P., 7, 49, 75
Goode, W. J., 8, 12, 16, 18, 60, 61,
    65, 118, 121, 134, 137, 202
Gorer, G., 56, 126, 134, 138
Gouldner, A. W., 192
Gurin, G., 151

Hansen, M., 195
Harris, A., 28
Harris, C., 145
Heraud, B. J., 145

227

Subject index

International Library of Sociology

Edited by
John Rex
University of Warwick

Founded by
Karl Mannheim

as The International Library of Sociology
and Social Reconstruction

*This Catalogue also contains other Social Science
series published by Routledge*

Routledge & Kegan Paul   London and Boston

68-74 Carter Lane London EC4V 5EL
9 Park Street Boston Mass 02108

Contents

● *Books so marked are available in paperback*
All books are in Metric Demy 8vo format (216 × 138mm approx.)

GENERAL SOCIOLOGY

Belshaw, Cyril. The Conditions of Social Performance. *An Exploratory Theory. 144 pp.*

Brown, Robert. Explanation in Social Science. *208 pp.*

Cain, Maureen E. Society and the Policeman's Role. *About 300 pp.*

Gibson, Quentin. The Logic of Social Enquiry. *240 pp.*

Homans, George C. Sentiments and Activities: *Essays in Social Science. 336 pp.*

Isajiw, Wsevold W. Causation and Functionalism in Sociology. *165 pp.*

Johnson, Harry M. Sociology: *a Systematic Introduction. Foreword by Robert K. Merton. 710 pp.*

Mannheim, Karl. Essays on Sociology and Social Psychology. *Edited by Paul Keckskemeti. With Editorial Note by Adolph Lowe. 344 pp.*
Systematic Sociology: *An Introduction to the Study of Society. Edited by J. S. Erös and Professor W. A. C. Stewart. 220 pp.*

Martindale, Don. The Nature and Types of Sociological Theory. *292 pp.*

● **Maus, Heinz.** A Short History of Sociology. *234 pp.*

Mey, Harald. Field-Theory. *A Study of its Application in the Social Sciences. 352 pp.*

Myrdal, Gunnar. Value in Social Theory: *A Collection of Essays on Methodology. Edited by Paul Streeten. 332 pp.*

Ogburn, William F., and **Nimkoff, Meyer F.** A Handbook of Sociology. *Preface by Karl Mannheim. 656 pp. 46 figures. 35 tables.*

Parsons, Talcott, and **Smelser, Neil J.** Economy and Society: *A Study in the Integration of Economic and Social Theory. 362 pp.*

● **Rex, John.** Key Problems of Sociological Theory. *220 pp.*

Stark, Werner. The Fundamental Forms of Social Thought. *280 pp.*

FOREIGN CLASSICS OF SOCIOLOGY

● **Durkheim, Emile.** Suicide. *A Study in Sociology. Edited and with an Introduction by George Simpson. 404 pp.*
Professional Ethics and Civic Morals. *Translated by Cornelia Brookfield. 288 pp.*

● **Gerth, H. H.,** and **Mills, C. Wright.** From Max Weber: *Essays in Sociology. 502 pp.*

Tönnies, Ferdinand. Community and Association. *(Gemeinschaft und Gesellschaft.) Translated and Supplemented by Charles P. Loomis. Foreword by Pitirim A. Sorokin. 334 pp.*

SOCIAL STRUCTURE

Andreski, Stanislav. Military Organization and Society. *Foreword by Professor A. R. Radcliffe-Brown. 226 pp. 1 folder.*

● **Cole, G. D. H.** Studies in Class Structure. *220 p.*

Coontz, Sydney H. Population Theories and the Economic Interpretation. *202 pp.*

Coser, Lewis. The Functions of Social Conflict. *204 pp.*

Dickie-Clark, H. F. Marginal Situation: *A Sociological Study of a Coloured Group. 240 pp. 11 tables.*

Glass, D. V. (Ed.). Social Mobility in Britain. *Contributions by J. Berent, T. Bottomore, R. C. Chambers, J. Floud, D. V. Glass, J. R. Hall, H. T. Himmelweit, R. K. Kelsall, F. M. Martin, C. A. Moser, R. Mukherjee, and W. Ziegel. 420 pp.*

Glaser, Barney, and **Strauss, Anselm L.** Status Passage. *A Formal Theory. 208 pp.*

Jones, Garth N. Planned Organizational Change: *An Exploratory Study Using an Empirical Approach. 268 pp.*

Kelsall, R. K. Higher Civil Servants in Britain: *From 1870 to the Present Day. 268 pp. 31 tables.*

König, René. The Community. *232 pp. Illustrated.*

● **Lawton, Denis.** Social Class, Language and Education. *192 pp.*

McLeish, John. The Theory of Social Change: *Four Views Considered. 128 pp.*

Marsh, David C. The Changing Social Structure in England and Wales, 1871-1961. *272 pp.*

Mouzelis, Nicos. Organization and Bureaucracy. *An Analysis of Modern Theories. 240 pp.*

Mulkay, M. J. Functionalism, Exchange and Theoretical Strategy. *272 pp.*

Ossowski, Stanislaw. Class Structure in the Social Consciousness. *210 pp.*

SOCIOLOGY AND POLITICS

Crick, Bernard. The American Science of Politics: *Its Origins and Conditions. 284 pp.*

Hertz, Frederick. Nationality in History and Politics: *A Psychology and Sociology of National Sentiment and Nationalism. 432 pp.*

Kornhauser, William. The Politics of Mass Society. *272 pp. 20 tables.*

Laidler, Harry W. History of Socialism. *Social-Economic Movements: An Historical and Comparative Survey of Socialism, Communism, Co-operation, Utopianism; and other Systems of Reform and Reconstruction. 992 pp.*

Mannheim, Karl. Freedom, Power and Democratic Planning. *Edited by Hans Gerth and Ernest K. Bramstedt. 424 pp.*

Mansur, Fatma. Process of Independence. *Foreword by A. H. Hanson. 208 pp.*

Martin, David A. Pacificism: *an Historical and Sociological Study. 262 pp.*

Myrdal, Gunnar. The Political Element in the Development of Economic Theory. *Translated from the German by Paul Streeten. 282 pp.*

Verney, Douglas V. The Analysis of Political Systems. *264 pp.*

Wootton, Graham. Workers, Unions and the State. *188 pp.*

FOREIGN AFFAIRS: THEIR SOCIAL, POLITICAL AND ECONOMIC FOUNDATIONS

Bonné, Alfred. State and Economics in the Middle East: *A Society in Transition. 482 pp.*
Studies in Economic Development: *with special reference to Conditions in the Under-developed Areas of Western Asia and India. 322 pp. 84 tables.*
Mayer, J. P. Political Thought in France from the Revolution to the Fifth Republic. *164 pp.*

CRIMINOLOGY

Ancel, Marc. Social Defence: *A Modern Approach to Criminal Problems. Foreword by Leon Radzinowicz. 240 pp.*
Cloward, Richard A., and **Ohlin, Lloyd E.** Delinquency and Opportunity: *A Theory of Delinquent Gangs. 248 pp.*
Downes, David M. The Delinquent Solution. *A Study in Subcultural Theory. 296 pp.*
Dunlop, A. B., and **McCabe, S.** Young Men in Detention Centres. *192 pp.*
Friedlander, Kate. The Psycho-Analytical Approach to Juvenile Delinquency: *Theory, Case Studies, Treatment. 320 pp.*
Glueck, Sheldon, and **Eleanor.** Family Environment and Delinquency. *With the statistical assistance of Rose W. Kneznek. 340 pp.*
Lopez-Rey, Manuel. Crime. *An Analytical Appraisal. 288 pp.*
Mannheim, Hermann. Comparative Criminology: *a Text Book. Two volumes. 442 pp. and 380 pp.*
Morris, Terence. The Criminal Area: *A Study in Social Ecology. Foreword by Hermann Mannheim. 232 pp. 25 tables. 4 maps.*
Trasler, Gordon. The Explanation of Criminality. *144 pp.*

SOCIAL PSYCHOLOGY

Bagley, Christopher. The Social Psychology of the Child with Epilepsy. *320 pp.*
Barbu, Zevedei. Problems of Historical Psychology. *248 pp.*
Blackburn, Julian. Psychology and the Social Pattern. *184 pp.*
● **Fleming, C. M.** Adolescence: *Its Social Psychology: With an Introduction to recent findings from the fields of Anthropology, Physiology, Medicine, Psychometrics and Sociometry. 288 pp.*
● The Social Psychology of Education: *An Introduction and Guide to Its Study. 136 pp.*
Homans, George C. The Human Group. *Foreword by Bernard DeVoto. Introduction by Robert K. Merton. 526 pp.*
Social Behaviour: *its Elementary Forms. 416 pp.*

Klein, Josephine. The Study of Groups. *226 pp. 31 figures. 5 tables.*
Linton, Ralph. The Cultural Background of Personality. *132 pp.*
Mayo, Elton. The Social Problems of an Industrial Civilization. *With an appendix on the Political Problem. 180 pp.*
Ottaway, A. K. C. Learning Through Group Experience. *176 pp.*
Ridder, J. C. de. The Personality of the Urban African in South Africa. *A Thematic Apperception Test Study. 196 pp. 12 plates.*
● **Rose, Arnold M.** (Ed.). Human Behaviour and Social Processes: *an Inter-actionist Approach. Contributions by Arnold M. Rose, Ralph H. Turner, Anselm Strauss, Everett C. Hughes, E. Franklin Frazier, Howard S. Becker, et al. 696 pp.*
Smelser, Neil J. Theory of Collective Behaviour. *448 pp.*
Stephenson, Geoffrey M. The Development of Conscience. *128 pp.*
Young, Kimball. Handbook of Social Psychology. *658 pp. 16 figures. 10 tables.*

SOCIOLOGY OF THE FAMILY

Banks, J. A. Prosperity and Parenthood: *A Study of Family Planning among The Victorian Middle Classes. 262 pp.*
Bell, Colin R. Middle Class Families: *Social and Geographical Mobility. 224 pp.*
Burton, Lindy. Vulnerable Children. *272 pp.*
Gavron, Hannah. The Captive Wife: *Conflicts of Household Mothers. 190 pp.*
George, Victor, and **Wilding, Paul.** Motherless Families. *220 pp.*
Klein, Josephine. Samples from English Cultures.
   1. Three Preliminary Studies and Aspects of Adult Life in England. *447 pp.*
   2. Child-Rearing Practices and Index. *247 pp.*
Klein, Viola. Britain's Married Women Workers. *180 pp.*
   The Feminine Character. *History of an Ideology. 244 pp.*
McWhinnie, Alexina M. Adopted Children. *How They Grow Up. 304 pp.*
Myrdal, Alva, and **Klein, Viola.** Women's Two Roles: *Home and Work. 238 pp. 27 tables.*
Parsons, Talcott, and **Bales, Robert F.** Family: *Socialization and Interaction Process. In collaboration with James Olds, Morris Zelditch and Philip E. Slater. 456 pp. 50 figures and tables.*

SOCIAL SERVICES

Bastide, Roger. The Sociology of Mental Disorder. *Translated from the French by Jean McNeil. 264 pp.*
Carlebach, Julius. Caring For Children in Trouble. *266 pp.*
Forder, R. A. (Ed.). Penelope Hall's Social Services of Modern England. *352 pp.*
George, Victor. Foster Care. *Theory and Practice. 234 pp.*
   Social Security: *Beveridge and After. 258 pp.*

● **Goetschius, George W.** Working with Community Groups. *256 pp.*
Goetschius, George W., and **Tash, Joan.** Working with Unattached Youth. *416 pp.*
Hall, M. P., and **Howes, I. V.** The Church in Social Work. *A Study of Moral Welfare Work undertaken by the Church of England. 320 pp.*
Heywood, Jean S. Children in Care: *the Development of the Service for the Deprived Child. 264 pp.*
Hoenig, J., and **Hamilton, Marian W.** The De-Segration of the Mentally Ill. *284 pp.*
Jones, Kathleen. Lunacy, Law and Conscience, *1744-1845: the Social History of the Care of the Insane. 268 pp.*
Mental Health and Social Policy, 1845-1959. *264 pp.*
King, Roy D., Raynes, Norma V., and **Tizard, Jack.** Patterns of Residential Care. *356 pp.*
Leigh, John. Young People and Leisure. *256 pp.*
Morris, Pauline. Put Away: *A Sociological Study of Institutions for the Mentally Retarded. 364 pp.*
Nokes, P. L. The Professional Task in Welfare Practice. *152 pp.*
Timms, Noel. Psychiatric Social Work in Great Britain (1939-1962). *280 pp.*
● Social Casework: *Principles and Practice. 256 pp.*
Trasler, Gordon. In Place of Parents: *A Study in Foster Care. 272 pp.*
Young, A. F., and **Ashton, E. T.** British Social Work in the Nineteenth Century. *288 pp.*
Young, A. F. Social Services in British Industry. *272 pp.*

SOCIOLOGY OF EDUCATION

Banks, Olive. Parity and Prestige in English Secondary Education: a Study in Educational Sociology. *272 pp.*
Bentwich, Joseph. Education in Israel. *224 pp. 8 pp. plates.*
● **Blyth, W. A. L.** English Primary Education. *A Sociological Description.*
1. Schools. *232 pp.*
2. Background. *168 pp.*
Collier, K. G. The Social Purposes of Education: *Personal and Social Values in Education. 268 pp.*
Dale, R. R., and **Griffith, S.** Down Stream: *Failure in the Grammar School. 108 pp.*
Dore, R. P. Education in Tokugawa Japan. *356 pp. 9 pp. plates*
Evans, K. M. Sociometry and Education. *158 pp.*
Foster, P. J. Education and Social Change in Ghana. *336 pp. 3 maps.*
Fraser, W. R. Education and Society in Modern France. *150 pp.*
Grace, Gerald R. Role Conflict and the Teacher. *About 200 pp.*
Hans, Nicholas. New Trends in Education in the Eighteenth Century. *278 pp. 19 tables.*
● Comparative Education: *A Study of Educational Factors and Traditions. 360 pp.*

Hargreaves, David. Interpersonal Relations and Education. *432 pp.*
● Social Relations in a Secondary School. *240 pp.*
Holmes, Brian. Problems in Education. *A Comparative Approach. 336 pp.*
King, Ronald. Values and Involvement in a Grammar School. *164 pp.*
● **Mannheim, Karl,** and **Stewart, W. A. C.** An Introduction to the Sociology of Education. *206 pp.*
Morris, Raymond N. The Sixth Form and College Entrance. *231 pp.*
● **Musgrove, F.** Youth and the Social Order. *176 pp.*
● **Ottaway, A. K. C.** Education and Society: *An Introduction to the Sociology of Education. With an Introduction by W. O. Lester Smith. 212 pp.*
Peers, Robert. Adult Education: *A Comparative Study. 398 pp.*
Pritchard, D. G. Education and the Handicapped: *1760 to 1960. 258 pp.*
Richardson, Helen. Adolescent Girls in Approved Schools. *308 pp.*
Simon, Brian, and **Joan** (Eds.). Educational Psychology in the U.S.S.R. *Introduction by Brian and Joan Simon. Translation by Joan Simon. Papers by D. N. Bogoiavlenski and N. A. Menchinskaia, D. B. Elkonin, E. A. Fleshner, Z. I. Kalmykova, G. S. Kostiuk, V. A. Krutetski, A. N. Leontiev, A. R. Luria, E. A. Milerian, R. G. Natadze, B. M. Teplov, L. S. Vygotski, L. V. Zankov. 296 pp.*
Stratta, Erica. The Education of Borstal Boys. *A Study of their Educational Experiences prior to, and during Borstal Training. 256 pp.*

SOCIOLOGY OF CULTURE

Eppel, E. M., and **M.** Adolescents and Morality: *A Study of some Moral Values and Dilemmas of Working Adolescents in the Context of a changing Climate of Opinion. Foreword by W. J. H. Sprott. 268 pp. 39 tables.*
● **Fromm, Erich.** The Fear of Freedom. *286 pp.*
The Sane Society. *400 pp.*
● **Mannheim, Karl.** Diagnosis of Our Time: *Wartime Essays of a Sociologist. 208 pp.*
Essays on the Sociology of Culture. *Edited by Ernst Mannheim in co-operation with Paul Kecskemeti. Editorial Note by Adolph Lowe. 280 pp.*
Weber, Alfred. Farewell to European History: *or The Conquest of Nihilism. Translated from the German by R. F. C. Hull. 224 pp.*

SOCIOLOGY OF RELIGION

Argyle, Michael. Religious Behaviour. *224 pp. 8 figures. 41 tables.*
Nelson, G. K. Spiritualism and Society. *313 pp.*

Stark, Werner. The Sociology of Religion. *A Study of Christendom.*
Volume I. *Established Religion. 248 pp.*
Volume II. *Sectarian Religion. 368 pp.*
Volume III. *The Universal Church. 464 pp.*
Volume IV. *Types of Religious Man. 352 pp.*
Volume V. *Types of Religious Culture. 464 pp.*
Watt, W. Montgomery. Islam and the Integration of Society. *320 pp.*

SOCIOLOGY OF ART AND LITERATURE

Beljame, Alexandre. Men of Letters and the English Public in the Eighteenth
Century: *1660-1744, Dryden, Addison, Pope. Edited with an Introduction
and Notes by Bonamy Dobrée. Translated by E. O. Lorimer. 532 pp.*
Jarvie, Ian C. Towards a Sociology of the Cinema. *A Comparative Essay
on the Structure and Functioning of a Major Entertainment Industry.
405 pp.*
Rust, Frances S. Dance in Society. *An Analysis of the Relationships between
the Social Dance and Society in England from the Middle Ages to the
Present Day. 256 pp. 8 pp. of plates.*
Schücking, L. L. The Sociology of Literary Taste. *112 pp.*
Silbermann, Alphons. The Sociology of Music. *Translated from the German
by Corbet Stewart. 222 pp.*

SOCIOLOGY OF KNOWLEDGE

Mannheim, Karl. Essays on the Sociology of Knowledge. *Edited by Paul
Kecskemeti. Editorial note by Adolph Lowe. 353 pp.*
Stark, Werner. The Sociology of Knowledge: *An Essay in Aid of a Deeper
Understanding of the History of Ideas. 384 pp.*

URBAN SOCIOLOGY

Ashworth, William. The Genesis of Modern British Town Planning: *A Study
in Economic and Social History of the Nineteenth and Twentieth Centuries.
288 pp.*
Cullingworth, J. B. Housing Needs and Planning Policy: *A Restatement of
the Problems of Housing Need and 'Overspill' in England and Wales.
232 pp. 44 tables. 8 maps.*
Dickinson, Robert E. City and Region: *A Geographical Interpretation.
608 pp. 125 figures.*
The West European City: *A Geographical Interpretation. 600 pp. 129 maps.
29 plates.*
● The City Region in Western Europe. *320 pp. Maps.*

9

Humphreys, Alexander J. New Dubliners: *Urbanization and the Irish Family. Foreword by George C. Homans. 304 pp.*

Jackson, Brian. Working Class Community: *Some General Notions raised by a Series of Studies in Northern England. 192 pp.*

Jennings, Hilda. Societies in the Making: *a Study of Development and Redevelopment within a County Borough. Foreword by D. A. Clark. 286 pp.*

Kerr, Madeline. The People of Ship Street. *240 pp.*

● **Mann, P. H.** An Approach to Urban Sociology. *240 pp.*

Morris, R. N., and **Mogey, J.** The Sociology of Housing. *Studies at Berinsfield. 232 pp. 4 pp. plates.*

Rosser, C., and **Harris, C.** The Family and Social Change. *A Study of Family and Kinship in a South Wales Town. 352 pp. 8 maps.*

RURAL SOCIOLOGY

Chambers, R. J. H. Settlement Schemes in Africa: *A Selective Study. 268 pp.*

Haswell, M. R. The Economics of Development in Village India. *120 pp.*

Littlejohn, James. Westrigg: *the Sociology of a Cheviot Parish. 172 pp. 5 figures.*

Williams, W. M. The Country Craftsman: *A Study of Some Rural Crafts and the Rural Industries Organization in England. 248 pp. 9 figures. (Dartington Hall Studies in Rural Sociology.)*

The Sociology of an English Village: *Gosforth. 272 pp. 12 figures. 13 tables.*

SOCIOLOGY OF INDUSTRY AND DISTRIBUTION

Anderson, Nels. Work and Leisure. *280 pp.*

● **Blau, Peter M.,** and **Scott, W. Richard.** Formal Organizations: *a Comparative approach. Introduction and Additional Bibliography by J. H. Smith. 326 pp.*

Eldridge, J. E. T. Industrial Disputes. *Essays in the Sociology of Industrial Relations. 288 pp.*

Hetzler, Stanley. Technological Growth and Social Change. *Achieving Modernization. 269 pp.*

Hollowell, Peter G. The Lorry Driver. *272 pp.*

Jefferys, Margot, *with the assistance of Winifred Moss.* Mobility in the Labour Market: *Employment Changes in Battersea and Dagenham. Preface by Barbara Wootton. 186 pp. 51 tables.*

Millerson, Geoffrey. The Qualifying Associations: *a Study in Professionalization. 320 pp.*

Smelser, Neil J. Social Change in the Industrial Revolution: *An Application of Theory to the Lancashire Cotton Industry, 1770-1840. 468 pp. 12 figures. 14 tables.*

Williams, Gertrude. Recruitment to Skilled Trades. *240 pp.*

Young, A. F. Industrial Injuries Insurance: *an Examination of British Policy. 192 pp.*

ANTHROPOLOGY

Ammar, Hamed. Growing up in an Egyptian Village: *Silwa, Province of Aswan. 336 pp.*

Brandel-Syrier, Mia. Reeftown Elite. *A Study of Social Mobility in a Modern African Community on the Reef. 376 pp.*

Crook, David, and **Isabel.** Revolution in a Chinese Village: *Ten Mile Inn. 230 pp. 8 plates. 1 map.*

The First Years of Yangyi Commune. *302 pp. 12 plates.*

Dickie-Clark, H. F. The Marginal Situation. *A Sociological Study of a Coloured Group. 236 pp.*

Dube, S. C. Indian Village. *Foreword by Morris Edward Opler. 276 pp. 4 plates.*

India's Changing Villages: *Human Factors in Community Development. 260 pp. 8 plates. 1 map.*

Firth, Raymond. Malay Fishermen. *Their Peasant Economy. 420 pp. 17 pp. plates.*

Gulliver, P. H. Social Control in an African Society: a Study of the Arusha, Agricultural Masai of Northern Tanganyika. *320 pp. 8 plates. 10 figures.*

Ishwaran, K. Shivapur. *A South Indian Village. 216 pp.*

Tradition and Economy in Village India: *An Interactionist Approach. Foreword by Conrad Arensburg. 176 pp.*

Jarvie, Ian C. The Revolution in Anthropology. *268 pp.*

Jarvie, Ian C., and **Agassi, Joseph.** Hong Kong. *A Society in Transition. 396 pp. Illustrated with plates and maps.*

Little, Kenneth L. Mende of Sierra Leone. *308 pp. and folder.*

Negroes in Britain. *With a New Introduction and Contemporary Study by Leonard Bloom. 320 pp.*

Lowie, Robert H. Social Organization. *494 pp.*

Mayer, Adrian C. Caste and Kinship in Central India: *A Village and its Region. 328 pp. 16 plates. 15 figures. 16 tables.*

Smith, Raymond T. The Negro Family in British Guiana: *Family Structure and Social Status in the Villages. With a Foreword by Meyer Fortes. 314 pp. 8 plates. 1 figure. 4 maps.*

DOCUMENTARY

Meek, Dorothea L. (Ed.). Soviet Youth: *Some Achievements and Problems. Excerpts from the Soviet Press, translated by the editor. 280 pp.*

Schlesinger, Rudolf (Ed.). Changing Attitudes in Soviet Russia.
2. *The Nationalities Problem and Soviet Administration. Selected Readings on the Development of Soviet Nationalities Policies. Introduced by the editor. Translated by W. W. Gottlieb. 324 pp.*

11

SOCIOLOGY AND PHILOSOPHY

Barnsley, John H. The Social Reality of Ethics. *A Comparative Analysis of Moral Codes. 448 pp.*

Douglas, Jack D. (Ed.). Understanding Everyday Life. *Toward the Reconstruction of Sociological Knowledge. Contributions by Alan F. Blum. Aaron W. Cicourel, Norman K. Denzin, Jack D. Douglas, John Heeren, Peter McHugh, Peter K. Manning, Melvin Power, Matthew Speier, Roy Turner, D. Lawrence Wieder, Thomas P. Wilson and Don H. Zimmerman. 358 pp.*

Jarvie, Ian C. Concepts and Society. *216 pp.*

Roche, Maurice. Phenomenology, Language and the Social Sciences. *About 400 pp.*

Sklair, Leslie. The Sociology of Progress. *320 pp.*

International Library of Social Policy

General Editor Kathleen Janes

Jones, Kathleen. Mental Health Services. *A history, 1744-1971. About 500 pp.*

Thomas, J. E. The English Prison Officer since 1850: *A Study in Conflict. 258 pp.*

Primary Socialization, Language and Education

General Editor Basil Bernstein

Bernstein, Basil. Class, Codes and Control. *2 volumes.*
 1. *Theoretical Studies Towards a Sociology of Language. 254 pp.*
 2. *Applied Studies Towards a Sociology of Language. About 400 pp.*

Brandis, Walter, and **Henderson, Dorothy.** Social Class, Language and Communication. *288 pp.*

Cook, Jenny. Socialization and Social Control. *About 300 pp.*

Gahagan, D. M., and **G. A.** Talk Reform. *Exploration in Language for Infant School Children. 160 pp.*

Robinson, W. P., and **Rackstraw, Susan, D. A.** A Question of Answers. *2 volumes. 192 pp. and 180 pp.*

Turner, Geoffrey, J., and **Mohan, Bernard, A.** A Linguistic Description and Computer Programme for Children's Speech. *208 pp.*

Reports of the Institute of Community Studies and the Institute of Social Studies in Medical Care

Cartwright, Ann. Human Relations and Hospital Care. *272 pp.*
  Parents and Family Planning Services. *306 pp.*
  Patients and their Doctors. *A Study of General Practice. 304 pp.*
Dunnell, Karen, and Cartwright, Ann. Medicine Takers, Prescribers and Hoarders. *About 140 pp.*
● Jackson, Brian. Streaming: *an Education System in Miniature. 168 pp.*
Jackson, Brian, and Marsden, Dennis. Education and the Working Class: *Some General Themes raised by a Study of 88 Working-class Children in a Northern Industrial City. 268 pp. 2 folders.*
Marris, Peter. Widows and their Families. *Foreword by Dr. John Bowlby. 184 pp. 18 tables. Statistical Summary.*
  Family and Social Change in an African City. *A Study of Rehousing in Lagos. 196 pp. 1 map. 4 plates. 53 tables.*
  The Experience of Higher Education. *232 pp. 27 tables.*
Marris, Peter, and Rein, Martin. Dilemmas of Social Reform. *Poverty and Community Action in the United States. 256 pp.*
Marris, Peter, and Somerset, Anthony. African Businessmen. *A Study of Entrepreneurship and Development in Kenya. 256 pp.*
Runciman, W. G. Relative Deprivation and Social Justice. *A Study of Attitudes to Social Inequality in Twentieth Century England. 352 pp.*
Townsend, Peter. The Family Life of Old People: *An Inquiry in East London. Foreword by J. H. Sheldon. 300 pp. 3 figures. 63 tables.*
Willmott, Peter. Adolescent Boys in East London. *230 pp.*
  The Evolution of a Community: *a study of Dagenham after forty years. 168 pp. 2 maps.*
Willmott, Peter, and Young, Michael. Family and Class in a London Suburb. *202 pp. 47 tables.*
Young, Michael. Innovation and Research in Education. *192 pp.*
● Young, Michael, and McGeeney, Patrick. Learning Begins at Home. *A Study of a Junior School and its Parents. 128 pp.*
Young, Michael, and Willmott, Peter. Family and Kinship in East London. *Foreword by Richard M. Titmuss. 252 pp. 39 tables.*

Medicine, Illness and Society
General Editor W. M. Williams

Robinson, David. The Process of Becoming Ill.
Stacey, Margaret. *et al.* Hospitals, Children and Their Families. *The Report of a Pilot Study. 202 pp.*

Routledge Social Science Journals

The British Journal of Sociology. *Edited by Terence P. Morris. Vol. 1, No. 1, March 1950 and Quarterly. Roy. 8vo. Back numbers available. An international journal with articles on all aspects of sociology.*

Economy and Society. *Vol. 1, No. 1. February 1972 and Quarterly. Metric Roy. 8vo. A journal for all social scientists covering sociology, philosophy, anthropology, economics and history.*

Printed in Great Britain by Lewis Reprints Limited
Brown Knight & Truscott Group, London and Tonbridge   21972

Motherless Families

The problems that fatherless families present to their members and to society have frequently been discussed and described. Until very recently, however, motherless families and their difficulties have largely been ignored despite the fact that the problem is widespread. This book shows how, with the slow disappearance of the extended family and the support that it could offer in such situations, society has found itself responsible for these incomplete families. The authors cover the situation of about six hundred families in the East Midlands where the father was caring for his children on his own. They examine the father's feelings about his new circumstances, the problems he faces and how he copes with them. They look at the ways in which the social services, the modified extended family and the immediate community react to the father's position. They also consider the children's adaptation to the motherless situation and their new relationships with the father or a mother substitute. In the final chapter the authors examine the ways in which social class and social values affect the definition of social problems and the formulation of social policy.

Both administrators and practitioners in the social services, as well as students of related subjects, will welcome the research contained in this book, and will find the authors' conclusions of particular help in their approach to the problems of all types of one-parent families.